OVID WITH LOVE

APHRODITE (Venus) and EROS. Terracotta from TANAGRA, IV century B.C. Seattle Museum of Art. Photo R.V. Schoder, S.J.

OVID WITH LOVE

SELECTIONS FROM ARS AMATORIA I AND II

OXFORD TEXT, COMMENTARY, VOCABULARY, INTRODUCTION

BY

P. MURGATROYD

BOLCHAZY-CARDUCCI PUBLISHERS

The Latin selections reprinted in this textbook are taken from the Oxford edition of E. J. Kenney. Acknowledgement is here made for the permission granted by Professor Kenney and the Oxford University Press.

Cover Design
Adam Phillip Velez

Cover Illustration
Leon Danilovics

Bolchazy-Carducci Publishers, Inc.
1000 Brown Street
Wauconda, IL 60084 USA
www.bolchazy.com

Printed in the United States of America
Fourth Printing, 2002
by United Graphics

ISBN 0-86516-015-5

UXORI CARISSIMAE (MEAE)

Professor Murgatroyd is also the author of *Tibullus I: A Commentary on the First Book of the Elgies of Albius Tibullus*

CONTENTS

List of Selections viii

Introduction 1

Variants from the Oxford Classical Text 23

Text 25

Commentary... 49

Vocabulary 199

LIST OF SELECTIONS

BC Edition	Oxford Edition
Selections Book I	*Ars Amatoria Book I*
1-8	1-8
9-18	25-34
19-24	35-40
25-46	41-52, 57-66
47-92	89-134
93-120	135-162
121-134	163-176
135-152	229-230, 237-252
153-158	263-268
159-220	269-326, 341-344
221-252	437-468
253-270	469-486
271-286	487-500, 503-504
287-304	505-506, 509-524
305-348	525-568
349-370	569-578, 591-592, 595-600, 603-606
371-436	607-614, 619-624, 631-636, 645-646, 659-666, 669-704
437-454	705-722
455-470	755-770
471-472	771-772
Selections Book II	*Ars Amatoria Book II*
1-18	1-4, 9-20, 97-98
19-26	99-106
27-62	107-108, 111-144
63-74	145-146, 151-160
75-116	177-178, 197-202, 209-242
117-132	295-306, 311-314
133-150	315, 318-319, 322-336
151-178	339-342, 345-352, 357-372
179-200	373-378, 385-396, 409-412
201-216	427-432, 435-436, 439-446
217-234	493-510
235-286	511-512, 537-540, 543-544, 547-548, 553-556, 559-596
287-298	733-744

The *Ars Amatoria* can be read and enjoyed on several levels,
and it is my hope that this edition will bridge a number of those
levels.   It is aimed primarily at British sixth-formers and first-
year university students elsewhere.   However, I have tried to
make it suitable for less-advanced readers too by adding a vocab-
ulary and making a particular arrangement of material in the notes.
The first paragraphs of all notes contain only remarks which assist
basic understanding of the poetry (résumé, grammar, references etc.).
Accordingly, younger pupils could be told to use this edition read-
ing only those first paragraphs, and teachers could supply further
information from the rest of the commentary as they see fit.
(Even in the case of older pupils, as there is so much to what
Ovid writes, it might be advisable to separate the processes of
comprehension and literary criticism.)   Stylistic and metrical
features receive much attention, as is only fair and proper in
view of their importance in the *Ars*.   My remarks on these aspects
are full for the first 92 lines, so that students may realize just
how ubiquitous Ovid's technical skills are and observe them in op-
eration in both didactic and narrative passages;   it is also my
hope that thus even the slowest may learn to spot these features
with ease.   Subsequently only especially noteworthy instances are
at first pointed out and finally merely alluded to (to encourage
pupils to make their own investigations).   These comments are
generally grouped together in the notes so that advanced students
can be told to ignore the more obvious points when the appropriate
stage of proficiency has been attained.

I covered 770 lines with my class in the course, and such a
length is, I think, necessary for a worthwhile acquaintance with
the *Ars*.   Of course, users of this book are free to omit lines and
sections as they wish.   I found the business of selection very
difficult (especially in the case of book II), although there are
parts of the *Ars* which can be readily omitted because they would
probably not be particularly congenial or immediately intelligible
to younger students.   In the selections made I have tried to con-
vey a fair impression of the actual precepts and of the general
variety and diversity of the poem.   In my attempt to bridge levels
I have given a full introduction.   With the less advanced it may
be found desirable to omit some sections there or at least to take
pupils through them.   My purpose in the notes was to facilitate
(succinctly) an understanding of the Latin and to make the work
come alive for the reader (which meant that I concentrated in par-
ticular on bringing out the humour and ingenuity).   I have con-
sulted past commentators, but the only one I found to be of any
help was Hollis (on book I).   In an edition of this nature a blan-
ket acknowledgement here seemed sufficient.   I am aware that many
of the interpretations which I offer are unconventional, not least
due to my belief that there is generally some point to what a poet
of Ovid's calibre writes.   It did not seem desirable to clutter
up the commentary with lengthy arguments and references for well-
known facts, and, in any case, I hope that my views (which were
only reached after much thought and which have been subjected to
subsequent scrutiny) have common sense and sensibility on their
side.   Of course, readers are always at liberty to reject them
and have recourse to the standard explanations so readily applied
by scholars, such as Ovid's fondness for padding and rhetorical
expansion.

It remains to record my debts of thanks.   I would like to
acknowledge the kind permission of Professor E.J. Kenney and the
Oxford University Press to base my text on the Oxford Classical
Texts edition of the *Ars Amatoria* (1965 reprint).   I was particu-
larly fortunate to be able to draw upon the scholarship and exper-
ience of David Raven, who generously agreed to look through a first
draft of this work at a time when he was very busy.   He examined
it with his usual meticulous care and attention and effected a
large number of improvements (especially with regard to the amount
of grammatical and syntactical help given).   Of course, he should
not be held responsible for any of the views expressed in this edi-
tion nor for any errors of omission or commission.

January, 1980.   P. Murgatroyd.

Ovid – born 43 B.C. ⟩ 59
        died 17 A.D.

Ars published ~~the~~ – several years
                before 8 A.D.
First published around ~~9 A.D.~~ 1 B.C. (1st Book)
        published w/ Book 3 1 A.D.

The *Ars Amatoria* and the *Remedia Amoris* during quite recent
times virtually enjoyed the status of banned books, rigorously
excluded from the syllabuses of schools and universities.   The
Ars in particular had acquired the reputation of being a Latin
Kama Sutra or *Perfumed Garden* and was roundly condemned, especially
by pious and upright Victorians.   "Perhaps the most immoral poem
ever written", "shameless compendium in profligacy", "of 'The Art
of Love' the less, perhaps, that is said the better", "base level
of sensuality", "vade mecum in wantonness" critics used to exclaim,
and then they would hurriedly move on to devote the rest of their
discussion to the beauty of (some of) the mythical digressions in
the poem or the interesting insights into Roman social life that
it affords.

Such criticism is unfair and inaccurate.   As a more recent
scholar, L.P. Wilkinson, has pointed out, "the prurient will read
on with increasing disappointment, and may never reach their first
meagre reward at the end of Book II" (there is also a rather naughty
bit at the end of Book III).   In the past thirty years or so many
scholars and a few teachers have come to realize again that the
Ars is neither pornographic nor offensive.   On the contrary, it
is one of the cleverest and most amusing of Ovid's poems, one of
the best works of a poet who is very different from impressions of
him normally gathered at school by reading innocuous and rather
boring selections from the *Fasti*, *Tristia* and *Epistulae Ex Ponto*.
In fact Ovid is a very appealing writer - elegant, sophisticated,
often outrageously funny and in many ways very modern.

① OVID'S LIFE

Ovid (full name: Publius Ovidius Naso) came from an estab-
lished equestrian (middle-class) family and was born in 43 B.C. at
Sulmo, an Italian town about ninety miles from Rome.   He was sent
to Rome to be educated, where he would have studied Greek and
Latin language and literature, followed by rhetoric, and later
finished his education by touring Athens, Sicily and Asia Minor.
Ovid became interested in poetry while still a boy, and during his
rhetorical training he showed himself a good speaker, but already
his compositions seemed like free verse (*1). His literary pro-
clivities were fired by the presence in Rome of the great poets
of the day, whom the young Ovid worshipped. His father wanted
him to pursue a conventional and respectable occupation, but Ovid
rebelled, and after holding some minor offices he gave up public
life for a career as a poet. He had given his first reading from
his poetry when aged about eighteen, and he soon became famous and
successful.   Much admired now by younger poets, he devoted him-
self to the pleasures of writing and moving in intellectual and
literary circles. Ovid was a prolific and versatile author: in
addition to the *Ars Amatoria* he wrote the *Amores* (love elegies),
Heroides (imaginary love letters from and to heroines of mythol-
ogy), *Medea* (a lost tragedy), *Medicamina Faciei* (a treatise on
cosmetics), *Remedia Amoris* (a didactic poem like the *Ars*, but this
time on how to terminate a love-affair), *Fasti* (a poetic calen-
dar), *Metamorphoses* (a long poem in hexameters which recounts a
series of mythological stories involving change) and in exile verse-
letters called the *Tristia* and *Epistulae Ex Ponto* as well as the
Ibis (a vehement invective against an unnamed personal enemy).

Ovid's enjoyable way of life in smart society came to an abrupt end in 8 A.D. with his banishment for an offence against the Establishment.   The emperor Augustus exiled him to Tomis on the Black Sea (in modern Roumania).   Ovid himself tells us that a poem and a mistake were responsible (*2).   The poem was the *Ars Amatoria*. Although the *Ars* had been published several years earlier and had not apparently aroused imperial displeasure then, and although Ovid had explicitly stated that it was not intended for married women (*3), the poem was charged with undermining public morality and teaching adultery, which was now a criminal offence.   It also seems likely that Ovid's flippant and rather irreverent attitude in the *Ars* to various Roman sacred cows would not have gone down well with the emperor.   The mistake made by Ovid, which was apparently a more serious matter (*4), is a mystery.   The poet himself says that he witnessed something unintentionally, but he never says exactly what that something was (one popular theory is that it was connected with the escapades of Augustus' granddaughter Julia, who, perhaps significantly, was exiled for adultery in the same year as Ovid).   Ovid never did win recall but spent the rest of his life in misery and frustration far from sophisticated Rome in a place where no Latin (and only a barbarous form of Greek) was spoken, exposed to the discomforts of bitterly cold weather and the dangers of raids by hostile tribes. He finally died in 17 A.D. aged 59 (*5).

② THE AUGUSTAN PERIOD

Ovid was born a year after the assassination of Julius Caesar, came to Rome to be educated round about the time of the battle of Actium and spent most of his adult life under the principate of Augustus and his final few years under that of Tiberius.   This means that Ovid knew little of the Republic and that he was what is called an "Augustan" poet, a poet who wrote when Augustus was emperor.   The Augustan poets lived through the era that saw the end of the Civil Wars and the end of the Republican form of government, when Octavian, Julius Caesar's grandnephew and adopted son, defeated his rivals for supremacy, Antony and Cleopatra, at the battle of Actium (31 B.C.) and shortly afterwards became the first Roman emperor (or *princeps*, as he was styled), adopting the name Augustus.   In his principate there ensued a period of comparative peace, order and political calm in Rome, although on the frontiers of the empire fighting with foreign enemies continued.   Externally Augustus improved the appearance of Rome by an ambitious programme of restoring old buildings and constructing new ones.   Internally he tried to bring about a moral and religious reform by passing laws against extravagance and immorality (for instance adultery was made a public crime), repairing temples and reviving ancient rites and ceremonies.

This was also a period of great literary achievement, when Livy wrote his famous history and most of the finest Latin poetry was produced.   Apart from Ovid there were three other gifted elegists (Gallus, Tibullus and Propertius), there was Horace, the best lyric poet of the day, and, of course, there was Virgil, author of the *Eclogues*, *Georgics* and *Aeneid* and generally considered to be the greatest poet ever produced by Rome.   Although

each of these poets is distinctive and individual, they all held
in common certain views on the nature of poetry.   In these views
they were largely influenced by another group of authors, the
"Hellenistic" (or "Alexandrian") poets, Greeks writing from about
the time of the death of Alexander the Great (323 B.C.) to the latter
part of the first century B.C., whose most famous members were
Callimachus, Theocritus and Apollonius of Rhodes.   Following
their lead, the Augustans produced sophisticated poetry, gener-
ally characterized by scholarship, cleverness, painstaking care
and high technical skill.   The Augustan poets were intellec-
tuals and cultured men, who were interested in religion, history
and geography, steeped in mythology and intimately acquainted
with the works of their literary predecessors (both Greek and
Roman).   Such erudition (*doctrina*) is present throughout their
writings and in the opinion of the authors themselves constituted
a vital feature of poetry.   The other main aspect of their over-
all sophistication is the close attention they paid to metre,
style and language.   They refined the various metres in which
they were working and showed much care and sensitivity in their
handling of sound and rhythm.   Numerous stylistic devices adorned
their work, and often did more than merely adorn, and they were
capable of producing a telling word or phrase and were well aware
of the tone and fine nuances of vocabulary.

       All of this made for elegant and professional poetry, but,
of course, this kind of sophistication can have its drawbacks.
Such scholarship can result in difficulty and obscurity (especi-
ally in the case of Propertius), and such polish can be charged
with excessive artificiality and superficiality (charges often
levelled at Virgil's *Eclogues* and Ovid).   To an extent perhaps
the criticism is justified, but, by way of compensation, there
are very real technical qualities in the poetry, and in addition
the humanity of Virgil and Horace should not be ignored, nor the
range and depth of feeling in Tibullus and Propertius, nor for
that matter Ovid's wit and humour.

3   LATIN LOVE-POETRY BEFORE OVID

       The first Latin love poet of any real importance was Gaius
Valerius Catullus (approx. 84-54 B.C.).   Most of his poetry is
concerned with love, in particular his affair with Lesbia.   The
name "Lesbia" was probably a pseudonym for Clodia, an aristo-
cratic married woman several years older than the poet, famous
for her beauty and accomplishments, but also notorious for her
lust and profligacy.   She is the woman whom Cicero attacked in
his speech *Pro Caelio*, in which he gives a vivid (if, no doubt,
rather exaggerated) picture of her way of life.   Although, of
course, it is always impossible to tell exactly to what extent
love poetry reflects actual emotions and experiences and how
much of it is embroidered or even invented, it seems that in the
early days of their affair Catullus was supremely happy and op-
timistic, but before long rivals appeared and Lesbia's infideli-
ties increased, until her behaviour moved the poet to extreme
bitterness and anger, and finally after a great internal struggle
he renounced her.   His poems (in a variety of metres) portray
vividly and movingly a whole range of emotions reflecting these
events - passion, verging on obsession, for Lesbia, sheer joy and

delight at first, suspicions and anxiety later, and finally des-
pair, rage and torment.   Dependent on mood, his writing moves from
tenderness and beauty to forceful outspokenness and scathing irony,
while his style and language vary from high poetry to gross abuse
and obscenity.

There is an air of freshness and spontaneity to Catullus'
poems, but his writing did have an intellectual as well as an emo-
tional side to it, and obviously this intellectual side of his work
was of extreme importance in the poet's eyes.   In many ways
Catullus was a forerunner of the Augustan poets.   He was a mem-
ber (probably a leading member) of a group of friends called the
"New Poets" (or "Neoterics"), who were responsible for a revo-
lution in Roman poetry.   They expanded the range of serious poetry,
adding love, wine and friends to its subjects;   they produced
writing that was intensely personal and subjective;   they paid
close attention to technique, linguistic innovation and experi-
mentation in metre and form;   they produced learned, allusive and
intellectual poetry, attaching much importance to *doctrina*.   In
these respects they were influenced by the Hellenistic (or Alex-
andrian) poets, and they bequeathed these Hellenistic leanings to
the Augustans.

The next important name in Latin love poetry is Gaius Corne-
lius Gallus, the first of the elegists.   Unfortunately only one
line of his works survives (*6), and so our knowledge of his
poetry is severely restricted.   He was born round about 69 B.C.
and after distinguishing himself as a soldier and administrator
was made the first Prefect of Egypt by Augustus.   Later, however,
he was relieved of this post in disgrace and committed suicide in
26 B.C. He wrote four books of love elegies (probably entitled
Amores)addressed to his mistress Lycoris (a pseudonym, we are told,
for the Greek actress Cytheris).   It is probable that mythology
played a part in his poems (*7), and his friend Virgil's tenth
Eclogue, which was in part based on Gallus' own poetry (*8), sugg-
ests that Lycoris was cruel to him.   Beyond this nothing is
certain.

Sextus Propertius was born in about 50 B.C. and died some
time between 16 B.C. and 2 A.D.   Cynthia was the name of his
girlfriend, and it is she and the theme of love which dominate
the first three of his four books.   We are informed that "Cynthia"
was a pseudonym for Hostia (*9), but her exact status is hard to
decide (she may or may not be depicted as a married woman).
Propertius has been described as the first neurotic of European
literature, and, although he could write in a detached and witty
manner, he does more often show involvement, usually intense and
passionate involvement, in his amatory relations.   The feelings
in his poems tend to run to extremes, occasionally extremes of
happiness, but most frequently extremes of despair, anguish and
misery.   Yet at the same time he was aware that others too were
in love, and, more important, his own experiences and sufferings
(not to mention his knowledge of earlier love poetry) meant that
he was particularly qualified to pass remarks on the whole phenom-
enon of love to the less sophisticated.   So we often find him
taking on the pose of an expert, making learned observations
and offering advice to the world in general or friends in

particular.

Propertius is also a notoriously difficult poet. His
language, grammar and imagery are often very bold, and his pro-
gression of thought can be abrupt.   The resultant effect is
complex, flamboyant and individual, if at times obscure, and
Propertius often reaches heights to which the other elegists
never even aspire.   His difficulty is increased (for us at any
rate) by his *doctrina*.   None of the elegists is as ready to
introduce learned allusions (especially to mythology).   Al-
though Propertius does at times seem simply to show off his
knowledge, he can use these erudite references to good effect -
to produce background-colouring, to avoid the more obvious or
prosaic mode of expression, to back up a point that he is mak-
ing or to elevate his mistress and his love-affair.   Such
scholarship was very important to Propertius, as he himself
acknowledges, and gives his work a particular colouring. This
is the type of very ingenious and allusive poetry that came
back in vogue in the twentieth century.

Albius Tibullus (approx. 50-19 B.C.) is altogether more
restrained.   In his short life he wrote only two books of
elegies.   In the first book his mistress (not a married woman)
is called Delia, which is said to be a pseudonym for Plania(*9),
and he also has a boyfriend called Marathus, while in the second
he has a new girlfriend called Nemesis (also apparently unmarried).
Love is his commonest theme, and in his poetry we see a wide range
of emotions (generally less violent than those of Propertius).
In line with these feelings we find a range of attitudes to love.
Most often the tone is one of involvement and the poet's behaviour
is humble and obsequious towards his girl or boy, but Tibullus at
times took stern, superior and amused stances too.   Although
there are occasional outbursts of anger, in his writing he comes
over as a sensitive, thoughtful and rather gentle person, with a
tendency towards melancholy and a longing for days gone by.

Doctrina appears less frequently and less obtrusively in
Tibullus than in the other elegists.   His style shows a similar
restraint.   Generally speaking his poetry is a good example of
"artistic simplicity" - it seems simple on the surface, but this
simplicity is deliberate and produced by a great deal of skill,
and usually there is much more to what he writes than appears at
first sight.   Tibullus is subtle and unostentatious, and his
writing is characterized by lucidity, sensitivity, a lightness
of touch and a gentle charm and grace, generally free from the
flamboyance of Propertius and the dazzling virtuosity of Ovid.

Something else that distinguishes Tibullus from the other
elegists is the air of greater thoughtfulness and depth to his
poetry.   The countryside is an important theme (unlike Proper-
tius and Ovid, he likes to set his love-affair with Delia there),
and although his writing suggests a fondness for the Italian
country itself, what seems to have particularly attracted him
was the idea of its honest toil, modest standard of living and
simple country gods.   Closely bound up with his love for the
countryside is Tibullus' moralizing.   A sentiment not unnatu-
ral for the period in which he was living was his detestation

of war and love of peace.   Connected with this was his hatred
of greed, since he believed that the desire to acquire wealth
in the form of booty was a major cause of war.   Religion is
another important and kindred feature of Tibullan poetry.   He
appears as a pious and devout man, who firmly believes in the
gods.   Although he refers most often to the Olympians (especi-
ally the deities of love), he seems to have been particularly
attracted to the ancient Italian rustic gods and the old Roman
household-gods (Lares and Penates).   In fact, Tibullus states
that he finds the piety and morality of the past (either in the
early days of Rome or in the mythical Golden Age) preferable to
the life-style of contemporary Rome, and he bases his own ideal
way of life on that (*10).

(4)   OVID AS A LOVE-POET

Ovid presents a marked change from Catullus, Propertius
and Tibullus.   In his love-poetry (*Amores, Heroides, Ars Ama-
toria* and *Remedia Amoris*) one characteristic stands out above
all - his sophistication, which is even more developed and
widespread than in the other elegists.   Ovid hardly ever lets
the mask of elegance and refinement slip, and his whole atti-
tude to love is that of a superior expert and somewhat blasé
connoisseur, not without a degree of urbane cynicism.   This
tone is evident throughout the *Ars*, but earlier too: in
Amores 1.5, for instance, when his mistress Corinna comes to
see him in a revealing dress he pulls it off, describing her
rather feeble resistance as merely token or a tease (*victa
est non aegre proditione sua*, 16), and when she now stands be-
fore him naked, although not unmoved, he gives a calm appraisal
of her attractions, finally tiring of needlessly listing all
her good points (17ff.).

In line with this sophisticated pose is Ovid's general air
of detachment, based on experience and expertise.   Although he
shows insight into the psychology of the lover and (especially
in the *Heroides* and book three of the *Ars*) of women, he him-
self seldom seems deeply involved in or disturbed by love.   He
often analyses amatory phenomena in a rather clinical fashion,
and, unlike his intense and passionate predecessors, he makes
little of the hardships of the lover, frequently accepting them
with relish and even turning them into a joke (often at his own
expense).   So he appears in his poetry as a civilized and slight-
ly mocking man of the world, who regards love as something not
to be taken too seriously or solemnly, as an interesting and
generally rather pleasant game.   In the *Ars* he actually pro-
vides a set of rules for the players.

A truly sophisticated man can hardly fail to be amused from
time to time by love and the antics of lovers, and Ovid is fre-
quently flippant and frivolous.   He is quick to see the humour
in an amatory situation.   So his advice to short girls on how
to appear to their best advantage is: *si brevis es, sedeas, ne
stans videare sedere* (*11) ("if you are short, sit down; other-
wise when you stand up people will think you are sitting down").
His humour can be quite outrageous, as when he makes the rather
serious and sordid business of being suspected (rightly) of

having an affair with his mistress' maid highly entertaining:
in two adjoining poems (*Amores* 2.7 and 2.8) he first strongly
denies the charge on oath to his mistress, then points out to
the maid that his perjury has saved them, and demands that she
reward him by going to bed with him, adding that if she refuses
he will reveal everything to her mistress. This flippant atti-
tude is evident in Ovid's language too, as he delights in play-
ing with words and producing clever and provocative puns.
For instance, he says that just as soldiers find it advantage-
ous to attack when their enemy is asleep, so lovers too engage
in night-operations: *nempe maritorum somnis utuntur amantes/
et sua sopitis hostibus arma movent* (*12) ("of course, lovers
make use of the sleep of husbands and ply their weapons while
their enemy is slumbering"). The wit often lies in the
thought too. So in *Amores* 2.15, a poem accompanying the gift
of a ring to his mistress, he indulges in a clever and amusing
fantasy in which by being magically changed into the ring he
can manage all sorts of things (dropping off her finger into
her bra, being kissed by her when she uses the ring to seal a
letter (he hopes that then he will not be sealing his own fate)
and staying with her always, even when she takes a bath).
This levity also extended to the morality, conventions and
respected professions of Rome (see, e.g., the digression on
the rape of the Sabine women in your selection), and at times
Ovid was even irreverent at the expense of the emperor him-
self (*13).

    Ovid's technical mastery is another aspect of his sophis-
tication. Most of his poems in the *Amores* and *Heroides* are
structurally elegant, and in the *Ars* and *Remedia Amoris* he
takes pains to order his material neatly and clearly. Care
also went into the arrangement of individual poems or sections,
often to produce contrast or correspondence in tone, motif or
setting. Similar refinement is evident in his style and
metre, especially in the smoothness of his verse and the ingen-
uity of his expression (see further section 8 below), and
Ovid was very skilful at producing vivid, swift-moving narra-
tive and epigrammatic turns of phrase (e.g. *casta est quam nemo
rogavit* (*14) = "the chaste girl is the one that nobody has
asked" and *successore novo vincitur omnis amor* (*15) = "every
love is ousted by a new love"). Ovid also handled a large
number of amatory themes and situations, and he was always
eager to add novel details, give old ones a new twist and pres-
ent a full treatment.

    The final feature of his overall sophistication, his
doctrina, Ovid shared with his contemporaries and Catullus.
Ovid too was a very erudite and scholarly writer, and he was
particularly fond of literary and mythological allusions.
With his tendency to ingenuity and fullness he can at times
become carried away in his lists of learned references (*16),
just as at times he overdoes things in piling up arguments,
examples and illustrations. But his learning is generally
apt and interesting, often ingenious and amusing, and at times
the whole point is the twist that he gives to a myth or a line
from another author. So, for instance, in *Aeneid* 6 Aeneas
was solemnly warned that the descent to the Underworld is easy

but the return is not (*sed revocare gradum superasque evadere ad auras,/hoc opus, hic labor est* (*17) = "but to recall your steps and pass out to the air above - this is the task, this the toil"). The reminiscence of Virgil's final phrase there and its transference to an outrageous new context is responsible for so much of the humour in the following Ovidian remark to the lover: *hoc opus, hic labor est, primo sine munere iungi* (*18) ("this is the task, this the toil - to copulate without giving a present first").

So much, then, for Ovid, the last Roman to write love-poetry worthy of the name. One seldom feels that he is a passionate or infatuated lover; rather, he appears to be playing around with motifs, characters and situations cleverly and dexterously. This has led to criticism that he is shallow and insincere and to the claim that his love-poetry lacks something that is found in his Roman predecessors. Certainly his elegies do not contain the emotional range and depth depicted in Catullus, Propertius and Tibullus, but it is inane to criticize his poetry for absence of reality and sincerity simply because he seldom *seems* involved, just as it is foolish to claim categorically that the other three love-poets are faithfully recording true events and feelings simply because they usually do *seem* involved. We have no way of telling exactly the amount of fact and fiction in the poetry of any one of them, and, for all we know, in real life Ovid may have actually been a rather detached and blasé type of lover. What we do know is that Ovid consciously aimed at producing poetry that would entertain rather than deeply move and that he presented to the world this picture of himself as the urbane and flippant connoisseur deliberately. Whether one prefers that character to the figure of the intense and sentimental lover is largely a matter of personal taste, but historically there was a good reason for Ovid's choice. After the generally serious and emotional approach of his three Latin predecessors Ovid was in danger of boring his readers by producing the same sort of stuff. Intelligently he decided to do something new, and so he refined and made his own the figure of the sophisticated and amused expert, thereby, I think, making an important and worthwhile contribution to Latin love-poetry.

⑤ THE ARS AMATORIA

The *Ars Amatoria* and *Remedia Amoris* were written round about the time of the birth of Christ (*19). Originally Ovid planned the *Ars* in two books, and it was to consist of advice to men on how to conduct a successful love-affair, divided under the headings of finding a girl, winning her and keeping her (*20). At a later stage (*21) he added a third book containing similar advice for women. (Taking this process of reversal one stage further, he then produced the *Remedia Amoris*, a single book on how to terminate a love-affair successfully.)

The *Ars* (and the *Remedia*) technically belongs to a genre called "didactic". Briefly a didactic poem was one that gave

> instruction on a particular skill or area of knowledge

instruction concerning a particular skill or branch of know-
ledge.   The Greeks invented the genre, and its first expo-
nent was Hesiod (8th or 7th century B.C.), whose *Works and
Days* concerns agriculture and combines tips on farming with
proverbial sayings, moralizing and digressions.   Later Greek
didactic works (especially common among the Hellenistic poets)
were on the subject of theology and the nature of the universe,
agriculture again, venomous reptiles, antidotes to poison and
astronomy.   The Romans picked up this genre, and there are
two famous Latin examples - Lucretius' *De Rerum Natura* (Epi-
curean philosophy), produced in the Republican period, and,
still a number of years before the *Ars*, Virgil's *Georgics*
(on farming).   In addition there were some rather boring did-
actic poems on hunting (*22) and astronomy and astrology (*23)
written in the Augustan period, as well as some on less seri-
ous subjects such as etiquette, games, pottery (*24) and cos-
metics (Ovid's own *Medicamina Faciei Femineae*).   Didactic,
then, was a well-established genre, and much in vogue during
Ovid's own lifetime.

    Instruction on the subject of love was not new: it had
already occurred in Roman elegy (*25) and even earlier (*26).
As is so often the case with Ovid, his originality lies not
so much in the idea itself as in the way in which he expands
upon it, producing for the first time a full didactic poem on
the subject.   Of course, the *Ars* is not seriously intended
as a practical handbook, but is humorous in both intent and
execution.   The whole concept of the poem is a joke.   The
general view of love at this time (as occasionally now) was
that it was irrational, a bewildering and rather chaotic ex-
perience, a phenomenon virtually impossible to control.   Tradi-
tionally the lover was totally in the grip of his passion, in
a mental turmoil, completely helpless and forced to go against
the dictates of good sense.   Yet in the *Ars* Ovid lays down
rules for love and teaches it systematically with a very rat-
ional and scientific approach.   So in books I and II he
makes the three main divisions noted above, then sub-divides
and presents each individual precept in a detached, learned
and carefully ordered fashion (*27).   There is additional
humour in the fact that the Romans generally regarded love
as a very trivial thing and love-poetry as one of the humblest
forms of literature, but for this "worthless" subject Ovid in
the *Ars* (with deliberate inconsistency) chooses a serious and
rather lofty genre (didactic).   In fact, the *Ars* is not so
much a didactic poem as a mock-didactic poem.   One way in
which a parody works is by mocking its original by placing
it in a frivolous context, and this is exactly what Ovid does
in the *Ars Amatoria*.   Instead of instruction on how to tell
the different constellations or on the physical composition
of the universe the poem contains hints on the most likely
places for picking up a mistress or how to chat up a girl.
He makes the parody even closer by imitating some of the
characteristic features of didactic.   So he often uses that
genre's elevated language and its terms and formulae (e.g.
common expressions to introduce a new point such as *principio*,
nunc age, *adde quod*, *interea* and *ergo* - all found in Lucretius
and Virgil).   Similarly he picks up some of the set-pieces

of didactic, such as the list of contents (*28), the recapit-
ulation (*29) and the conclusion (*30).   Like the didactic
poets, he introduces analogies from other occupations (*31),
from nature (*32) and from mythology (*33), and, like them,
he varies his advice with picturesque digressions (e.g. the
rape of the Sabine women, the stories of Pasiphae, Ariadne
and the affair between Mars and Venus).   So too he often
quotes or alludes to specific details, ideas, phrases, lines
and passages in his didactic predecessors.   This mock-didac-
tic element gives the *Ars* its framework and holds it together,
as well as adding to the humour.

        Although it might seem that the whole joke of the *Ars*
and the whole idea of instruction on love would be enough to
engage and interest the reader, the poem does go on for some
2,330 lines, and in view of its length there was a danger of
monotony.   Ovid fully realized this and did his best to avoid
it.   All his general characteristics mentioned in the prev-
ious section are present in the *Ars* and continually enliven
it.   His pose as the connoisseur and detached expert, his (of-
ten outrageous) frivolity, his great technical skills (includ-
ing his narrative powers) and his learning are all very much
in evidence.   At times scandalously cynical remarks increase
the fun (34), and at times he teases and intrigues the reader
by disguising or concealing his real point for several lines.
So too the expert's psychological insight is frequently evident
(e.g. the reader is told to conceal his infidelities from most
girls, but to reveal them to some - the type that actually
need a rival to stir them up).   In addition, in the narrative
pieces his delight in the grotesque is sometimes apparent and
adds greatly to the interest.   So, for instance, he gives his
version of the story of Pasiphae, who fell in love with a
bull (*35), and takes pleasure in depicting at length what he
thinks the woman would have felt and done in this bizarre and
rather absurd situation: she cuts the finest grass for her
bull-lover; she wishes that she had horns; she is enraged
when some heifer takes her lover's eye and immediately has
her taken away and set to ploughing or sacrificed to the gods.
Another entertaining aspect of the *Ars* is the way in which
it can take a satirical turn and pass some penetrating social
observations, as when Ovid talks about the small number of
really cultured girls and the much larger number of girls
who are not cultured but wish that they were, or when he ex-
plains the tricks of women for extorting money from the lover,
such as having numerous birthdays, begging for little pres-
ents continually and pretending to have lost a precious ear-
ring that needs replacing.   I might add that when one looks
a little deeper into the poem it is often possible to see an
underlying element of humanity (Ovid does recommend overall
civilized conduct in relations with the girl, albeit with an
ulterior motive).   Finally, of course, there always the vivid
glimpses of Roman life so dear to the Victorians that the poem
contains (the resort of Baiae (a sort of Roman Brighton), the
forums, crowds, games, fashions, triumphs and the theatre).
The mixture of these several elements and the way in which now
one, now another is brought into particular prominence success-

fully hold the attention and make for constant variety.

(6)   SCANSION

Quantity   : To scan one must first be able to recognize short
(◡) and long (–) syllables.

A syllable is *short* if it ends in a short vowel
alone or a short vowel plus one consonant only (not foll-
owed by another consonant in the same or a following word):
e.g. *mensă* (nominative), *ămăt ĕăm*.

A syllable is *long* if its vowel is long by nat-
ure or is followed by two or more consonants (whether
in the same word or not (*36)) or a double letter (z
and x): e.g. *mēnsā* (ablative), *rēx*, *tūm lĭcet*.   Dipthongs
(ae, ai, au, ei, eu, oe when pronounced as one syllable)
are long by nature: e.g. *mēnsāe*.

Correct pronunciation is generally the only
guide to determining whether a vowel is long or short by
nature (see Kennedy's *Revised Latin Primer*, where long
vowels are marked), but, in any case, a line can usually
be made to scan by trial and error.

N.B.   The letter h is ignored in scansion (so put a
line through it).

The letter i may be a vowel (as in *ineptus*) or
a consonant (as in *iam*).

For scansional purposes qu counts as a single con-
sonant (e.g. *mēnsăquĕ*).

When a short vowel is followed by certain combin-
ations of consonants (provided that they both occur in
the same word/syllable) the syllable may be long or short.
These combinations are: bl, br, cl, chl, cr, chr, dr, fl,
fr, gl, gr, pl, pr, tr, thr (it will be easiest to remem-
ber the final letters: l and r): e.g. *pătres* or *pātres*
(*37).

Elision   : If a word ending in a vowel or a vowel plus m
is followed by a word beginning with a vowel (or, of
course, h plus a vowel), the first vowel is cut off and
ignored for scansion (so put a line through it): e.g.
illă ĕrăt, mēnsăm hŭmĕrōs (*38).

Hexameter : The hexameter consists of six units (feet).

A foot in the hexameter has two variations: the
spondee (two longs – –) and the dactyl (a long followed
by two shorts – ◡ ◡).

In the hexameter each of the first four feet may
be either a spondee or a dactyl, but the fifth foot is

almost always a dactyl and the sixth foot a spondee (or
a long followed by a short ($-\smile$): in most metres the
final syllable can be long or short).

Beginners find it easiest to mark in the last
two feet, then work out the rest of the line by marking
in syllables which must be long and next making up feet
on a trial and error basis.

Always check that you do have six feet and that
each foot is actually either a spondee or a dactyl.

If you make a mistake, try to see where it is
and start again.

The word caesura means a break between words
within a foot. Obviously a caesura may occur in any
foot. But each hexameter must have a main (central)
caesura, normally marked by a double line ($\parallel$). In
the hexameter this main caesura is usually in the third
foot, most commonly after the first syllable of the
foot (i.e. $-\parallel-$ or $-\parallel\smile\smile$); alternatively after the
second syllable of a dactyl (i.e. $-\smile\parallel\smile$). If there is
no caesura in the third foot, the main caesura is after
the first syllable of the fourth foot.

Examples:

(i) quis tibi, saeve puer, dedit hoc in carmina
     iuris.
(ii) conticuere omnes intentique ora tenebant
(iii) inde toro pater Aeneas sic orsus ab alto
(iv) et quorum pars magna fui. quis talia fando
(v) unius in miseri exitium conversa tulere

Beginners should find it useful to follow this
procedure in scanning hexameters:

1   cross out the letter h and elisions;
2   mark in the final two feet;
3   mark in syllables that must be long in the
   first four feet;
4   make up the first four feet on a trial and
   error basis;
5   check that you have six feet and that all
   are dactyls or spondees;
6   mark in the main caesura.

Pentameter : The pentameter is always the even-numbered, in-
dented line. Its name means "of five feet", but it is
better regarded as falling into two halves of 2½ feet
each ($-\overset{\smile}{\smile}\mid-\overset{\smile}{\smile}\mid-\parallel-\smile\smile\mid-\smile\smile\mid-$).

Each of the first two feet may be either a dactyl
or a spondee, but the rest of the line is fixed as in the
diagram above (again the final syllable can be long or
short).

Beginners find it easiest to work from the end
of the line and mark in all except the first two feet,
and then to mark in syllables that must be long and make
up the first two feet by trial and error.

Always check that you do have 2½ plus 2½ feet.

If you make a mistake, try to see where it is
and start again.

The main caesura always occurs exactly half
way through the line (after the first 2½ feet).

Examples:

  (i) et teneat culti iugera multa soli
  (ii) libatum agricolae ponitur ante deo
  (iii) et vidi nullo concutiente mori
  (iv) ut domus hostiles praeferat exuvias
  (v) cum mea ridebunt vana magisteria

Beginners should find it useful to follow this
procedure in scanning pentameters:

1   cross out the letter h and elisions;
2   mark in all except the first two feet;
3   mark in syllables that must be long in
    the first two feet;
4   make up the first two feet by trial and
    error;
5   check that you have 2½ plus 2½ feet;
6   mark in the main caesura.

7. METRICAL AND STYLISTIC EFFECTS

One of the most noteworthy aspects of Ovid's poetry is
its great technical skill.   The ease and facility of his
verse and the ingenuity of his arrangement of words are truly
remarkable and form an integral part of his qualities as a
poet.   A full study of Ovid's metre and style is beyond the
scope of this book, but it did seem worthwhile to indicate
the main points of interest.   Readers should be warned that
much of what follows is subjective (especially in the case
of metrical effects).   It is not always easy to be sure that
what one sees in the poetry was deliberate, and often the
reader has to be guided by his own sensibility.   However,
Ovid was a supreme artist, and I suspect that modern scholars
actually miss much of his skill and cleverness.

The elegiac couplet of Catullus (the first important
writer of Latin elegy that has survived in any quantity) was
in many ways very different from that of Ovid.   For instance,
Catullus' elegies typically contained pentameters ending in
words of various lengths, had numerous elisions and were
rather spondaic by nature, with sentences often extending
over a number of couplets.   Propertius and Tibullus, who seem
to have found their predecessor's handling of metre either

rather clumsy or unsuitable to their own tone and approach,
began a process of reaction and development, and this proc-
ess culminated in Ovid.   The Propertian and Tibullan ten-
dency towards a disyllabic ending in the pentameter reaches
its logical conclusion in Ovid, who almost invariably ends
his pentameters thus;   his elegiacs also contain few elisions
and a much higher preponderance of dactyls;   so too his sen-
tences rarely extend beyond a couplet - in fact couplets
often consist of a number of short clauses.   All of this
means that the Ovidian elegiac couplet is rather rigid in its
format (although Ovid takes great pains to avoid monotony),
but it also means that it has a smoothness and lightness
eminently suitable to the tone of his poetry, while with the
shorter sense-unit he excelled in producing balance, contrast
and similarly ingenious points of style.

    A number of metrical effects enhance Ovid's verse.
Alliteration (the repetition of the same initial letter in
closely succeeding words) is common.   Often it is used
simply to produce pleasant music or an intricate pattern of
sound:

    (i) *monte minor collis, campis erat altior aequis;*
                                      *(A.A.*2.71)
    (ii) *arma dedi vobis;   dederat Vulcanus Achilli:*
                                      *(A.A.*2.741)

At times it seems to have a more serious purpose.   So there
is sadness in the repeated m in the following line from Ovid's
funeral-elegy for Tibullus:

       Memnona si mater, mater ploravit Achillem
                                 *(Am.*3.9.1)

Again, after Ovid has recommended that the lover at the races
should lift up a girl's cloak if it is trailing on the ground,
there seems to be excitement in the alliteration of p and c
when he goes on to say:

       protinus, officii pretium, patiente puella
         contingent oculis crura videnda tuis.
                              *(A.A.*1.155f.)

Alliteration can also add a certain vigour and forcefulness,
as when Ovid advises the lover to be free with promises:

       nec timide promitte: trahunt promissa puellas;
         pollicito testes quoslibet adde deos.
                              *(A.A.*1.631f.)

or when Daedalus says to Minos:

       si non vis puero parcere, parce seni   *(A.A.*2.30)

    Another common metrical effect is assonance (rhyming
vowel-sounds).   Like alliteration, often its purpose is simply
to produce pleasant music, as in the second half of the pen-

tameter in the following couplet:

> *dum fallax servus, durus pater, improba lena*
> *vivent et meretrix blanda, Menandros erit;*
> (Am.1.15.17f.)

Assonance too can be used for a deeper purpose.   Note the
(mock-) sad o and ae sounds in the following lines on the
death of Corinna's parrot:

> *quid referam timidae pro te pia vota puellae,*
> *vota procelloso per mare rapta Noto?*
> (Am.2.6.43f.)

An advanced use of the above effects is onomatopoeia,
whereby words sound like what they are describing.   The re-
peated p sound in the following line suggests the beating
of feathery breasts:

> *ite, piae volucres, et plangite pectora pinnis*
> (Am.2.6.3)

Similarly when Ovid describes Ariadne beating her breasts and
the sudden appearance of noisy Bacchanals the sounds in the
Latin reproduce the actual sounds:

> *iamque iterum tundens mollissima pectora palmis*
> *"perfidus ille abiit: quid mihi fiet?" ait.*
> *"quid mihi fiet?" ait; sonuerunt cymbala toto*
> *litore et adtonita tympana pulsa manu.*
> (A.A.1.535-8)

Another musical effect is rhyme, which takes a variety
of forms in Ovid.   For instance, there is "internal rhyme"
(rhyme between the word immediately before the caesura and
the final word of the line).   Sometimes the same internal
rhyme is found in both hexameter and pentameter:

> *nam modo Threicio Borea, modo currimus Euro;*
> *saepe tument Zephyro lintea, saepe Noto.*
> (A.A.2.431f.)

There is sometimes rhyme between the first and last words of
the line too:

> (i) *ardet, et in vultu pignora mentis habet;*
> (A.A.2.378)
> (ii) *invenit, et lumen quod fuit ante, redit:*
> (A.A.2.442)

More intricate patterns of rhyme also occur:

> (i) *evocat antiquis proavos atavosque sepulcris*
> (Am.1.8.17)
> (ii) *hos petit in socio bella puella viro:*
> (Am.1.9.6)
> (iii) *culta Palaestino septima festa Syro.* (A.A.1.416)

The final metrical feature to be covered in this brief
account is rhythm.   Although Ovid did in general prefer his
verse to be dactylic, at times the dactyls seem to be per-
forming a function beyond that of simply making the verse
light.   So they convey the speed and excitement of the Romans
and the panic of their quarry in the following passage on the
rape of the Sabine women:

> *protinus exiliunt animum clamore fatentes*
> *virginibus cupidas iniciuntque manus;*
> *ut fugiunt aquilas, timidissima turba, columbae*
> *utque fugit visos agna novella lupos,*
> *sic illae timuere viros sine more ruentes;*
> *constitit in nulla qui fuit ante color.*
>   *(A.A.*1.115-120)

Again, in *Amores* 1.5 Ovid describes an afternoon seduction
of Corinna, and the dactylic nature of the poem's final line
suggests well the poet's buoyancy and lightheartedness:

> *proveniant medii sic mihi saepe dies!*
>   *(Am.*1.5.26)

Spondaic lines generally have the opposite effect.   So in
his elegy addressed to Dawn they represent slowness and weari-
ness:

> *te surgit quamvis lassus veniente viator*
> *et miles saevas aptat ad arma manus;*
>   *(Am.*1.13.13f.)

His funeral-elegy for Tibullus opens with a heavily spondaic
couplet that conveys a suitable air of sadness and solemn-
ity:

> *Memnona si mater, mater ploravit Achillem,*
> *et tangunt magnas tristia fata deas,*
>   *(Am.*3.9.1f.)

Stylistic effects also abound in Ovid.   Particularly
common are balance (of parallels) and contrast (of oppo-
sites).   Balance may extend to one line only:

> *saevus uterque puer, natus uterque dea.*
>   *(A.A.*1.18)

or to more than one line:

> *fertilior seges est alienis semper in agris,*
> *vicinumque pecus grandius uber habet.*
>   *(A.A.*1.349f.)

So too contrast may be made within a single line:

> *altera maesta silet, frustra vocat altera matrem;*
>   *(A.A.*1.123)

or a couplet:

> *qui totiens socios, totiens exterruit hostes,*
>   *creditur annosum pertimuisse senem; (A.A.1.13f.)*

or even more than one couplet:

> *luce deas caeloque Paris spectavit aperto,*
>   *cum dixit Veneri "vincis utramque, Venus."*
> *nocte latent mendae...*   (A.A.1.247-9)

At times Ovid even produces a balance and a contrast within
the same couplet:

> *utque viro furtiva venus, sic grata puellae:*
>   *vir male dissimulat: tectius illa cupit.*
>   (A.A.1.275f.)

Chiasmus is a similar point of style and is achieved by
arranging words, clauses, details or ideas in an ABBA pat-
tern.   Thus in the following couplet we find the order:
serious love, dalliance, dalliance, serious love:

> *illic invenies quod ames, quod ludere possis,*
>   *quodque semel tangas, quodque tenere velis.*
>   (A.A.1.91f.)

Another ingenious arrangement is the tricolon crescendo
(a group of three in which each succeeding member is
longer than the last):

> *hic modus;   haec nostro signabitur area curru;*
> *haec erit admissa meta premenda rota.*
>   (A.A.1.39f.)

The reverse process is known as a tricolon diminuendo (each
of the three members is shorter than the last):

> *principio, quod amare velis, reperire labora,*
>   *qui nova nunc primum miles in arma venis;*
> *proximus huic labor est placitam exorare puellam;*
>   *tertius, ut longo tempore duret amor.*
>   (A.A.1.35-38)

Juxtaposition is the name given to the process of plac-
ing words next to each other for special effect.   Ovid
juxtaposes words to give emphasis:

> *ipsa nemus tacito clam pede fortis init.*
>   (A.A.3.712)

(note here the way that stealth is brought out by the group-
ing together of *tacito* and *clam*).   By placing persons next
to each other in the word-order Ovid reflects the actual
connection between people in real life:

> *Hippolytum Phaedra, nec erat bene cultus, amavit;*
>   (A.A.1.511)

Similarly the collocation *oculos oculis* suggests well the

interlocking gaze of ardent lover and girl in the following
line:

>   *atque oculos oculis spectare fatentibus ignem:*
>   *(A.A.*1.573)

Ovid also likes to juxtapose opposites, such as the soft back
of a girl and the hard knee of the man sitting behind her in
the following pentameter:

>   *respice praeterea, post vos quicumque sedebit,*
>   *ne premat opposito mollia terga genu.*
>   *(A.A.*1.157f.)

(note also that, as in the word-order, the back and the knee
would be actually touching). So too unwillingness and will-
ingness are placed next to each other:

>   *haec quoque, quam poteris credere nolle, volet.*
>   *(A.A.*1.274)

A more ingenious and complex example occurs when the colour
white is followed by white and then by red:

>   *candida, candorem roseo suffusa rubore,*
>   *ante fuit...*   *(Am.*3.3.5f.)

"Framing" is the term applied to another skilful arrange-
ment of words (the positioning of a noun and an adjective
agreeing with it at far ends of the line):

>   (i) *purpureus Bacchi cornua pressit Amor,* *(A.A.*1.232)
>   *(ii) officio est illi poena reperta suo;* *(Am.*3.3.38)

The "golden line" takes this process a little further. A
golden line is made up of a pair of nouns with a pair of
adjectives in agreement separated from their nouns by a
verb, as in the following examples:

>   (i) *ferreus adsiduo consumitur anulus usu,*
>   *(A.A.*1.473)
>   (ii) *nec tepidus pluvias concitat Auster aquas;*
>   *(A.A.*3.174)

Ovid was also fond of repeating words. Anaphora
(the repetition of a word or phrase at the beginning of
successive clauses, sentences, couplets or lines) may be
used simply as a rather neat point of style in itself, as
in the following couplet:

>   *plaudite Neptuno, nimium qui creditis undis...*
>   *plaude tuo Marti, miles...*   *(Am.*3.2.47-9)

But it can also be employed to impart emphasis. So when
Ovid advises the lover to keep away from girls on days when
it is customary to give presents he drives home his point
by repeating *tunc:*

differ opus: tunc tristis hiems, tunc Pliades instant,
tunc tener aequorea mergitur Haedus aqua;
tunc bene desinitur;   tunc si quis creditur alto,
vix tenuit lacerae naufraga membra ratis.
                                              *(A.A.*1.409-12)

Anaphora may indicate emotional intensity, as when Ovid explains
that in contemporary Rome friendship and good faith are mere
empty names:

nomen amicitia est, nomen inane fides.
                                              *(A.A.*1.740)

In the following lines (of Daedalus looking for his drowned
son Icarus) the repetition indicates emotional intensity and
also represents the actual echoing of the father's cries of
"Icare":

at pater infelix, nec iam pater, "Icare" clamat,
"Icare," clamat, "ubi es, quove sub axe volas?"
"Icare" clamabat...   *(A.A.*2.93-5)

The other forms of repetition in Ovid are too numerous and
varied to discuss in detail or classify here, but listed be-
low are examples of the commonest variations:

(i) *Memnona si mater, mater ploravit Achillem*
                                     *(Am.*3.9.1)
(ii) *cum tibi sint fratres, fratres ulciscere laesos,*
                                     *(A.A.*1.195)
(iii) *quid referam timidae pro te pia vota puellae,*
      vota procelloso per mare rapta Noto?
                                     *(Am.*2.6.43f.)
(iv) *ut iam fallaris, tuta repulsa tua est.*
      sed cur fallaris...   *(A.A.*1.346f.)
(v)   *et qui spectavit vulnera, vulnus habet:*
                                     *(A.A.*1.166)
(vi) *it comes armentis, nec ituram cura moratur*
                                     *(A.A.*1.301)
(vii)   *ne dederit gratis quae dedit, usque dabit.*
                                     *(A.A.*1.454)
(viii)   *multa dedit populo vulnera, multa dabit.*
                                     *(A.A.*1.262)
(ix)   *quo facilis dominae mens sit et apta capi;*
      mens erit apta capi tum, cum...   *(A.A.*1.358f.)
(x) *spectatum veniunt, veniunt spectentur ut ipsae;*
                                     *(A.A.*1.99)
(xi) *nam timor unus erat, facies non una timoris:*
                                     *(A.A.*1.121)
(xii) *tuta frequensque via est, per amici fallere nomen:*
      tuta frequensque licet sit via, crimen habet.
                                     *(A.A.*1.585f.)
(xiii) *utque fit, in gremium pulvis si forte puellae*
       deciderit, digitis excutiendus erit;
      etsi nullus erit pulvis, tamen excute nullum:
                                     *(A.A.*1.149-51)
(xiv) *cum surgit, surges;   donec sedet illa, sedebis:*
                                     *(A.A.*1.503)

(xv)   *qui canit arte, canat; qui bibit arte, bibat.*
                                             (A.A.2.506)
(xvi)   *ut ameris, amabilis esto;*
                                             (A.A.2.107)
(xvii) *si non accipiet scriptum, inlectumque remittet,*
       lecturam spera...   *(A.A.1.469f.)*
(xviii)   *semibovemque virum semivirumque bovem,*
                                             (A.A.2.24)

Particularly worth noting is the repetition of a word
at the beginning and end of a line:

     pauper amet caute: timeat maledicere pauper,
                                             (A.A.2.167)

or at the start and close of a couplet:

     Iuppiter ad veteres supplex heroidas ibat:
     corrupit magnum nulla puella Iovem. (A.A.1.713f.)

With his ingenuity Ovid even managed to open and close a coup-
let with the same group of words:

   (i) *ante veni quam vir; nec quid, si veneris ante,*
       possit agi video, sed tamen ante veni.
                                             (Am.1.4.13f.)

   (ii) *militat omnis amans, et habet sua castra Cupido;*
        Attice, crede mihi, militat omnis amans.
                                             (Am.1.9.1f.)

One final point worth mentioning is emphatic position.
A word could be given emphasis by being placed at the begin-
ning or end of sentences, clauses and lines.

8   FURTHER READING

EDITIONS OF THE ARS

H. Bornecque	*L'Art d'Aimer* (Budé) Paris, 1924 (with notes)
P. Brandt	*De Arte Amatoria Libri Tres* repr. Hildesheim, 1963 (with commentary)
M.J. Griggs	*Ovid Ars Amatoria Selections* London, 1971 (with commentary)
A.S. Hollis	*Ovid Ars Amatoria Book I* Oxford, 1977 (with full commentary)
E.J. Kenney	*Amores, Medicamina Faciei Femineae* etc. Oxford Classical Text, 1965
F.W. Lenz	*Ars Amatoria* Turin, 1969
F.W. Lenz	*Ars Amatoria* Berlin, 1969 (with commentary)

TRANSLATIONS OF THE ARS

J.H. Mozley	*The Art of Love, and Other Poems* (Loeb) London, 1929 (1969)

P. Turner   *Ovid The Technique of Love. Remedies for
                    Love* London, 1968 (highly recommended)

METRE

M.C. Platnauer   *Latin Elegiac Verse* Cambridge, 1951 (repr.
                    1971 Archon)
D.S. Raven   *Latin Metre.   An Introduction* London, 1965

WORKS ON OVID

J. Barsby   *Ovid: Amores Book I* (text and commentary)
                    Oxford, 1973
J. Barsby   *Ovid* (Greece & Rome New Surveys in the Clas-
                    sics 12) Oxford, 1978
J.W. Binns (ed.)   *Ovid* (Greek and Latin Studies) London, 1973
H. Fraenkel   *Ovid, A Poet Between Two Worlds* repr. Berke-
                    ley, 1969
N.I. Herescu (ed.) *Ovidiana* Paris, 1958
A.G. Lee   *Ovid's Amores* London, 1968 (an excellent
                    translation plus text)
A.G. Lee   *Tenerorum Lusor Amorum* in *Critical Essays
                    on Roman Literature. Elegy & Lyric* (ed.
                    Sullivan) London, 1962
N. Rudd   *Lines of Enquiry* (chaps. 1 and 7) Cambridge,
                    1976
J.C. Thibault   *The Mystery of Ovid's Exile* Berkeley, 1964
L.P. Wilkinson   *Ovid Recalled* Cambridge, 1955
L.P. Wilkinson   *Ovid Surveyed* (an abridgement of the above)
                    Cambridge, 1962

GENERAL WORKS

A.A. Day   *The Origins of Latin Love-Elegy* repr.
                    Hildesheim, 1972
J. Higginbotham (ed.)
                    Greek and Latin Literature (chaps. 3
                    and 5) London, 1969
S. Lilja   *The Roman Elegists' Attitude to Women*
                    Helsinki, 1965
G. Luck   *The Latin Love Elegy* New York, 1960
J.K. Newman   *Augustus and the New Poetry* Collection Lato-
                    mus 88 (1967)
J.P. Sullivan (ed.)
                    *Critical Essays on Roman Literature.
                    Elegy and Lyric* London, 1962

9   NOTES ON THE INTRODUCTION

*1   Seneca *Contr.* 2.2.8.
*2   *Tristia* 2.207.
*3   e.g. *A.A.* 1.31ff.
*4   *Ex Ponto* 3.3.72.
*5   Biographers of Ovid are fortunate in that a great num-
     ber of details about his life are contained in his own
     writings, especially *Tristia* 2 (a lengthy apologia) and
     4.10 (an autobiography).   The above account is based
     largely on these two poems.

*6   *uno tellures dividit amne duas.*   In addition a papyrus
      with fragments of elegiac poetry almost certainly by
      Gallus has recently been discovered in Egypt.
*7   Parthenius of Nicaea dedicated to Gallus a collection
      of love-stories for use in his poetry.
*8   See Servius on *Ecl.*10.46.
*9   Apuleius *Apology* 10.
*10   There are a further two books of poems attributed to
      Tibullus, but they are now generally believed to be the
      work of other members of Messalla's (the patron of
      Tibullus) circle of poets.   These books include six
      rather disappointing elegies by a certain Lygdamus con-
      cerning a woman called Neaera and eleven charming short
      elegies on the subject of the love of the girl Sulpicia
      for a young man called Cerinthus.
*11   *A.A.*3.263.
*12   *Am.*1.9.25f.
*13   e.g. *Am.*1.2.51f., *A.A.*1.171ff.   It should not be assumed
      on the basis of this that Ovid was an outright opponent
      of the Establishment.   Rather, his wit and humour were
      all-embracing, and the solemn, the revered and the con-
      ventional offered particularly tempting targets.
*14   *Am.*1.8.43.
*15   *Rem.*462.
*16   e.g. *Am.*3.12.21ff.
*17   Virgil *Aen.*6.128f.
*18   *A.A.*1.453.
*19   On the question of date see Barsby *Ovid* (Greece and Rome
      New Surveys in the Classics 12), 4f.
*20   *A.A.*1.35-40.
*21   See *A.A.*2.745f.
*22   Grattius *Cynegetica.*
*23   Manilius *Astronomica.*
*24   See Ovid *Tristia* 2.471ff.
*25   Tibullus 1.4, 1.6, 1.8, Propertius passim (especially
      4.5), Ovid *Am.*1.4, 1.8.
*26   e.g. Moschus frag. 2, Bion frag. 13 (Gow), Plautus
      Mostellaria 157ff.
*27   Many sections begin with a clear statement of a general
      principle, followed by methods of application and analo-
      gies and/or examples.
*28   *A.A.*1.35ff.
*29   *A.A.*1.263ff., 2.1ff.
*30   *A.A.*2.732ff., 3.809ff.
*31   e.g. *A.A.*1.3f.
*32   e.g. *A.A.*1.57f.
*33   e.g. *A.A.*1.5ff.   Such analogies are found in earlier
      elegy, but they have particular point in the *Ars.*
*34   It should be noted that Ovid's cynicism is never malic-
      ious or intended seriously, and many of his comments
      (and calculating tips) at the expense of women are com-
      pletely reversed in book III, when he approaches this
      game of love from the opposite (female) point of view.
*35   *A.A.*1.289ff.
*36   Occasionally a short final vowel remains short before
      two consonants beginning the next word, but in nearly
      every case the combination of consonants involved is

one of those listed on page 14 under *N.B.*
*37 But if these consonants follow a vowel that is long by
   nature or belong to different parts of a compound, the
   syllable is long (e.g. *mātres* (from *māter*) and *ābrumpo*).
*38 Sometimes a final vowel or vowel plus m is not elided.
   This phenomenon is called hiatus and in elegy is most
   common after the interjections *o, a* and *heu*.

VARIANTS FROM THE OXFORD CLASSICAL TEXT

1.17	venerem for Venerem
1.44	semicolon for full stop at end of line
1.91	sollemni for sollemnia
1.165	venus for Venus
1.168	semicolon for full stop at end of line
1.170	full stop for colon at end of line
1.280	full stop for comma at end of line
1.407	veneris for Veneris
1.451	veneris for Veneris
2.104	comma for full stop at end of line
2.133	comma added at end of line
2.135	comma added at end of line
2.154	full stop for semicolon at end of line
2.162	full stop for colon at end of line
2.184	full stop for semicolon at end of line
2.208	full stop for semicolon at end of line
2.286	full stop for semicolon at end of line

OVID WITH LOVE

SELECTIONS FROM ARS AMATORIA I AND II

LATIN TEXT

P. OVIDI NASONIS ARTIS
AMATORIAE
LIBER PRIMVS

Si quis in hoc artem populo non nouit amandi,
  hoc legat et lecto carmine doctus amet.
arte citae ueloque rates remoque mouentur,
  arte leues currus: arte regendus Amor.
5 curribus Automedon lentisque erat aptus habenis,   5
  Tiphys in Haemonia puppe magister erat:
me Venus artificem tenero praefecit Amori;
  Tiphys et Automedon dicar Amoris ego.

non ego, Phoebe, datas a te mihi mentiar artes,   25
10 nec nos aeriae uoce monemur auis,
nec mihi sunt uisae Clio Cliusque sorores
  seruanti pecudes uallibus, Ascra, tuis;
usus opus mouet hoc: uati parete perito;
  uera canam. coeptis, mater Amoris, ades.   30
15 este procul, uittae tenues, insigne pudoris,
  quaeque tegis medios instita longa pedes:
nos Venerem tutam concessaque furta canemus
  inque meo nullum carmine crimen erit.

PRINCIPIO, quod amare uelis, reperire labora,   35
20 qui noua nunc primum miles in arma uenis;
proximus huic labor est placitam exorare puellam;
  tertius, ut longo tempore duret amor.
hic modus; haec nostro signabitur area curru;
  haec erit admissa meta premenda rota.   40

25 Dvm licet et loris passim potes ire solutis,
  elige cui dicas 'tu mihi sola places.'
haec tibi non tenues ueniet delapsa per auras;
  quaerenda est oculis apta puella tuis.

Line Numbers on the *Left* are those of this Edition; these Numbers Correspond to the Numbers in the Commentary. The Numbers on the *Right* are those of the Oxford Edition.

scit bene uenator, ceruis ubi retia tendat;   45
    scit bene, qua frendens ualle moretur aper;
aucupibus noti frutices; qui sustinet hamos,
    nouit quae multo pisce natentur aquae:
tu quoque, materiam longo qui quaeris amori,
    ante frequens quo sit disce puella loco.   50
non ego quaerentem uento dare uela iubebo,
    nec tibi ut inuenias longa terenda uia est.
Gargara quot segetes, quot habet Methymna racemos,   57
    aequore quot pisces, fronde teguntur aues,
quot caelum stellas, tot habet tua Roma puellas:
    mater in Aeneae constitit urbe sui.   60
seu caperis primis et adhuc crescentibus annis,
    ante oculos ueniet uera puella tuos;
siue cupis iuuenem, iuuenes tibi mille placebunt:
    cogeris uoti nescius esse tui.
seu te forte iuuat sera et sapientior aetas,   65
    hoc quoque, crede mihi, plenius agmen erit.

sed tu praecipue curuis uenare theatris;   89
    haec loca sunt uoto fertiliora tuo.   90
illic inuenies quod ames, quod ludere possis,
    quodque semel tangas, quodque tenere uelis.
ut redit itque frequens longum formica per agmen,
    granifero solitum cum uehit ore cibum,   95
aut ut apes saltusque suos et olentia nactae
    pascua per flores et thyma summa uolant,
sic ruit ad celebres cultissima femina ludos;
    copia iudicium saepe morata meum est.
spectatum ueniunt, ueniunt spectentur ut ipsae;
    ille locus casti damna pudoris habet.   100
primus sollicitos fecisti, Romule, ludos,
    cum iuuit uiduos rapta Sabina uiros.
tunc neque marmoreo pendebant uela theatro,
    nec fuerant liquido pulpita rubra croco;
illic quas tulerant nemorosa Palatia frondes   105
    simpliciter positae scena sine arte fuit;
in gradibus sedit populus de caespite factis,
    qualibet hirsutas fronde tegente comas.
respiciunt oculisque notant sibi quisque puellam

quam uelit, et tacito pectore multa mouent;   110

dumque rudem praebente modum tibicine Tusco

70   ludius aequatam ter pede pulsat humum,

in medio plausu (plausus tunc arte carebant)

rex populo praedae signa †petenda† dedit.

protinus exiliunt animum clamore fatentes   115

uirginibus cupidas iniciuntque manus;

75   ut fugiunt aquilas, timidissima turba, columbae

utque fugit uisos agna nouella lupos,

sic illae timuere uiros sine lege ruentes;

constitit in nulla qui fuit ante color.   120

— nam timor unus erat, facies non una timoris:

80   pars laniat crines, pars sine mente sedet;

altera maesta silet, frustra uocat altera matrem;

haec queritur, stupet haec; haec manet, illa fugit.

ducuntur raptae, genialis praeda, puellae,   125

et potuit multas ipse decere timor.

85   si qua repugnarat nimium comitemque negarat,

sublatam cupido uir tulit ipse sinu

atque ita 'quid teneros lacrimis corrumpis ocellos?   130

quod matri pater est, hoc tibi dixit 'ero.'

Romule, militibus scisti dare commoda solus:

90   haec mihi si dederis commoda, miles ero.

scilicet ex illo sollemni more theatra

nunc quoque formosis insidiosa manent.

• • •

nec te nobilium fugiat certamen equorum: 135

multa capax populi commoda Circus habet.

95   nil opus est digitis per quos arcana loquaris,

nec tibi per nutus accipienda nota est;

proximus a domina nullo prohibente sedeto;

iunge tuum lateri qua potes usque latus;   140

100   et bene, quod cogit, si nolis, linea iungi,

quod tibi tangenda est lege puella loci.

hic tibi quaeratur socii sermonis origo,

et moueant primos publica uerba sonos:

cuius equi ueniant facito studiose requiras,   145

nec mora, quisquis erit cui fauet illa, faue.

105   at cum pompa frequens caelestibus ibit eburnis,

tu Veneri dominae plaude fauente manu;

utque fit, in gremium puluis si forte puellae

deciderit, digitis excutiendus erit;   150
etsi nullus erit puluis, tamen excute nullum:
110   quaelibet officio causa sit apta tuo;
pallia si terra nimium demissa iacebunt,
collige et inmunda sedulus effer humo:
protinus, officii pretium, patiente puella   155
contingent oculis crura uidenda tuis.
115   respice praeterea, post uos quicumque sedebit,
ne premat opposito mollia terga genu.
parua leuis capiunt animos: fuit utile multis
puluinum facili composuisse manu;   160
profuit et tenui uentos mouisse tabella
120   et caua sub tenerum scamna dedisse pedem.

hos aditus Circusque nouo praebebit amori
sparsaque sollicito tristis harena foro.
illa saepe puer Veneris pugnauit harena   165
et, qui spectauit uulnera, uulnus habet:
125   dum loquitur tangitque manum poscitque libellum
et quaerit posito pignore, uincat uter,
saucius ingemuit telumque uolatile sensit
et pars spectati muneris ipse fuit.   170
quid, modo cum belli naualis imagine Caesar
130   Persidas induxit Cecropiasque rates?
nempe ab utroque mari iuuenes, ab utroque puellae
uenere, atque ingens orbis in Vrbe fuit.
quis non inuenit turba, quod amaret, in illa?   175
eheu, quam multos aduena torsit amor!

135   dant etiam positis aditum conuiuia mensis;   229
est aliquid praeter uina, quod inde petas.   230
uina parant animos faciuntque caloribus aptos;   237
cura fugit multo diluiturque mero.
tunc ueniunt risus, tum pauper cornua sumit,
140   tum dolor et curae rugaque frontis abit.   240
tunc aperit mentes aeuo rarissima nostro
simplicitas, artes excutiente deo.
illic saepe animos iuuenum rapuere puellae,
et Venus in uinis ignis in igne fuit.
145   hic tu fallaci nimium ne crede lucernae: 245
iudicio formae noxque merumque nocent.

luce deas caeloque Paris spectauit aperto,
    cum dixit Veneri 'uincis utramque, Venus.'
nocte latent mendae uitioque ignoscitur omni,
    horaque formosam quamlibet illa facit.   250
consule de gemmis, de tincta murice lana,
    consule de facie corporibusque diem.

        ■ ■ ■

HACTENVS, unde legas quod ames, ubi retia ponas,   263
    praecipit imparibus uecta Thalea rotis.
nunc tibi quae placuit, quas sit capienda per artes,   265
    dicere praecipuae molior artis opus.
quisquis ubique, uiri, dociles aduertite mentes
    pollicitisque fauens uulgus adeste meis.

        ■ ■ ■

prima tuae menti ueniat fiducia, cunctas
    posse capi: capies, tu modo tende plagas.   270
uere prius uolucres taceant, aestate cicadae,
    Maenalius lepori det sua terga canis,
femina quam iuueni blande temptata repugnet;
    haec quoque, quam poteris credere nolle, uolet.
utque uiro furtiua Venus, sic grata puellae;   275
    uir male dissimulat, tectius illa cupit.

conueniat maribus ne quam nos ante rogemus,
    femina iam partes uicta rogantis aget.
mollibus in pratis admugit femina tauro,
    femina cornipedi semper adhinnit equo: 280
parcior in nobis nec tam furiosa libido;
    legitimum finem flamma uirilis habet.
Byblida quid referam, uetito quae fratris amore
    arsit et est laqueo fortiter ulta nefas?
Myrrha patrem, sed non qua filia debet, amauit,   285
    et nunc obducto cortice pressa latet;
illius lacrimis, quas arbore fundit odora,
    unguimur, et dominae nomina gutta tenet.
forte sub umbrosis nemorosae uallibus Idae
    candidus, armenti gloria, taurus erat   290
signatus tenui media inter cornua nigro;
    una fuit labes, cetera lactis erant.
illum Cnosiadesque Cydoneaeque iuuencae
    optarunt tergo sustinuisse suo.
Pasiphae fieri gaudebat adultera tauri;   295

150
155
160
165
170
175
180
185

inuida formosas oderat illa boues.
nota cano; non hoc, centum quae sustinet urbes,
quamuis sit mendax, Creta negare potest.
ipsa nouas frondes et prata tenerrima tauro
fertur inadsueta subsecuisse manu;   300
it comes armentis, nec ituram cura moratur
coniugis, et Minos a boue uictus erat.
quo tibi, Pasiphae, pretiosas sumere uestes?
ille tuus nullas sentit adulter opes.
quid tibi cum speculo montana armenta petenti?   305
quid totiens positas fingis inepta comas?
crede tamen speculo, quod te negat esse iuuencam:
quam cuperes fronti cornua nata tuae!
siue placet Minos, nullus quaeratur adulter;
siue uirum mauis fallere, falle uiro.   310
in nemus et saltus thalamo regina relicto
fertur, ut Aonio concita Baccha deo.
a, quotiens uaccam uultu spectauit iniquo
et dixit 'domino cur placet ista meo?
aspice ut ante ipsum teneris exultet in herbis;   315
nec dubito quin se stulta decere putet'!
dixit et ingenti iamdudum de grege duci
iussit et inmeritam sub iuga curua trahi,
aut cadere ante aras commentaque sacra coegit
et tenuit laeta paelicis exta manu;   320
paelicibus quotiens placauit numina caesis
atque ait exta tenens 'ite, placete meo'!
et modo se Europen fieri, modo postulat Ion,
altera quod bos est, altera uecta boue!
hanc tamen impleuit uacca deceptus acerna   325
dux gregis, et partu proditus auctor erat.
omnia feminea sunt ista libidine mota;   341
acrior est nostra plusque furoris habet.
ergo age, ne dubita cunctas sperare puellas:
uix erit e multis, quae neget, una, tibi.

■ ■ ■

cera uadum temptet rasis infusa tabellis,   437
cera tuae primum conscia mentis eat;
blanditias ferat illa tuas imitataque amantum
uerba, nec exiguas, quisquis es, adde preces.   440
Hectora donauit Priamo prece motus Achilles;
flectitur iratus uoce rogante deus.

promittas facito, quid enim promittere laedit?
    pollicitis diues quilibet esse potest.
Spes tenet in tempus, semel est si credita, longum;   445
230   illa quidem fallax, sed tamen apta, dea est.
si dederis aliquid, poteris ratione relinqui:
    praeteritum tulerit perdideritque nihil.
at quod non dederis, semper uideare daturus:
    sic dominum sterilis saepe fefellit ager.   450
235 sic, ne perdiderit, non cessat perdere lusor,
    et reuocat cupidas alea saepe manus.
hoc opus, hic labor est, primo sine munere iungi:
    ne dederit gratis quae dedit, usque dabit.
ergo eat et blandis peraretur littera uerbis   455
240   exploretque animos primaque temptet iter:
littera Cydippen pomo perlata fefellit,
    insciaque est uerbis capta puella suis.
disce bonas artes, moneo, Romana iuuentus,
    non tantum trepidos ut tueare reos: 460
245 quam populus iudexque grauis lectusque senatus,
    tam dabit eloquio uicta puella manus.
sed lateant uires, nec sis in fronte disertus;
    effugiant uoces uerba molesta tuae.
quis, nisi mentis inops, tenerae declamat amicae?   465
250   saepe ualens odii littera causa fuit.
sit tibi credibilis sermo consuetaque uerba,
    blanda tamen, praesens ut uideare loqui.

■ ■ ■

si non accipiet scriptum inlectumque remittet,
    lecturam spera propositumque tene.   470
255 tempore difficiles ueniunt ad aratra iuuenci,
    tempore lenta pati frena docentur equi.
ferreus adsiduo consumitur anulus usu,
    interit adsidua uomer aduncus humo.
quid magis est saxo durum, quid mollius unda?   475
260   dura tamen molli saxa cauantur aqua.
Penelopen ipsam, persta modo, tempore uinces:
    capta uides sero Pergama, capta tamen.
legerit et nolit rescribere, cogere noli;
    tu modo blanditias fac legat usque tuas.   480
265 quae uoluit legisse, uolet rescribere lectis:
    per numeros ueniunt ista gradusque suos.

    forsitan et primo uéniet tibi littera tristis
        quaeque roget ne se sollicitare uelis;
    quod rogat illa, timet; quod non rogat, optat, ut instes: 485
270   insequere, et uoti postmodo compos eris.

■ ■ ■

    interea, siue illa toro resupina feretur,
        lecticam dominae dissimulanter adi;
    neue aliquis uerbis odiosas offerat auris,
        qua potes, ambiguis callidus abde notis.   490
275 seu pedibus uacuis illi spatiosa teretur
        porticus, hic socias tu quoque iunge moras,
    et modo praecedas facito, modo terga sequaris,
        et modo festines et modo lentus eas.
    nec tibi de mediis aliquot transire columnas   495
280   sit pudor aut lateri continuasse latus,
    nec sine te curuo sedeat speciosa theatro:
        quod spectes, umeris adferet illa suis.
    illam respicias, illam mirere licebit,
        multa supercilio, multa loquare notis;   500
285 cum surgit, surges; donec sedet illa, sedebis: 503
        arbitrio dominae tempora perde tuae.

■ ■ ■

    sed tibi nec ferro placeat torquere capillos,   505
        nec tua mordaci pumice crura teras;
    forma uiros neglecta decet; Minoida Theseus   509
290   abstulit, a nulla tempora comptus acu;   510
    Hippolytum Phaedra, nec erat bene cultus, amauit;
        cura deae siluis aptus Adonis erat.
    munditie placeant, fuscentur corpora Campo;
        sit bene conueniens et sine labe toga.
295 †lingua ne rigeat†; careant rubigine dentes;   515
        nec uagus in laxa pes tibi pelle natet;
    nec male deformet rigidos tonsura capillos:
        sit coma, sit trita barba resecta manu.
    et nihil emineant et sint sine sordibus ungues,
300   inque caua nullus stet tibi nare pilus.   520
    nec male odorati sit tristis anhelitus oris,
        nec laedat naris uirque paterque gregis.
    cetera lasciuae faciant concede puellae
        et si quis male uir quaerit habere uirum.

■ ■ ■

305   ecce, suum uatem Liber uocat: hic quoque amantis   525
       adiuuat et flammae, qua calet ipse, fauet.
    Cnosis in ignotis amens errabat harenis,
       qua breuis aequoreis Dia feritur aquis;
    utque erat e somno, tunica uelata recincta
310   nuda pedem, croceas inreligata comas,   530
    Thesea crudelem surdas clamabat ad undas,
       indigno teneras imbre rigante genas.
    clamabat flebatque simul, sed utrumque decebat;
       non facta est lacrimis turpior illa suis.
315   iamque iterum tundens mollissima pectora palmis   535
       'perfidus ille abiit: quid mihi fiet?' ait;
    'quid mihi fiet?' ait; sonuerunt cymbala toto
       litore et adtonita tympana pulsa manu.
    excidit illa metu rupitque nouissima uerba;
320   nullus in exanimi corpore sanguis erat.   540
    ecce, Mimallonides sparsis in terga capillis,
       ecce, leues Satyri, praeuia turba dei.
    ebrius, ecce, senex pando Silenus asello
       uix sedet et pressas continet arte iubas.
325   dum sequitur Bacchas, Bacchae fugiuntque petuntque,   545
       quadrupedem ferula dum malus urget eques,
    in caput aurito cecidit delapsus asello;
       clamarunt Satyri 'surge age, surge, pater.'
    iam deus in curru, quem summum texerat uuis,
330   tigribus adiunctis aurea lora dabat;   550
    et color et Theseus et uox abiere puellae,
       terque fugam petiit terque retenta metu est.
    horruit, ut steriles agitat quas uentus aristas,
       ut leuis in madida canna palude tremit.
335   cui deus 'en, adsum tibi cura fidelior' inquit;   555
       'pone metum, Bacchi Cnosias uxor eris.
    munus habe caelum: caelo spectabere sidus;
       saepe reges dubiam Cressa Corona ratem.'
    dixit et e curru, ne tigres illa timeret,
340   desilit (inposito cessit harena pede)   560
    implicitamque sinu, neque enim pugnare ualebat,
       abstulit: in facili est omnia posse deo.
    pars 'Hymenaee' canunt, pars clamant 'Euhion, euhoe';
       sic coeunt sacro nupta deusque toro.
345   ergo, ubi contigerint positi tibi munera Bacchi   565

atque erit in socii femina parte tori,
Nycteliumque patrem nocturnaque sacra precare
ne iubeant capiti uina nocere tuo.

■ ■ ■

hic tibi multa licet sermone latentia tecto
350   dicere, quae dici sentiat illa sibi,   570
blanditiasque leues tenui perscribere uino,
ut dominam in mensa se legat illa tuam,
atque oculos oculis spectare fatentibus ignem:
saepe tacens uocem uerbaque uultus habet.
355 fac primus rapias illius tacta labellis   575
pocula, quaque bibet parte puella, bibas;
et quemcumque cibum digitis libauerit illa,
tu pete, dumque petes, sit tibi tacta manus.
iurgia praecipue uino stimulata caueto   591
360   et nimium faciles ad fera bella manus.
si uox est, canta; si mollia bracchia, salta;   595
et, quacumque potes dote placere, place.
ebrietas ut uera nocet, sic ficta iuuabit:
fac titubet blaeso subdola lingua sono,
365 ut, quicquid facias dicasue proteruius aequo,
credatur nimium causa fuisse merum.   600
at cum discedet mensa conuiua remota,   603
ipsa tibi accessus turba locumque dabit.
insere te turbae leuiterque admotus eunti   605
370   uelle latus digitis et pede tange pedem.

■ ■ ■

conloquii iam tempus adest; fuge rustice longe
hinc Pudor: audentem Forsque Venusque iuuat.
non tua sub nostras ueniat facundia leges;
fac tantum cupias, sponte disertus eris.   610
375 est tibi agendus amans imitandaque uulnera uerbis;
haec tibi quaeratur qualibet arte fides.
nec credi labor est: sibi quaeque uidetur amanda;
pessima sit, nulli non sua forma placet.
blanditiis animum furtim deprendere nunc sit,   619
380   ut pendens liquida ripa subestur aqua.   620
nec faciem nec te pigeat laudare capillos
et teretes digitos exiguumque pedem:
delectant etiam castas praeconia formae;
uirginibus curae grataque forma sua est.

385   nec timide promitte: trahunt promissa puellas;   631
        pollicito testes quoslibet adde deos.
      Iuppiter ex alto periuria ridet amantum
        et iubet Aeolios inrita ferre Notos.
      per Styga Iunoni falsum iurare solebat   635
390   Iuppiter: exemplo nunc fauet ipse suo.
      fallite fallentes; ex magna parte profanum   645
        sunt genus: in laqueos, quos posuere, cadant.
      et lacrimae prosunt; lacrimis adamanta mouebis: 659
        fac madidas uideat, si potes, illa genas.   660
395   si lacrimae, neque enim ueniunt in tempore semper,
        deficient, uncta lumina tange manu.
      quis sapiens blandis non misceat oscula uerbis?
        illa licet non det, non data sume tamen.
      pugnabit primo fortassis et 'improbe' dicet;   665
400   pugnando uinci se tamen illa uolet.
      oscula qui sumpsit, si non et cetera sumit,   669
        haec quoque, quae data sunt, perdere dignus erit.   670
      quantum defuerat pleno post oscula uoto?
        ei mihi, rusticitas, non pudor ille fuit.
405   uim licet appelles: grata est uis ista puellis;
        quod iuuat, inuitae saepe dedisse uolunt.
      quaecumque est Veneris subita uiolata rapina,   675
        gaudet, et inprobitas muneris instar habet.
      at quae, cum posset cogi, non tacta recessit,
410   ut simulet uultu gaudia, tristis erit.
      uim passa est Phoebe, uis est allata sorori;
        et gratus raptae raptor uterque fuit.   680
      fabula nota quidem, sed non indigna referri,
        Scyrias Haemonio iuncta puella uiro.
415   iam dea laudatae dederat mala praemia formae
        colle sub Idaeo uincere digna duas;
      iam nurus ad Priamum diuerso uenerat orbe,   685
        Graiaque in Iliacis moenibus uxor erat;
      iurabant omnes in laesi uerba mariti,
420   nam dolor unius publica causa fuit.
      turpe, nisi hoc matris precibus tribuisset, Achilles
        ueste uirum longa dissimulatus erat.   690
      quid facis, Aeacide? non sunt tua munera lanae;
        tu titulos alia Palladis arte petes.

425   quid tibi cum calathis? clipeo manus apta ferendo est;
        pensa quid in dextra, qua cadet Hector, habes?
    reice succinctos operoso stamine fusos: 695
        quassanda est ista Pelias hasta manu.
    forte erat in thalamo uirgo regalis eodem;
430   haec illum stupro comperit esse uirum.
    uiribus illa quidem uicta est (ita credere oportet),
        sed uoluit uinci uiribus illa tamen.   700
    saepe 'mane' dixit, cum iam properaret Achilles:
        fortia nam posito sumpserat arma colo.
435   uis ubi nunc illa est? quid blanda uoce moraris
        auctorem stupri, Deidamia, tui?

■ ■ ■

    scilicet, ut pudor est quaedam coepisse priorem,   705
        sic alio gratum est incipiente pati.
    a, nimia est iuueni propriae fiducia formae,
440   expectat si quis, dum prior illa roget.
    uir prior accedat, uir uerba precantia dicat;
        excipiat blandas comiter illa preces.   710
    ut potiare, roga: tantum cupit illa rogari;
        da causam uoti principiumque tui.
445   Iuppiter ad ueteres supplex heroidas ibat;
        corrupit magnum nulla puella Iouem.
    si tamen a precibus tumidos accedere fastus   715
        senseris, incepto parce referque pedem.
    quod refugit, multae cupiunt; odere, quod instat:
450   lenius instando taedia tolle tui.
    nec semper Veneris spes est profitenda roganti;
        intret amicitiae nomine tectus amor.   720
    hoc aditu uidi tetricae data uerba puellae;
        qui fuerat cultor, factus amator erat.

■ ■ ■

455   finiturus eram, sed sunt diuersa puellis   755
        pectora; mille animos excipe mille modis.
    nec tellus eadem parit omnia: uitibus illa
        conuenit, haec oleis; hic bene farra uirent.
    pectoribus mores tot sunt, quot in ore figurae:
460   qui sapit, innumeris moribus aptus erit,   760
    utque leues Proteus modo se tenuabit in undas,
        nunc leo, nunc arbor, nunc erit hirtus aper.
    hi iaculo pisces, illi capiuntur ab hamis,
        hos caua contento retia fune trahunt:

465   nec tibi conueniet cunctos modus unus ad annos;   765
        longius insidias cerua uidebit anus.
    si doctus uideare rudi petulansue pudenti,
        diffidet miserae protinus illa sibi.
    inde fit ut, quae se timuit committere honesto,
470   uilis ad amplexus inferioris eat.   770

■ ■ ■

    Pars superat coepti, pars est exhausta, laboris;
        hic teneat nostras ancora iacta rates.

LIBER SECVNDVS

Dicite 'io Paean' et 'io' bis dicite 'Paean':
    decidit in casses praeda petita meos.
laetus amans donat uiridi mea carmina palma
    praelata Ascraeo Maeonioque seni.
quid properas, iuuenis? mediis tua pinus in undis   9
    nauigat, et longe, quem peto, portus abest.   10
non satis est uenisse tibi me uate puellam;
    arte mea capta est, arte tenenda mea est.
nec minor est uirtus, quam quaerere, parta tueri:
    casus inest illic, hoc erit artis opus.
nunc mihi, si quando, puer et Cytherea, fauete;   15
    nunc Erato, nam tu nomen Amoris habes.
magna paro, quas possit Amor remanere per artes,
    dicere, tam uasto peruagus orbe puer.
et leuis est et habet geminas, quibus auolet, alas;
    difficile est illis inposuisse modum.   20
non potuit Minos hominis conpescere pinnas,   97
    ipse deum uolucrem detinuisse paro.

■ ■ ■

fallitur, Haemonias si quis decurrit ad artes
    datque quod a teneri fronte reuellit equi.   100
non facient, ut uiuat amor, Medeides herbae
    mixtaque cum magicis nenia Marsa sonis:
Phasias Aesoniden, Circe tenuisset Vlixem,
    si modo seruari carmine posset amor.
nec data profuerint pallentia philtra puellis;   105
    philtra nocent animis uimque furoris habent.

■ ■ ■

sit procul omne nefas! ut ameris, amabilis esto;
    quod tibi non facies solaue forma dabit.
ut dominam teneas nec te mirere relictum,   111
    ingenii dotes corporis adde bonis.
forma bonum fragile est, quantumque accedit ad annos,
    fit minor et spatio carpitur ipsa suo.
nec uiolae semper nec hiantia lilia florent,   115
    et riget amissa spina relicta rosa;

35 et tibi iam uenient cani, formose, capilli,
        iam uenient rugae, quae tibi corpus arent.
    iam molire animum, qui duret, et adstrue formae:
        solus ad extremos permanet ille rogos.   120
    nec leuis ingenuas pectus coluisse per artes
40   cura sit et linguas edidicisse duas:
    non formosus erat, sed erat facundus Vlixes,
        et tamen aequoreas torsit amore deas.
    o quotiens illum doluit properare Calypso   125
        remigioque aptas esse negauit aquas!
45 haec Troiae casus iterumque iterumque rogabat;
        ille referre aliter saepe solebat idem.
    litore constiterant; illic quoque pulchra Calypso
        exigit Odrysii fata cruenta ducis.   130
    ille leui uirga (uirgam nam forte tenebat),
50   quod rogat, in spisso litore pingit opus.
    'haec' inquit 'Troia est' (muros in litore fecit),
        'hic tibi sit Simois; haec mea castra puta.
    campus erat' (campumque facit), 'quem caede Dolonis   135
        sparsimus, Haemonios dum uigil optat equos.
55 illic Sithonii fuerant tentoria Rhesi;
        hac ego sum captis nocte reuectus equis—'
    pluraque pingebat, subitus cum Pergama fluctus
        abstulit et Rhesi cum duce castra suo;   140
    tum dea 'quas' inquit 'fidas tibi credis ituro,
60   perdiderint undae nomina quanta, uides?'
    ergo age, fallaci timide confide figurae,
        quisquis es, aut aliquid corpore pluris habe.

                        ■ ■ ■

    dextera praecipue capit indulgentia mentes;   145
        asperitas odium saeuaque bella mouet.
65 este procul, lites et amarae proelia linguae;   151
        dulcibus est uerbis mollis alendus amor.
    lite fugent nuptaeque uiros nuptasque mariti
        inque uicem credant res sibi semper agi:
    hoc decet uxores, dos est uxoria lites;   155
70   audiat optatos semper amica sonos.
    non legis iussu lectum uenistis in unum;
        fungitur in uobis munere legis Amor.
    blanditias molles auremque iuuantia uerba
        adfer, ut aduentu laeta sit illa tuo.   160

75 si nec blanda satis nec erit tibi comis amanti,   177
   perfer et obdura: postmodo mitis erit.
  cede repugnanti: cedendo uictor abibis;   197
   fac modo, quas partes illa iubebit, agas.
  arguet: arguito; quicquid probat illa, probato;
80   quod dicet, dicas; quod negat illa, neges.   200
  riserit: adride; si flebit, flere memento:
   imponat leges uultibus illa tuis.
  ipse tene distenta suis umbracula uirgis,   209
   ipse fac in turba, qua uenit illa, locum.   210
85 nec dubita tereti scamnum producere lecto,
   et tenero soleam deme uel adde pedi.
  saepe etiam dominae, quamuis horrebis et ipse,
   algenti manus est calficienda sinu.
  nec tibi turpe puta (quamuis sit turpe, placebit)   215
90   ingenua speculum sustinuisse manu.
  ille, fatigata praebendo monstra nouerca
   qui meruit caelum, quod prior ipse tulit,
  inter Ioniacas calathum tenuisse puellas
   creditur et lanas excoluisse rudes.   220
95 paruit imperio dominae Tirynthius heros:
   i nunc et dubita ferre quod ille tulit.
  iussus adesse foro iussa maturius hora
   fac semper uenias nec nisi serus abi.
  occurras aliquo tibi dixerit: omnia differ;   225
100   curre, nec inceptum turba moretur iter.
  nocte domum repetens epulis perfuncta redibit:
   tunc quoque pro seruo, si uocat illa, ueni.
  rure erit et dicet uenias; Amor odit inertes:
   si rota defuerit, tu pede carpe uiam.   230
105 nec graue te tempus sitiensque Canicula tardet
   nec uia per iactas candida facta niues.
  militiae species amor est: discedite, segnes;
   non sunt haec timidis signa tuenda uiris.
  nox et hiems longaeque uiae saeuique dolores   235
110   mollibus his castris et labor omnis inest.
  saepe feres imbrem caelesti nube solutum
   frigidus et nuda saepe iacebis humo.
  Cynthius Admeti uaccas pauisse Pheraei
   fertur et in parua delituisse casa: 240
115 quod Phoebum decuit, quem non decet? exue fastus,

curam mansuri quisquis amoris habes.
■ ■ ■

sed te, cuicumque est retinendae cura puellae,   295
  attonitum forma fac putet esse sua.
siue erit in Tyriis, Tyrios laudabis amictus;
120 siue erit in Cois, Coa decere puta.
aurata est: ipso tibi sit pretiosior auro;
  gausapa si sumit, gausapa sumpta proba.   300
astiterit tunicata: 'moues incendia' clama,
  sed timida, caueat frigora, uoce roga.
125 conpositum discrimen erit: discrimina lauda;
  torserit igne comam: torte capille, place.
bracchia saltantis, uocem mirare canentis,   305
  et, quod desierit, uerba querentis habe.
tantum, ne pateas uerbis simulator in illis,   311
130 effice nec uultu destrue dicta tuo.
si latet, ars prodest; adfert deprensa pudorem
  atque adimit merito tempus in omne fidem.
■ ■ ■

saepe sub autumnum, cum formosissimus annus   315
  aere non certo corpora languor habet.   318
135 illa quidem ualeat, sed si male firma cubabit
  tum sere, quod plena postmodo falce metas.   322
nec tibi morosi ueniant fastidia morbi,
  perque tuas fiant, quae sinet ipsa, manus,
et uideat flentem, nec taedeat oscula ferre,   325
140 et sicco lacrimas conbibat ore tuas.
multa uoue, sed cuncta palam, quotiensque libebit,
  quae referas illi, somnia laeta uide.
et ueniat quae lustret anus lectumque locumque,
  praeferat et tremula sulphur et oua manu.   330
145 omnibus his inerunt gratae uestigia curae;
  in tabulas multis haec uia fecit iter.
nec tamen officiis odium quaeratur ab aegra;
  sit suus in blanda sedulitate modus:
neue cibo prohibe nec amari pocula suci   335
150 porrige; riualis misceat illa tuus.
■ ■ ■

dum nouus errat amor, uires sibi colligat usu;   339
  si bene nutrieris, tempore firmus erit: 340
quem taurum metuis, uitulum mulcere solebas;
  sub qua nunc recubas arbore, uirga fuit;

155   fac tibi consuescat: nil adsuetudine maius,   345
        quam, tu, dum capias, taedia nulla fuge:
      te semper uideat, tibi semper praebeat aures,
        exhibeat uultus noxque diesque tuos.
      cum tibi maior erit fiducia, posse requiri,
160   cum procul absenti cura futurus eris,   350
      da requiem: requietus ager bene credita reddit,
        terraque caelestes arida sorbet aquas:
      sed mora tuta breuis: lentescunt tempore curae   357
        uanescitque absens et nouus intrat amor:
165   dum Menelaus abest, Helene, ne sola iaceret,
        hospitis est tepido nocte recepta sinu.   360
      quis stupor hic, Menelae, fuit? tu solus abibas,
        isdem sub tectis hospes et uxor erant?
      accipitri timidas credis furiose columbas,
170   plenum montano credis ouile lupo.
      nil Helene peccat, nihil hic committit adulter: 365
        quod tu, quod faceret quilibet, ille facit.
      cogis adulterium dando tempusque locumque;
        quid, nisi consilio est usa puella tuo?
175   quid faciat? uir abest, et adest non rusticus hospes,
        et timet in uacuo sola cubare toro.   370
      uiderit Atrides; Helenen ego crimine soluo:
        usa est humani commoditate uiri.

■ ■ ■

      sed neque fuluus aper media tam saeuus in ira est,
180   fulmineo rabidos cum rotat ore canes,
      nec lea, cum catulis lactantibus ubera praebet,   375
        nec breuis ignaro uipera laesa pede
      femina quam socii deprensa paelice lecti:
        ardet et in uultu pignora mentis habet;
185   hoc bene compositos, hoc firmos soluit amores;   385
        crimina sunt cautis ista timenda uiris.
      nec mea uos uni donat censura puellae;
        di melius! uix hoc nupta tenere potest.
      ludite, sed furto celetur culpa modesto;
190   gloria peccati nulla petenda sui est.   390
      nec dederis munus, cognosse quod altera possit,
        nec sint nequitiae tempora certa tuae,
      et, ne te capiat latebris sibi femina notis,
        non uno est omnis conuenienda loco,

195 et, quotiens scribes, totas prius ipse tabellas   395
       inspice: plus multae, quam sibi missa, legunt.
     quae bene celaris, si qua tamen acta patebunt,   409
       illa licet pateant, tu tamen usque nega.   410
     tum neque subiectus solito nec blandior esto:
200   haec animi multum signa nocentis habent.

                              ■ ■ ■

     qui modo celabas monitu tua crimina nostro,   427
       flecte iter et monitu detege furta meo.
     nec leuitas culpanda mea est: non semper eodem
       impositos uento panda carina uehit.   430
205 nam modo Threicio Borea, modo currimus Euro;
       saepe tument Zephyro lintea, saepe Noto.
     sunt quibus ingrate timida indulgentia seruit   435
       et, si nulla subest aemula, languet amor;
     ut leuis absumptis paulatim uiribus ignis   439
210   ipse latet, summo canet in igne cinis,   440
     sed tamen extinctas admoto sulphure flammas
       inuenit et lumen, quod fuit ante, redit:
     sic, ubi pigra situ securaque pectora torpent,
       acribus est stimulis eliciendus amor.
215 fac timeat de te tepidamque recalface mentem;   445
       palleat indicio criminis illa tui.

                              ■ ■ ■

     haec ego cum canerem, subito manifestus Apollo   493
       mouit inauratae pollice fila lyrae.
     in manibus laurus, sacris induta capillis   495
220   laurus erat: uates ille uidendus adit.
     is mihi 'lasciui' dixit 'praeceptor Amoris,
       duc age discipulos ad mea templa tuos,
     est ubi diuersum fama celebrata per orbem
       littera, cognosci quae sibi quemque iubet.   500
225 qui sibi notus erit, solus sapienter amabit
       atque opus ad uires exiget omne suas:
     cui faciem natura dedit, spectetur ab illa;
       cui color est, umero saepe patente cubet;
     qui sermone placet, taciturna silentia uitet;   505
230   qui canit arte, canat; qui bibit arte, bibat.
     sed neque declament medio sermone diserti,
       nec sua non sanus scripta poeta legat.'
     sic monuit Phoebus: Phoebo parete monenti;
       certa dei sacro est huius in ore fides.   510

■ ■ ■

235 ad propiora uocor; quisquis sapienter amabit,
  uincet et e nostra, quod petet, arte feret.
 ardua molimur, sed nulla, nisi ardua, uirtus;   537
  difficilis nostra poscitur arte labor.
 riualem patienter habe: uictoria tecum
240 stabit, eris magni uictor in Arce Iouis.   540
 innuet illa: feras; scribet: ne tange tabellas;   543
  unde uolet, ueniat, quoque libebit, eat.
 hac ego, confiteor, non sum perfectus in arte; 547
  quid faciam? monitis sum minor ipse meis.
245 non semel hoc uitium nocuit mihi; doctior ille, 553
  quo ueniunt alii conciliante uiri.
 sed melius nescisse fuit: sine furta tegantur,   555
  ne fugiat fasso uictus ab ore pudor.
 crescit amor prensis: ubi par fortuna duorum est, 559
250 in causa damni perstat uterque sui.   560
 fabula narratur toto notissima caelo,
  Mulciberis capti Marsque Venusque dolis.
 Mars pater insano Veneris turbatus amore
  de duce terribili factus amator erat;
255 nec Venus oranti (neque enim dea mollior ulla est) 565
  rustica Gradiuo difficilisque fuit.
 a, quotiens lasciua pedes risisse mariti
  dicitur et duras igne uel arte manus!
 Marte palam simul est Vulcanum imitata, decebat,
260 multaque cum forma gratia mixta fuit.   570
 sed bene concubitus primo celare solebant;
  plena uerecundi culpa pudoris erat.
 indicio Solis (quis Solem fallere possit?)
  cognita Vulcano coniugis acta suae.
265 (quam mala, Sol, exempla moues! pete munus ab ipsa: 575
  et tibi, si taceas, quod dare possit, habet.)
 Mulciber obscuros lectum circaque superque
  disponit laqueos; lumina fallit opus.
 fingit iter Lemnon; ueniunt ad foedus amantes;
270 impliciti laqueis nudus uterque iacent;   580
 conuocat ille deos; praebent spectacula capti;
  uix lacrimas Venerem continuisse putant;
 non uultus texisse suos, non denique possunt
  partibus obscenis obposuisse manus.
275 hic aliquis ridens 'in me, fortissime Mauors, 585

si tibi sunt oneri, uincula transfer' ait.
uix precibus, Neptune, tuis captiua resoluit
    corpora; Mars Thracen occupat, illa Paphon.
hoc tibi perfecto, Vulcane, quod ante tegebant,
280   liberius faciunt, et pudor omnis abest.   590
saepe tamen demens stulte fecisse fateris,
    teque ferunt artis paenituisse tuae.
hoc uetiti uos este: uetat deprensa Dione
    insidias illas, quas tulit ipsa, dare.
285   nec uos riuali laqueos disponite nec uos   595
    excipite arcana uerba notata manu;

∎ ∎ ∎

Finis adest operi: palmam date, grata iuuentus,   733
    sertaque odoratae myrtea ferte comae.
quantus apud Danaos Podalirius arte medendi,   735
290   Aeacides dextra, pectore Nestor erat,
quantus erat Calchas extis, Telamonius armis,
    Automedon curru, tantus amator ego.
me uatem celebrate, uiri, mihi dicite laudes;
    cantetur toto nomen in orbe meum.   740
295   arma dedi uobis; dederat Vulcanus Achilli:
    uincite muneribus, uicit ut ille, datis.
sed, quicumque meo superarit Amazona ferro,
    inscribat spoliis NASO MAGISTER ERAT.

COMMENTARY

1-8   Ovid's poem will teach his readers how to be expert
lovers. Just as technique is necessary in sailing and driving
a chariot, so it is necessary in love, and Ovid possesses the
requisite technique in abundance.

        The lines form an apt introduction to the *Ars Amatoria*.
They state the theme of the poem, introduce its format (didactic)
and show Ovid already in his role as a cultured expert on love
with a frivolous turn of mind.   His ingenuity and technical
skill (see INTRODUCTION section 7) are also immediately appar-
ent.   Note especially the repetition of *hoc* in 1 and 2;
amandi (1) picked up by *amet* (2) and later by *Amor* (4), *Amori*
(7) and *Amoris* (8); *legat* taken up by *lecto* (2); the contrast
between amatory ignorance (1) and expertise (2); the emphatic
anaphora of *arte* (3-4), picking up *artem* (1) and echoed in *artif-
icem* (7); the contrast between vehicles on sea and land in 3-4;
the chiastic order of ships, chariots, chariots, ships in 3-6;
the picking-up of *currus* (4) in *curribus* (5); the balance in
the two famous experts in 5-6; the repetition of *erat* (5-6);
the chiastic order of Automedon, Tiphys, Tiphys, Automedon in
5-8; the juxtaposed *Amoris ego* in 8, suggesting Ovid's close
connection with Love; the (emphatic) positioning of parts of
ego at the opening and close of the couplet (7-8).   The fre-
quent repetition makes these lines pleasantly musical, and also
noteworthy are the rhyme between the first and last words in 1,
the alliteration of n and assonance of o in *populo non novit*
(1) and the alliteration of r, assonance of e and rhyme in
-*oque* in *veloque rates remoque* (3).   Thus Ovid opens with a
flourish.

1-2   The usual prose word-order in line 1 would be: *si quis
in hoc populo artem amandi non novit*.   The arrangement of words
in verse often differs from that in prose (not least because
the words had to be made to fit the metre), and it is always
very important to analyse exactly clauses and sentences when
reading poetry.   With <u>hoc</u> in line 2 understand *carmen* (from
carmine).   <u>legat</u> and <u>amet</u> are jussive subjunctives.   <u>doctus</u>
is used in an adverbial sense: "let him love expertly" (i.e.
be an expert in love).

        In the very first couplet Ovid introduces one of the

main sources of humour in the *Ars*, namely his rational and
scientific approach to irrational, emotional love (artem...
amandi, doctus amet). There is also humour in the fact that
it is here implied that love (conventionally frivolous and
trivial) is something rather serious and important and that tech-
nique in love is something desirable, and in the cocky asser-
tion that the *Ars* will be invariably successful.

    The element of parody is already evident in the commands
(naturally common in didactic) in line 2.

3-4   arte (all three times), veloque and remoque are abla-
tives of instrument/means (literally: "by technique are swift
ships propelled by sail and oar...").   With currus understand
moventur (from line 3), and with regendus understand *est* (such
omissions are common in poetry).   The (illogical) implication
is that if technique is required for sailing and for driving
a chariot, then it is also required for love.

    The clear lack of logic in Ovid's implication here is
entirely deliberate.   It is also rather amusing and cheeky of
Ovid to compare love to these more serious and demanding pur-
suits.   The use of an analogy from other occupations parodies
didactic (cf. e.g. Virgil *Georgics* 1.204ff.).

    Ovid's epithets are often rather otiose (cf. e.g. lentis
in 5), but here citae and leves suggest the difficulties and
dangers of managing a ship or chariot, just as it is supposed
to be a difficult and dangerous task to control Love.   In
addition, Love, who was a winged god, was also notoriously
swift.

5-6   Automedon was the charioteer of Achilles (the finest
Greek warrior in the Trojan War).   Tiphys was the helmsman of
the Argo (the ship in which Jason and the Argonauts sailed on
their quest for the Golden Fleece).   The Argo is described as
Haemonia puppe because it was built in Thessaly from Thessalian
trees and its captain Jason came from Thessaly.

    The mythological parallels here, apart from showing the
poet's learning (especially in the allusion to the Argo), parody
similar analogies from myth in didactic poetry (cf. e.g. Virgil
Georgics 3.258ff.).

7-8   artificem is in apposition to me ("Venus has set me, as
an expert, in charge of..."). dicar is most probably future
passive indicative (although it could be present subjunctive).
Tiphys and Automedon are both examples of people who were very
efficient at and famous for their craft (involving control of
something), so that in 8 Ovid is in effect saying "I shall be
extremely skilful in and renowned for my control of Love".

        artificem (from ars and facio) may well contain a pun:
it could also suggest the meaning "one who produces an ars"
(amatoria).

        The claims of expertise in 7 and 8 are intentionally
bold and extravagant.   There is further humour in the some-
what odd expression in the pentameter and in the fact that in
the reference to Tiphys and Automedon Ovid is impudently em-
ploying dignified figures from ancient myth in a trival and
undignified context.

9-18   Ovid really has no prophetic powers, nor has he been
inspired by the Muses: his poem is based on experience.   The
work should not be read by married women, since it is not in-
tended to promote adultery, which is against the law.

        This section contains further introductory remarks.   In
the first six lines Ovid continues in his role as a man of learn-
ing (both amatory and literary) with a sophisticated and cheeky
sense of humour, but in the final four lines he seems to restrain
himself somewhat and become a little more serious.   His stylis-
tic and metrical skills are still in evidence - especially the
juxtapositions ego, Phoebe and te mihi in 9, suggesting the con-
nection with Apollo that Ovid is denying in that line and pro-
ducing a chiastic order of Ovid, Apollo, Apollo, Ovid;   the
balance between 9 and 10 (prophetic skills denied);   the allit-
eration of m in 9 and n in 10;   the juxtaposed and repeated
forms of Clio in 11;   the alliteration of c and s in 11 and 12;
the balance between 9-10 and 11-12 (divine inspiration denied);
the jingle in parete perito (13);   the alliteration of p, c and
a in 13-14;   the contrast between ades (14) and este procul (15);
the balance between vittae and instita in 15-16;   the balance
between 17 and 18 (legality);   the alliteration of c in 17 and
18 (for the meaning of the technical terms here see INTRODUCTION

section 7).

9-10   Phoebus Apollo here appears in his role as the god of
prophecy who inspired seers (he was also the god of poetry and
music).   One of the ways in which the Romans foretold the fut-
ure was by observing the cries of birds such as the owl, the
raven and the crow.   The omen varied according to their note
and the place from which they sang.   mentiar may mean "fabri-
cate" (in which case datas is simply a participle agreeing with
artes) or "state falsely" (in which case understand *esse* with
datas, which forms the perfect passive infinitive in an accusa-
tive and infinitive construction).   nos stands for *ego* (as
nostro (23) stands for *meo*): this usage of *nos* (plural for
singular) is found in poetry and prose and is common in the
Ars.

        At this stage it is a little puzzling to find Ovid dis-
claiming prophetic skills.   The reference is to his coming
interpretation of amatory matters and correct prediction of how
the girl and reader will feel and behave, and the implication
seems to be that he will prove such an expert in his field that
he could get away with the claim that he is a prophet.   The
provocative immodesty is deliberate, as is the impertinent sug-
gestion that his knowledge about love could lead readers to
imagine that he is a (solemn, august and revered) prophet in-
spired by Apollo himself.

        The lines also show Ovid's learning: they look back to
two earlier passages in elegy (Propertius 1.9.5ff. *non me*
Chaoniae vincant in amore columbae/dicere, quos iuvenes quae-
que puella domet./me dolor et lacrimae merito fecere peritum
and Tibullus 1.8.1ff. *non ego celari possum, quid nutus amantis/*
quidve ferant miti lenia verba sono./nec mihi sunt sortes nec
conscia fibra deorum,/praecinit eventus nec mihi cantus avis:/
ipsa Venus magico religatum bracchia nodo/perdocuit multis non
sine verberibus).

11-12   Cliusque sorores: i.e. the other eight Muses.   Note the
unusual genitive form.   vallibus...tuis is a local ablative
(place where): in prose the preposition *in* would have been
added, but in poetry it is often omitted.   Ascra: a village
in Boeotia (in Greece) where the poet Hesiod was born and near

which the Muses appeared to him and inspired his poetry.

There is a reference here to *Theogony* 22ff., where
Hesiod describes this visit of the Muses.   Again Ovid is mak-
ing a scandalous implication: the *Ars* will be such excellent
didactic that his readers might believe that he is a second
Hesiod inspired by the Muses.   The comparison of Ovid the
didactic poet (on a flippant and trivial subject) to Hesiod the
archetypal didactic poet (on a serious and more weighty subject)
is a joke at the expense of the originator of the genre.   There
is also humour in Ovid's solemn denial that he has acted as a
shepherd: the urban and urbane poet is the last person one
could imagine in this role.

13-14   parete is addressed to Ovid's readers.   mater Amoris
refers to Venus, of course.

Ovid brings out his experience by the emphatic positions
(at the start and end of the line) of usus, perito and vera.

usus may well contain a pun: as well as meaning "experi-
ence" it can also (aptly enough here) denote sexual intercourse
(cf. e.g. Tibullus 1.9.55).

vati here is mock-solemn: *vates* is a stately word, used
of both poet and priest.

vera canam means that Ovid will write about matters that
he himself has experienced and so knows to be true.   The words
mischievously echo Hesiod (*Works and Days* 10: "and I, Perses,
would tell of true things").

There is also parody of didactic in coeptis, mater Amoris,
ades.   Considering the subject-matter, it seems natural enough
for Ovid to invoke Venus, but, no doubt, he also has in mind
the lengthy opening of the *De Rerum Natura*, where Lucretius
prayed to Venus for inspiration.   Here the invocation is much
briefer and the context a lot less serious.

15-16   vittae (headbands, usually made of wool) were a charac-
teristic feature of the Roman matron's dress.   insigne pudoris
is in apposition to vittae tenues.   The instita was techni-
cally a narrow band sewn on to the bottom of the *stola*, but
here (as the adjective longa shows) the word refers to the
stola itself, a long robe that extended down to the feet and

could only be worn by married women.   Ovid is here saying that
the *Ars* is not to be read by such women.

Since the *Lex Iulia* of 18 B.C. adultery had been a crim-
inal offence, so that Ovid here feels it necessary to avoid
trouble by openly declaring that the *Ars* is not intended to fos-
ter adultery (his declaration was ignored and he was charged
with teaching adultery: see INTRODUCTION section 1).   How-
ever, even now, it seems, Ovid cannot resist a sly joke. The
words este procul may well be intended to recall the cry to the
uninitiated to withdraw at the start of a religious ceremony
(cf. e.g. Virgil *Aeneid* 6.258 *procul, o procul este, profani).*
The idea would be that Ovid (cf. vati in 13) is celebrating
rites (of love) and that married women are excluded (since,
being uninitiated, they know nothing of love) and are actually
in danger of committing blasphemy.

17-18   For nos see on 9-10.

The paradox in concessaque furta (literally "and thefts
allowed by law") and the verbal play in carmine crimen erit
support the idea that Ovid cannot be totally serious even now.

19-24   List of contents: (i) finding the girl,(ii) winning her,
   (iii) keeping her.

Ovid here gives a succinct synopsis of the subject-
matter of books I (finding and winning the girl) and II (keep-
ing her), and, in doing so, parodies similar summaries in
earlier didactic (e.g. Virgil *Georgics* 1.1ff.).   The mock-
solemnity and the expert's orderly and detached approach to
chaotic, emotional love are also diverting.

Into only six lines Ovid packs a tricolon diminuendo
(19-22) immediately followed by a tricolon crescendo (23-24),
an echo of *labora* (19) in *labor* (21), emphatic anaphora of
hic (23-4), alliteration of n (20) and an intricate pattern of
sound in word-endings (24), including internal rhyme.

19-20   quod has a vague antecedent ("something", "an object"),
   which, as often, is not expressed in the Latin. Of course,
   Ovid really means "a girl" here: he uses the neuter to appear
   more clinical and detached. velis is either potential subjunc-
   tive or subjunctive in a generic relative clause (denoting the
   sort or type of thing) or subjunctive in a final relative

clause (expressing purpose).   The pentameter contains the old
image of the lover as a soldier (probably based on the actual
similarities between love and war, such as the fights between
lovers).   The image recurs throughout the *Ars*, and Ovid usually
pictures himself as the experienced veteran, as here.   See also
on 2.107-108.

principio is a common introductory term in Lucretius
(e.g. 1.503) and Virgil's *Georgics* (e.g.4.8).

laboro and *labor* (21) are frequently found in military
contexts, and, in view of the metaphor in the pentameter here,
it is likely that the words have a primarily military flavour.
However, the idea of the need for hard work in agriculture and
the use of the word *labor* often recur in Virgil's *Georgics* (cf.
also Hesiod *Works and Days* 382), and it seems likely that here
Ovid is also mischievously suggesting that hard work is necess-
ary in love too.

21-22   With tertius understand *labor est* (from 21).   ut ex-
presses purpose (= "to ensure that").   longo tempore is strict-
ly ablative of time within which, but translate: "for a long
time" (this ablative occasionally encroaches on the function
of the accusative of time how long).

There is a cool, matter-of-fact and clinical tone in the
reference here to these particularly delicate and difficult
matters, in which emotion rather than intellect dominates.

23-24   With hic modus understand *erit*.   For nostro see on 9-
10.   Basically Ovid is saying here that what he has mentioned
in 19-22 will be his subject-matter or "field".   He expresses
this by means of an image taken from chariot-driving.   An
area was literally an open space (also used, as here, of a
poet's "field" at *Amores* 3.15.18, *Fasti* 4.10), so that in the
hexameter haec...curru means "this is the field that I shall
cover".   A meta was a post fixed in the ground at either end
of a track, around which the charioteers had to turn, and they
tried to keep as close to it as they could, to make the dis-
tance covered as short as possible and to avoid being passed
on the inside.   Accordingly the pentameter means "I shall
keep very closely to my field, as I hurry along"(admissa...
rota).   Ovid adds the detail of the speeding wheel to suggest

the swiftness of his metre (predominantly dactylic) and of his
treatment of the subject (books I and II are comparatively
short for a contemporary didactic poem, and the reader is quickly
carried along by them).

    Such chariot-imagery (of the poet's progress) had a long
ancestry and was often employed in solemn and weighty poetry,
so that it is rather insolent of Ovid to apply it here to the
frivolous and trivial *Ars*. Probably he has particularly in
mind its use in didactic (e.g. Lucretius 6.92f., Virgil *Georgics*
2.541f.).

25-46   To acquire a mistress you must look for one and first
ascertain which places are frequented by women. You need go
no further than Rome, which is filled with females of all
ages.

    Ovid, logically enough, begins his advice at the
beginning, but to say that his pupil must actually look for a
girlfriend and first find out where to look is surely to state
the obvious. The joke lies in Ovid's apparently serious pre-
tence that it is not such obvious advice, that both points do
need making and that the second one in fact requires justifi-
cation by means of an analogy from other occupations. Simi-
larly, any Roman with a pair of eyes would hardly have been
likely to look somewhere else if he wanted a mistress, because
he must have been aware that there were many women of differ-
ent ages in the vast city of Rome, but Ovid (mock-) solemnly
informs his reader that there is no need to go off elsewhere
in search of a girl, and he emphasizes at length the great
number of women in Rome and the variety of their ages, as if
this was important new information that needed to be driven
home. There is added humour in the fact that at 37ff. the
poet is giving an ingenious amatory twist to a theme that was
rather common in contemporary literature and in the rhetori-
cal schools - the praise of Rome/Italy (cf. e.g. Varro *De Re
Rustica* 1.2.3ff., Virgil *Georgics* 2.136ff., Propertius 3.22,
Quintilian *Institutio Oratoria* 3.7.26). In such praises
emphasis was sometimes placed, as here, on the multiplicity
and variety of the place's good points.

25-26   loris...solutis: at present the reader is like a horse

given its head, but soon he will be kept from wandering and
held tightly under control (by a mistress).   cui: the vague
antecedent ("someone") is, as often, not expressed.   dicas
is subjunctive in a final relative clause (expressing purpose).

The hexameter contains an unusual amatory image.

Amusingly elige implies that falling in love is a matter
of cool, rational selection, rather than one of emotion and
passion.

'tu mihi sola places' is cited as a typical example of
the lover's line of chat (the phrase also occurs at Propertius
2.7.19 and Tibullus (?) 4.13.3).

The hexameter is a musical line with its alliteration
of l and p and its internal rhyme.   In 26 the juxtaposition
tu mihi (like haec tibi in 27) suggests the connection desired
by the lover.   Also, juxtaposition of pronouns is a favourite
conceit in sophisticated Latin authors.

27-28   oculis...tuis (ablative of instrument) goes with quae-
renda est, not with apta.

The (deliciously mock-serious) hexameter contains a form
of Roman proverbial expressions for a sudden, unexpected appear-
ance (usually of something welcome): cf. Tibullus 1.3.90 (of
his unannounced return to his mistress) *sed videar caelo missus
adesse tibi.*

quaerenda as first word in the line is emphatic by posi-
tion: Ovid is driving home the point that the reader himself
must make an effort.

There is alliteration in 27 and a sound-pattern in the
endings of the final four words in 28.

29-30   ubi has been postponed (such postponements are common
in poetry), and cervis (dative of disadvantage) goes with
retia tendat (deliberative subjunctive in an indirect question).

The analogy from other occupations parodies didactic.
It also mischievously compares love to those (conventionally)
more worthwhile and serious pursuits, suggesting that in love
too knowledge of the quarry's haunts is necessary.   The examples
given here and in the next couplet are especially apt because
imagery from hunting, fowling and fishing was frequently applied
to love (particularly of searching, chasing, trapping and

catching: cf. e.g. 47, Meleager's epigram (12.132) in the
Palatine Anthology and Plautus *Truculentus* 31ff.).

>   frendens adds a touch of vividness.

>   There is emphatic anaphora of scit bene and balance be-
tween hexameter and pentameter.

31-32   With noti understand *sunt*. (*is*) qui sustinet hamos (a
periphrasis for the fisherman) is the subject of novit.
natentur: the verb has its transitive sense here ("swim in").

>   Ovid avoids monotony in his examples (29-32) by the
variety in grammatical subject and the change in occupations
and quarry (creatures of land, air and water).

>   noti is picked up by novit (in emphatic position), again
bringing out the importance of knowledge, and there is a bal-
ance between the bird-catcher and the fisherman.

33-34   materiam and longo belong in the qui clause: this post-
ponement of *qui* is common in poetry.   The prose order in the
pentameter would be: *ante disce quo loco puella frequens sit.*
ante here is a temporal adverb.   puella and loco are singular
for plural (another common poetic usage).

>   materiam is a deliberately clinical and unemotional
term.

>   There is alliteration of q in 33.

35-36   With quaerentem understand *te*.   tibi is dative of the
agent with the gerundive terenda.   Understand *puellam* with
invenias.

>   Again burlesque is probably present: not surprisingly,
Virgil employed the verb *iubeo* several times in the *Georgics*
(e.g. 3.329).

>   quaerentem picks up quaeris (33), and there is balance
(no need for journey) and contrast (sea and land) between 35
and 36.

37-38   The expression in this couplet is very compressed:
habet is common to both clauses in the hexameter, and quot
and teguntur are common to both clauses in the pentameter
(i.e. understand *habent* with Gargara quot segetes, *teguntur*
with aequore quot pisces and *quot* with fronde teguntur aves).
Gargara(proverbial for its fertility) was the name of a
mountain-peak in the Ida range (near Troy) and of a town at

the base of the mountain.   Methymna was a city on the island
of Lesbos (off the coast of Asia Minor) famous for its wine.

The geographical references are intended to add variety
and interest.

The analogy from nature is another instance of parody
of didactic (cf. e.g. Lucretius 4.1197ff.).   Ovid avoids mono-
tony in his examples (in 37-39) by varying the construction,
by moving from land (37) to sea (38), to land again (38) and
to heaven (39), and by alternating between inanimate (37, 39)
and animate (38).

There is balance in 37 and in 38, and the pentameter
contains internal rhyme.

39-40   habet is common to both the quot and tot clauses.
mater refers to Venus.   Aeneas was, of course, the founder of
the Roman race, so that Rome can with reason be described as
his city.   The pentameter is a neat way of saying that Rome
is a city of love and amatory opportunities.

The hexameter may contain a learned reminiscence of
Herodas 1.32f.:   (Egypt contains) "women more in number - I
swear it by Persephone - than the sky boasts stars".

In 40 by emphasizing and cleverly playing on this
natural connection between the Romans' ancestor and love Ovid
puts both Aeneas and the capital city in a rather undignified
and frivolous light.   Such irreverent wit, one suspects, would
not have gone down well with the Establishment (especially since Aug-
ustus traced back his ancestry via the *gens Iulia* to Iulus (Ascanius)
and thence to his father Aeneas).   Aeneas was also the hero
of the recently published national epic the *Aeneid*.

The quadruple repetition of quot is answered by tot
(37-39), and there is repetition of habet (37 and 39) and in-
ternal rhyme in 39.

41-42   vera puella: *puella* could be applied to a woman of quite
mature years who was found attractive (especially in the sense
of "girlfriend", "mistress"); here Ovid is thinking of a
girl - hence the addition of vera.

There is internal rhyme in 41 and alliteration of v in
42.

43-44   iuvenem: a young woman (*not* a young man) in age between

primis...annis (41) and sera...aetas (45).   cogeris...tui:
i.e. you will not be able to decide which one you desire.

    The juxtaposed forms of *iuvenis* in 43 are followed by
internal rhyme in 44 (this is the fourth successive couplet
containing internal rhyme).

45-46   hoc goes with agmen, and plenius is the complement.
plenius here does not imply comparison (= "rather numerous").

    There is alliteration of s in 45, contrast between
the three different age-groups and balance in wishes satisfied
each time in 41-46.

47-58   The best place to acquire a girl is the theatre: the
smartest women flock there in great numbers, to see and be
seen.

    Ovid now gives some practical advice in an entertaining
passage.   Urbane assurance based on personal experience is
combined with subtle humour and a mild cynicism that gives the
lines a satirical flavour.   The whole is presented with much
elegance and ingenuity of expression.

47-48   In a passage omitted from this selection Ovid had listed
several suitable places and occasions for acquiring a woman
(various colonnades, temples, religious festivals and the law-
courts!); here he moves on to the best place of all. venare:
second person singular imperative of *venor* (deponent).   voto...
tuo is dative of reference/thing affected (= "for your wants")
or (just possibly) ablative of comparison (= "than you could
desire").

    The use of *tu* to reinforce a precept is in the formal
didactic manner (cf. e.g. Virgil *Georgics* 4.106f.).

    For the hunting imagery (venare) see on 29-30.

    Note the internal rhyme in the pentameter.

49-50   quod ames: for the use of the neuter and the omission
of the vague antecedent see on 19-20; ames is subjunctive in
a final relative clause (expressing purpose), as are possis,
tangas and velis.

    The expert clinically, and a little cynically, breaks
down attractive women at the theatre into two classes - those
suitable for a lengthy attachment or for a shorter encounter.

    This is a cleverly constructed couplet with its chiastic

arrangement of serious love, dalliance, dalliance, serious love, the repe-
titions of quod and quodque and the frequency of i and e in the
opening words of 49.

51-52   formica is singular for plural.   per (rather than *in*)
is a little puzzling at first.   Ovid must be envisaging the
foraging ants going to and fro *along* the lengthy column (as
though they themselves did not make up the column).   granifero
and solitum belong in the cum clause (this is another instance
of postposition).

The double simile (there is another one in the next coup-
let) was generally a characteristic of high style.   Part of
the fun in these lines lies in recognizing the sources of Ovid's
similes and seeing the twists that he gives to them.   The
present one was probably suggested by Virgil *Aeneid* 4.402-7,
where at a dramatic moment Aeneas' men leaving Carthage are
compared to a column of ants plundering a heap of grain and
carrying their spoil home.   Ovid here applies the epic-inspired
simile to *women* going *to* a place and uses it in a far more
trivial and less serious context.

There are several points of comparison.   The hexameter
suggests the large number of women bustling purposefully to the
theatre in a long line (cf. 55-56).   In the pentameter it
becomes clear that the ants have found for themselves a source
of sustenance: Ovid may well be implying rather cynically
that women go to the theatre because it provides the same type
of thing, i.e. in their case men to support and look after
them (see on 53-54 and cf. 57 veniunt spectentur ut ipsae).

This is another skilfully constructed couplet: there
is repetition of i, t, e, q and f in the hexameter and of -um
in the pentameter, which is also a golden line (for the mean-
ing of this term see INTRODUCTION section 7).

53-54
These lines could almost have been written by Virgil:
the simile is based on *Georgics* 4.53-55 (of bees) *illae*
continuo saltus silvasque peragrant/purpureosque metunt flores
et flumina libant/summa leves (cf. also for suos *Georgics* 4.22,
for olentia *Georgics* 4.30 and for nactae *Georgics* 4.77).
Again the reminiscence is put in a lightweight and more frivo-
lous context, and no doubt it amused Ovid to use Virgilian

didactic as illustrative material in his own didactic poem.

Like the bees, theatre-going women are purposeful and eager; again the pentameter may be intended to suggest that the women are after a man (as the bees are after pollen).

There is balance with the previous couplet, repetition of ut (from 51) and alliteration of s and p.

55-56   cultissima femina is singular for plural.   cultus here could refer to smartness of appearance or taste (or both).

It is entertaining to find even the expert at a loss in the pentameter.   Not surprisingly, it was a characteristic of didactic to cite personal experience (often introduced by vidi : cf. e.g. Lucretius 4.577f., Virgil Georgics 1.316ff.).

All variable feet except one are dactyls, possibly to suggest the bustling of the women and the excitement of the poet.   In addition alliteration of c and m is present.

57-58   spectatum is a supine in -um with a verb of motion to express purpose.   spectentur belongs inside the ut clause. The pentameter means that the place is detrimental or damaging to chastity: damna is plural for singular, casti...pudoris denotes the thing lost or damaged and habet means "contains".

The neatly epigrammatical hexameter cynically, if no doubt realistically in many cases, implies that women at the theatre are as keen to be picked up as men are to pick them up (spectentur ut ipsae; note also that spectatum is double-edged, referring to their intention to survey men as well as the show).   The line may be a reminiscence of and an attempt to improve on Plautus Poenulus 337 sunt illi aliae quas spectare ego et me spectari volo.   It contains a chiastic repetition of forms of specto and venio that produces much assonance and alliteration (continued in ut and ipsae/ille).

59-92   The theatre has always been the place for this type of thing ever since Romulus engineered the Rape of the Sabine Women there.

The section on the theatre continues, but Ovid here launches into an entertaining narrative that adds variety and shows his descriptive skills at their best: it is vivid, realistic, lively, full of detail and constantly enhanced by metrical effects and points of style.

There is also much humour in these lines.   Firstly,
parody is again in evidence: Ovid's digression here is in imi-
tation of the digressions in earlier didactic poetry (e.g.
Virgil *Georgics* 4.116ff.), and his use of the Rape of the
Sabine Women to account for the amatory associations of the
theatre is a burlesque of the Hellenistic aetion, a tale to
explain the origins of something (perhaps with an eye on the
aetion in didactic (e.g. Virgil *Georgics* 4.315ff.) in particu-
lar).   Ovid's treatment of the actual story is also diverting.
To appreciate it fully the reader should remember the brief,
dry and eminently respectable account of the Rape itself in the
contemporary historian Livy (1.9.10-12).   By way of contrast
Ovid produces a lengthy, light-hearted and irreverent version
of this old Roman legend.   He lingers somewhat mockingly on
the primitive crudity of the theatre at that time and of
Romulus' men, and he seems to take a positive delight in bring-
ing out the lustfulness and undignified conduct of those same
ancestors who in other authors are generally portrayed as stern,
upright and austerely dignified figures.   His mentions of
Romulus himself are brief and generally flippant (this is the
only place in the *Ars* where he figures, and here he appears as
the planner of a rape).   In addition the poet probably even
works in sly digs at contemporary segregation in the theatre
(67-68) and difficulties over recruitment (89-90).   Such levity,
embracing as it does Rome's early history and her revered founder,
is unlikely to have been well received by Romans of the old
school or by the emperor (especially since Augustus himself was
compared to and connected with Romulus and had at one time con-
templated assuming the name "Romulus": cf. e.g. Cassius Dio
53.16).

59-60   cum iuvit: the relation between the cum clause and the
hexameter is purely one of time, and the cum clause gives the
date at which the action of the main clause occurred, so that,
as always, the indicative (iuvit) is required.   Sabina is
singular for plural.

Ovid is giving a joking turn to the common literary theme

of the inventor.   Since fifth-century Greek tragedy (cf. e.g.
Aeschylus *Prometheus Vinctus* 442 ff.) writers had speculated on
who had been initially responsible for a particular art, skill
or artefact - here Ovid gives his conclusions on who was res-
ponsible for the erotic function of the theatre.

      Usually the Rape was placed at the chariot-races in the
Circus.   Ovid may have transferred it to the theatre because
he felt that he already had enough material that was lively for
his section on the races (93ff.) or it may be his intention to
poke fun at criticism of the theatre (cf. e.g. Tacitus *Annals*
14.20) as a deplorable foreign import conducive to promiscuity
(the implication here would be that such promiscuity at the
theatre had always been a feature of Roman life: cf. 91f.).

      The same internal rhyme is present in both hexameter
and pentameter, and 60 contains in addition assonance of u, i
and a, making it a particularly musical line.   There is also
an expressive juxtaposition (Sabina viros).

61-62   fuerant: the pluperfect is freely used in elegy for
the imperfect or perfect tense.   Ovid is here making a con-
trast with his own more sophisticated day, when the theatre
was actually a building, the spectators were protected from
the sun by awnings, there was a proper stage and it was sprayed
with a reddish-yellow mixture of saffron and wine, to produce
a pleasant smell.

      In these and the following lines Ovid presents his ver-
sion of another literary theme (primitive Rome).   The Augus-
tan poets liked to imagine what their city had been like in
its early days (cf. Virgil *Aeneid* 8.337ff., Tibullus 2.5.23ff.,
Propertius 4.1.1ff.).   They tended to emphasize its simplic-
ity (in contrast to the splendours to come) and the tone was
one of approval.   Ovid states elsewhere that he was no ad-
mirer of the past (*A.A.*3.121ff. *prisca iuvent alios, ego me
nunc denique natum/gratulor: haec aetas moribus apta meis,/
...quia cultus adest nec nostros mansit in annos/rusticitas
priscis illa superstes avis*), and the sophisticated, up-to-
date poet in this passage shows his irreverent amusement at
the former crudity of the place and its inhabitants.

This is another pleasant-sounding couplet: again the
same internal rhyme occurs in both hexameter and pentameter,
and there is in addition assonance of e in the hexameter and
of u, i and a in the pentameter.   Balance (between 61 and
62) and colour-contrast (in the juxtaposed rubra croco) are also
in evidence.

63-64   The subject is scena, sine arte performs the function of
an adjective (="artless") going with scena, and the complement
is frondes.   Palatia is a poetic plural (there was only one
Palatine hill).   A contrast is implied with the more elabor-
ate scenery of the theatre in Augustan times, and the hissing
suggests a degree of contempt.

There is a rather mocking emphasis on simplicity in
simpliciter and sine arte.

Alliteration of s occurs in the pentameter.

65-66   There is an ablative absolute in 65.   In Ovid's time
seats were made of wood or stone, and such crude sun-shades
were not necessary (see on 61-62).

Again the poet's amusement is evident: as well as the
details of the seats and the sun-shades, contemporary Romans
(especially lovers) attached importance to a neat hair-style
(cf. Ovid's own advice at 297-298), and shaggy hair was asso-
ciated with uncouth rustics and barbarians.

The pentameter shows Ovid's eye for picturesque de-
tail.

Note the balance between the (positive statements of
the) simplicity of the scenery (63-64) and of the rest of the
"theatre" (65-66).   There is internal rhyme and assonance of
e in 66, producing a melodious sound-pattern.

67-68   respiciunt: historic present (Ovid switches between
historic present, imperfect and perfect for the rest of the
narrative).   Respicio here may be used in the sense of "look
about" or "look behind".   With the latter sense there are a
number of possible situations.   The Romans may be looking be-
hind because they would then be facing those of the women who
were behind them and so be able to get a better view of their
attractions than those of the girls in front.   Again, perhaps

we are to assume that, either through their own choice or by
arrangement on the part of Romulus to facilitate the Rape, all
the Sabines were sitting together at the back. velit is pot-
ential subjunctive. tacito pectore: singular for plural (an-
other common poetic usage).

The men's behaviour here is a vivid and natural touch.
It is also rather funny: their eagerness and racing thoughts
are hardly compatible with the characteristics generally attri-
buted to them elsewhere in Latin authors.

If Ovid is picturing all the Sabine women sitting in a
body at the back (as women in the theatre did in his own day),
he may be making a sly jibe at the contemporary practice of
segregation of the sexes in the theatre introduced by Augustus:
the implication would be that such segregation never did prevent
promiscuity and that modern affairs struck up in this place in
spite of this hindrance have an ancient and hallowed precedent.

Multa movere is a solemn epic phrase (cf. Virgil *Aeneid*
3.34, 5.608, 10.890), here applied to the lewd thoughts of
Romulus' men.

Every variable foot in this couplet is a dactyl: the
rhythm may well be intended to convey excitement. There is also
suggestive juxtaposition (quisque puellam) and alliteration
(multa movent).

69-70   rudem...Tusco: the whole phrase is an ablative abso-
lute. Ovid selects the details of dancing to the accompaniment
of the flute in the Etruscan fashion (cf. Livy 7.2.4) and the
dance with the triple beat (cf. Horace *Odes* 4.1.28) because both
were connected with the early days of Rome and so are appro-
priate enough here.

The scene briefly pictured in this couplet adds colour
and life to Ovid's account. Again he stresses the lack of soph-
istication (rudem, aequatam...humum = the primitive *pulpita*).

There is alliteration of t in the hexameter and (sugges-
ting the noise of the foot beating the ground) of p in the pen-
tameter.

71-72   plausus and signa are plural for singular. The daggers
around petenda indicate that because the word makes little or

no sense here the editor believes that Ovid originally wrote
something else.   We depend for our text of the *Ars* on manu-
scripts going back to the ninth century A.D. which were copied
out by scribes.   Anyone who has to reproduce by hand a long
portion of Latin (or any other language) is liable through in-
attention to make mistakes (e.g. misreading, misspelling or
omitting words), and petenda is probably just one of the quite
numerous errors in our manuscripts of the *Ars*. Many modern
scholars think that originally Ovid had *signa petita* (= "the
signal they had been looking for"), but others disagree. Do
not translate petenda.

There is a mocking aside in the hexameter (even the
applause was primitive in those days).   Ovid has lingered en-
ough on the crudity of early Rome, and dramatically in the pen-
tameter the action really starts.

The frequency of p in this couplet may be intended to
reproduce the actual sound of applause.   Ovid also juxtaposes
forms of *plausus* in 71.

73-74   iniciuntque: the -que would normally be attached to
virginibus but is often postponed like this in elegy.

The noisy and lecherous eagerness of the ancient Romans
here hardly shows them in a very dignified light.   clamore is
a good point of detail.

There is much assonance of i and u here (continued in the
next couplet), and the many dactyls in these and the following
lines suggest well the speed, excitement and panic of the situ-
ation.

75-76   timidissima turba is in apposition to columbae. agna
novella is singular for plural.

For the double simile see on 51-52.   Line 75 (mischiev-
ously) contains a variant on a simile common in loftier genres
such as epic and tragedy (the *hawk* chasing doves: cf. e.g.
Homer *Iliad* 22.139ff., Aeschylus *Supplices* 223f., Virgil *Aeneid*
11.721ff.).   In view of similarities of detail and background-
situation line 76 is probably based on the Hellenistic poet
Theocritus (*Idyll* 11.24, a lover to a girl who runs from him,
"you flee as a sheep does when it has caught sight of a grey

wolf").

The main point of comparison is fear of the assailant
(timuere (77); note that not all the girls flee: see 80 and
82), and in both similes the girls are equated with weak and
helpless prey and the men with fierce predators.   In addition
the doves suggest the girls' pallor (cf. 78) and the lambs their
youth.

This elegant couplet contains balance (flight from preda-
tors) and contrast (air and land) between hexameter and penta-
meter, anaphora (*ut* and *fugio*), alliteration of t in 75 and a
musical pattern of endings in the final four words of 76.

77-78   timuere is an alternative form for *timuerunt*.   sine lege:
"wildly" (*lex* here means "control").   nulla is here used as a
noun ("no woman").   qui fuit ante: color is the antecedent
(i.e. the noun to which qui refers).

Again the wild rush of the Romans is undignified.

The girls' sudden pallor in the pentameter is another good
point of detail.

timuere picks up timidissima (75).

79-80   erat is common to both timor and facies...timoris.   Some
word such as *sed* has been omitted before facies.   sine mente:
cf. the English expression "mindless".

Ovid was interested in human (especially female) psy-
chology, and in this and the following couplet he allows his
imagination full rein over the girls' reactions.   The Sabines
are frozen in a great variety of poses in this detailed, drama-
tic, clear and lively tableau (whose effect is heightened by
asyndeton and short staccato phrases).

This is an ingenious couplet (the contrasts within both
hexameter and pentameter, the repetition of *timor* (picking up
timuere,77), *unus* and pars, the chiastic order of timor unus...
una timoris and the assonance and alliteration in the second
half of 80).

81-82   haec...haec; haec...illa: "one girl...another...;
one...another...".

The girl calling for her mother is a particularly
graphic and realistic detail,not without humour.

This couplet actually outdoes the previous one in ingenuity: apart from the number and variety of reactions packed into only two lines, it contains repetition of altera and haec, juxtaposition (haec; haec), chiastic order of pronoun, verb, verb, pronoun in both the hexameter and the first half of the pentameter, chiastic order of silence, noise, noise, silence (altera maesta.../ ...stupet haec) and simple contrast in haec manet, illa fugit.

83-84   genialis praeda is in apposition to raptae...puellae potuit...timor: "it could be that/I dare say that their very fear was becoming to many of them".

The arrangement of participle (or adjective), appositional phrase, noun in 83 is a device from Hellenistic poetry (cf. Hedylus *Palatine Anthology* 5.199.5) which was picked up by the Augustans (cf.180).

For the amused connoisseur's comment in the pentameter cf. *Fasti* 5.608 (of Europa carried off by Jupiter in bull form) *et timor ipse novi causa decoris erat.*

Internal rhyme is combined with alliteration of p in 83.

85-86   repugnarat (= *repugnaverat*) and negarat (= *negaverat*) are contracted forms. With comitemque negarat understand *se* (i.e. "and refused to be friendly").

It is a rather embarrassing situation for his ancestors that Ovid invents here. Again the Romans' eagerness and arousal are in evidence (cupido: cf. 74).

There is internal rhyme and alliteration of n in the hexameter.

87-88   ita ("as follows") goes with dixit and introduces the quote. It can be omitted in translation. quid: "why". quod is the relative.

Ovid amuses himself by going into indelicate detail and actually giving a (vivid) quote of his ancestors' undignified attempt at persuasion. Note especially the way in which he makes the old Romans speak like contemporary lovers in the hexameter (*tener* of parts of the girl's body and the affectionate diminutive *ocellus* are common in elegy (cf. e.g. Tibullus 1.1.68, Propertius 1.1.1); for tears spoiling the eyes cf. Tibullus 2.6.43) and use a rather funny euphemism in the pentameter.

There is internal rhyme in 87, while in 88 there is bal-
ance, repetition of parts of *sum* and the expressive juxtapos-
ition matri pater.

89-90   scisti is a contracted form of *scivisti*.   commoda:
"fringe-benefits".   solus here denotes pre-eminence (= "above
all others"): cf. Propertius 1.7.11 (of his unfaithful mis-
tress) *me laudent doctae solum placuisse puellae*. haec mihi
belongs inside the si clause.   dederis is future perfect.

The address to Romulus here recalls line 59 and provides
ring-structure within the digression.

Augustus at this time had been having difficulty in re-
cruiting soldiers and in an attempt to improve enlistment had
to increase their retirement-pay (an example of a *commodum*,
i.e. something additional to their regular pay).   Probably
Ovid is here being tactlessly flippant about this problem:
he may well be saying that Romulus had a better idea than Aug-
ustus of the fringe-benefits to offer troops (girls) and that
with such inducements there would be no enlistment-problems —
in fact Ovid would join up himself.   The pentameter is impud-
ently ironical, since Ovid had avoided the customary term of
military service (cf. *Amores* 1.15.3f.) and obviously had no
intention of entering the army.   The line is reminiscent of
Tibullus 2.6.7 (to Cupid) *quod si militibus parces, erit hic
quoque miles*.

As well as internal rhyme in 89 (this is the fourth
successive hexameter containing such rhyme) there are repe-
titions (of *miles*, *dare* and *commodum*).

91-92   ex illo stands for *ex illo tempore* ("from that time",
"ever since then").   sollemni more: "by hallowed tradition".
formosis: "for pretty girls" (*formosa* is used as a noun here).

This concluding couplet looks back to 59-60, reminding
the reader of the relevance of the digression and neatly round-
ing off the section.

scilicet here parodies the use of that word by earlier
didactic poets (cf. e.g. Lucretius 1.377, Virgil *Georgics*
2.61).

<u>sollemni more</u> is a final bit of cheek.

93-120   The Circus Maximus with its chariot-races is also a good
place for acquiring a girlfriend.   Sit right next to a girl and
strike up a casual conversation;   then hint at your inclina-
tions by applauding Venus in the procession of gods and perform
various minor services for the woman.

These lines are drawn from an earlier poem of Ovid's,
Amores 3.2, in which he depicts himself picking up a girl at
the chariot-races.   Usually the present passage is compared un-
favourably with *Amores* 3.2, but, although it does lack the drama
and much of the cleverness and vividness of its predecessor, it
does have some points in its favour: it presents the situation
from a new angle (didactic), it contains some novel details
(the cushion in 118 and the stool in 120, which looks like an
improvement on *Amores* 3.2.63f.) or twists (the pretence of
interest in the racing in 103, the more subtle use of the app-
lause for Venus in 106, the non-existent dust in 109), and it
is still lively and entertaining enough (especially for those
who have not read the earlier poem).   In addition he produces
a greatly abbreviated version here (*Amores* 3.2 is 84 lines long).

For the sake of variety this section differs in several
respects from the preceding one: it is not outrageous, not so
consistently and deeply amusing, and, although some metrical
and stylistic features are present here, they are not so dazzling
and numerous as in the previous lines;   we are now back to did-
actic too, and straight didactic at that - a series of commands
unaccompanied by analogies or descriptive passages (probably to
parody portions of unrelieved advice in didactic, such as Hesiod
Works and Days 706ff., Virgil *Georgics* 1.259ff.);   in addition,
Ovid here is telling his pupil not only where but also how to
acquire a girl, and in this respect he is anticipating at
length his own second main division of the *Ars* (see on 19-24;
this may well be in imitation of passages in earlier didactic
where subject-matter was anticipated or repeated: e.g. Virgil
Georgics 2.195ff., on herds, which were supposed to be covered
in book 3, Hesiod *Works and Days* passim).

There is much ingenuity in Ovid's advice here (the tips themselves, the number and variety of them).   There is also a logical progression.   Ovid recommends a slow and smooth build-up, and this is only one of several instances of his shrewd appreciation of female mentality evident in these lines.

93-94   Circus: i.e. the Circus Maximus, reputedly built at the time of the kings and subsequently enlarged by Julius Caesar. In Ovid's day the storied groups of seats could hold some 150,000 spectators (capax populi).

The Circus is recommended because of the large crowd it attracts (= more opportunities for the potential lover), and for its seating-arrangement (97ff.).

commoda (which picks up 89f. and provides a link between sections) is here yet another deliberately dry and unemotional term.

95-96   nil is here used adverbially ("not at all").   loquaris: subjunctive in a final relative clause (expressing purpose).   The point of this couplet is explained by the following lines: in the Circus there is no need for secret communication by signs from a distance (as there is elsewhere) - you can, and should, sit right next to her (97-98) and converse with her openly (101ff.).

Nods and sign-language (especially conveyed by fingers) are commonly mentioned in elegy, particularly at dinner-parties (where the girl was usually accompanied by her boyfriend or husband): cf. *Amores* 1.4.17ff.   (Ovid to his girl in this situation) *me specta nutusque meos vultumque loquacem:/excipe furtivas et refer ipsa notas./ verba superciliis sine voce loquentia dicam;/verba leges digitis, verba notata mero./ cum tibi succurret Veneris lascivia nostrae,/purpureas tenero pollice tange genas;/si quid erit, de me tacita quod mente quereris,/pendeat extrema mollis ab aure manus;/cum tibi, quae faciam, mea lux, dicamve, placebunt,/versetur digitis anulus usque tuis;/tange manu mensam, tangunt quo more precantes,/optabis merito cum mala multa viro.*   See also *Heroides* 17.75ff., Plautus *Asinaria* 792ff., Terence *Heauton Timorumenos* 372f.

97-98   nullo is here used as a noun ("no one").   sedeto: an old

form of the imperative second person singular (= *sede*). lateri
refers to the girl's side. qua potes: "as much as you can".
In contrast to the theatre (see on 67-68) there was no segrega-
tion of the sexes in the Circus.

Logically the poet begins the encounter at the races by
making the reader take a seat next to the girl.

In sedeto Ovid uses a solemn, archaic form of the impera-
tive that was common in didactic poetry (cf. e.g. Virgil *Georgics*
2.197, 408ff.) and other prescriptive Latin (e.g. *The Twelve
Tables*, Cicero *De Legibus*).

99-100   et bene, quod.../quod: with bene understand *est* ("and
it's a good thing that.../that"). si nolis: literally "even
if you were to be unwilling" (si is concessive). linea: seats
were marked out by lines on the benches, so that there was no
actual barrier between bodies and under normal (crowded) condi-
tions people would be forced to push up against their neigh-
bours. With iungi understand *latera*.

Note the irony in si nolis. The expression in 100,
which suggests that there is actually a regulation in the Cir-
cus that girls must be touched, is also rather comic.

101-102   hic: "at this point". tibi: dative of the agent (this
construction is mainly poetical except with the perfect passive
and the gerundive). et moveant...sonos: i.e. start the con-
versation with remarks for all to hear.

Ovid now moves on to the opening gambit of striking up
a casual and seemingly innocent conversation. Thereby he
recommends a gradual and smooth build-up (none of the clumsy
grabs or abrupt declarations that might put the girl off):
this is good psychology.

There is extensive alliteration and assonance in this
couplet.

103-104   cuius...requiras = *facito studiose requiras cuius
equi veniant*. facito = *fac* (for the form see on 97-98).
Commands are often expressed by *fac/facito* with a dependent
subjunctive (*ut* is generally omitted) - so here facito...
requiras. studiose is vocative, where, of course, the nom-
inative would be regular. This (originally Greek) construc-

tion is normally explained as attraction into the vocative case.
The adjective here is used adverbially ("eagerly"). cuius equi
veniant is an indirect question depending on requiras. nec mora:
understand *sit* (= "immediately"). *erit*: future tense (so too
below) because Ovid is giving advice concerning a situation that
will arise in the future.

    The hexameter helpfully suggests how the reader can start
a casual chat, and the pentameter shows him how to capitalize
on it. Supporting the same team as the girl (and so forging
a bond with her) is rather a good idea, and Ovid here shrewdly
advises his pupil to pretend to be a real racing-fan (studiose)
as a general rule, so as not to be too obvious (he himself had
opened *Amores* 3.2 by boldly admitting to the girl *non ego nobil-
ium sedeo studiosus equorum*).

105-106 pompa: before the races there was a procession in which
were carried many statues of the gods (frequens caelestibus...
eburnis), including Venus (cf. *Amores* 3.2.43ff.). manu is
singular for plural.

    With another gentle progression the reader is now told
to give the girl a hint about his reason for starting the con-
versation in the first place. From *Amores* 3.2.47ff. it is
plain that the spectators applauded their own patron deities
in the procession, so that the reader's applause for Venus here
should make his amatory inclinations a little clearer to the
woman (though not in a direct, clumsy fashion). (At *Amores*
3.2.55ff., on which this passage is based, Ovid applauds
Venus asking for her blessing on his attempt to pick up the girl,
but here context makes it clear that the main reason for the
reader's applause is that noted above.)

    For the mock-didactic tu see on 47-48.

107-108 si has been postponed from the start of the line ("and
if, as does happen,...").

    The reader is now advised to go a little further. For
the rest of the section Ovid usefully lists various minor ser-
vices that can be performed. Again this is good psychology:
the acts would show the man's interest in and concern for the
girl, would tend to win her over to him (cf. 117) and would

also imply that, given the chance, he would be the type of thought-
ful, devoted lover that so many women like.

    The pentameter is a particularly musical line with its
assonance, alliteration and rhyme (between first and last words).

109-110   With nullum understand *pulverem* (i.e. brush off non-existent
dust). causa here means "excuse" ("let any excuse serve for a
courteous act on your part").

    An ingenious and entertaining twist (not found in *Amores* 3.2)
is given to the previous couplet in the hexameter. The repeti-
tions of *nullus, pulvis* and *excutio* add to the cleverness.

    nullum and quaelibet are given emphasis by their posi-
tions.

111-112   pallia: plural for singular. The *pallium* was a (Greek)
cloak commonly worn by freedwomen and courtesans in Rome. Again
si has been postponed.

113-114   officii pretium is (accusative) in apposition to the
whole sentence ("as a reward for..."). crura videnda goes with
contingent (literally: "the seeing of (her) legs will be granted
to your eyes").

    Rather amusingly the expert here offers a more immediate
reward in addition to the long term benefits.

    The dactyls and alliteration suggest excitement.

115-116   post vos quicumque sedebit (i.e. *quicumque post vos sede-
bit*) belongs inside the ne clause as the subject of premat.
terga: plural for singular, referring to the girl's back.

    This is a particularly vivid and realistic detail.

    praeterea here mimics the use of that word in earlier
didactic (cf. e.g. Lucretius 1.225, Virgil *Georgics* 1.204).

    In terga genu we see a juxtaposition of opposites (hard
knee and soft back) and word-order reflecting the actual con-
junction of knee and back.

117-118   parva = "small attentions". levis: alternative form for
leves.

    There is a touch of cynicism in the epigrammatical parva
levis capiunt animos.

    The claim that the poet's advice was based on tried and
tested methods (fuit utile multis) was frequent in didactic

poetry (cf. especially Virgil *Georgics* 3.398 *multi etiam excretos
prohibent a matribus haedos*).   Similarly the claim that the did-
actic poet was passing on something useful was also common, and
the expressions *est utile* and *prodest* (119) had already been
employed in this connection (cf. e.g. Lucretius 1.331, Virgil
Georgics 4.267).

There is a tricolon diminuendo in lines 117-120 (fuit
utile...pedem).

119-120   ventos movisse: "to have stirred breezes/a breeze".
scamna: plural for singular.

For profuit see on 117-118.

121-134   Love-affairs have often started at gladiatorial shows,
and similarly the vast crowd that attended Augustus' recent mock
sea-battle provided a host of opportunities in this sphere.

By way of contrast to the previous section the poem at
this point returns strictly to advice on where to find a girl,
abandoning the series of unrelieved commands;   similarly
Ovid's technical skills are now more in evidence, and there is
much wit in the thought too.   Ovid's remarks on gladiatorial
contests (121-128) contain ingenious paradox and inversion, and
in the lines that he devotes to the idea that love-affairs often
start there we see yet another way in which he expands and adds
interest to the rather unpromising raw material for this part
of the poem, i.e. the actual places suitable for acquiring a
woman (cf. the digression in the section on the theatre (59ff.)
and the anticipatory advice in the passage on the chariot
races above).   The couplets on Augustus' naval show (129-134)
are generally rather flippant, and it is a particularly amusing
twist on Ovid's part to view the show itself and the crowds it
attracted as providing a good opportunity for finding a girl
rather than as a glorious and impressive spectacle (needless
to say, Augustus would not have found this funny).

(Those who find offensive Ovid's levity here in conn-
ection with gladiatorial shows should remember that stern
moralizing is hardly the purpose of the *Ars* and censure of the
shows themselves would be both irrelevant and distracting.
In addition, as far as we can tell, very few Romans of the

period saw anything objectionable in the contests, and so to
most of his contemporaries and to Ovid himself no doubt this
frivolous treatment of the subject would not have seemed in
poor taste.)

121-122   sollicito is rather boldly applied to the forum itself:
its real reference is most probably to the tenseness of the
spectators in the forum (it could also refer to the anxiety of
the gladiators fighting in the forum).   tristis refers to
the sand's gloomy connotations (of death): the sand was sprink-
led to absorb spilt blood.   foro: although a permanent (stone)
amphitheatre did exist at this period, gladiatorial shows were
still sometimes given in a forum.

The section begins with something of a paradox: the
shows with their tense atmosphere and sombre associations pro-
vide openings for love-affairs (contrast the conditions con-
sidered suitable for love at 138ff.).

Circusque.../sparsaque: this use of -que...-que (the
first -que is really redundant) is especially common in epic.

123-124   puer Veneris: Cupid.   The couplet is metaphorical:
the assault of love on a person's heart and his struggle to
resist it are often described as an attack by and fight with
the god of love Cupid (pugnavit), and similarly when a per-
son fell in love he was said to have been wounded by Cupid's
arrow(s) (vulnus habet).   vulnera refers to the gladiators'
wounds.   The subject of habet is (is) qui spectavit vulnera.

With a clever and entirely novel inversion Ovid depicts
a fight between Cupid and a spectator (instead of two gladia-
tors) in which the spectator is wounded (instead of watching
gladiators being wounded).   Note also that in the hexameter
Ovid may be playing on the fact that gladiators were sometimes
called Eros or Cupid, and habet in the pentameter probably con-
tains a reference to the common cry "habet" or "hoc habet"
("he's got it") by the crowd when one of the combatants was
wounded (instead of the spectator crying "habet" of another,
the word is actually applied to the spectator, who has rec-
eived a wound himself).

There is rhyme between the first and last words in

both the hexameter and the pentameter, framing (see INTRODUCTION
section 7), alliteration and repetition in 123, as well as con-
trast, juxtaposition and repetition in 124.

125-126   Suetonius (*Divus Augustus* 44) tells us that Augustus in-
troduced segregation of the sexes at gladiatorial shows, but
obviously 127 makes better and easier sense if the man here is
talking to and touching a girl: perhaps regulations were relaxed
when the show was in a forum, or Ovid may have written this be-
fore Augustus introduced his rule.   tangitque manum: this may
refer to some other accidental (?) brushing of hands, but most
probably the man is pointing to or reaching for the programme,
touching her hand in the process.   posito pignore: ablative
absolute with causal force.   vincat uter (=*uter vincat*) is an
indirect question depending on quaerit.

      These realistic details add life to Ovid's account.

      This musical couplet contains a tetracolon (group of four)
crescendo.

127-128   For the metaphor in saucius and telumque volatile see on
123-124.   spectati muneris: "of the show he had been watching".

      We see here the same type of inversion as in 123-124,
with the addition of the graphic (and rather comic) groan from
the spectator instead of the gladiator.

      There is mock-solemnity in the hexameter (especially in
the phrase telumque volatile, taken from loftier genres: e.g.
Lucretius 1.970).

      A tricolon crescendo is here added to the last coup-
let's tetracolon crescendo, not to mention the internal rhyme
and repetition.

129-130   quid, modo cum: "what about when recently...".   imagine
is an ablative of manner ("with a semblance of...").   Caesar:
i.e. Augustus ("Caesar" was inherited as a *cognomen* from Julius
Caesar by Augustus and was also adopted by succeeding emperors).
The reference in this couplet is to a show put on in Rome by
Augustus in 2 B.C. on an artificial lake.   It represented the
famous battle of Salamis (480 B.C.) in which the Greek fleet,
whose largest contingent by far was supplied by the Athenians
(hence Cecropias), had defeated the much stronger fleet of the

Persian invaders.

Cecropiasque is an instance of *doctrina*: Cecrops was said to have been the first king of Attica and the founder of Athens, so that *Cecropius* was used by Latin poets to mean "Athenian".

131-132   ab utroque mari...ab utroque: mari is common to both phrases.   The land-masses of the earth were supposed to be encompassed by a vast sea (*Oceanus*), so that the Latin here means from either side of this sea, i.e. from the furthest east and the furthest west.   venere: an alternative form for *vener-unt*.   Urbe: Rome.

nempe here may well be intended to mimic the use of that word by Lucretius (1.385, 2.487, 908, 4.1173, 1174).

Although vast crowds did attend such spectacles (cf. e.g. Suetonius *Divus Iulius* 39, Tacitus *Annals* 12.56), Ovid is obviously exaggerating in this couplet.   However, this exaggeration is not to compliment Augustus on the fame and popularity of his show but to point out the numerous opportunities for picking up a girlfriend (133-134).

There is rather frivolous verbal play in the pentameter's ingens orbis in Urbe.

133-134   quod amaret: for quod see on 19-20; amaret is subjunctive in a final relative clause.

Note the clever and amusing switches from the hexameter in the pentameter (the lover moves from an active to a passive role, there is a change from the rational view of love (quod) to emotional love (torsit), and the happy tone of 133 gives way to (mock-) sadness in 134).

There is mock-solemnity in the many spondees.

135-152   Openings are provided by dinner-parties too, since wine puts people in a mood for love.   However, caution is necessary in selecting a girl there, as drink and artificial light impair one's judgement.

This is another diverting section and one that again shows Ovid striving for variety and expanding upon his basic material in different ways.   In the first part of the passage (down to 144) we see once more the joke of the poet dilating with mock-

seriousness on something that was perfectly obvious and well-
known.   Although affairs very often started at dinner-parties
in love-poetry (e.g. Tibullus 1.6.18ff., Ovid *Heroides* 16.243ff.,
17.75ff.) and apparently in real life (e.g. Horaces *Odes* 3.6.
25ff.), Ovid pretends that the point needs emphasizing (it is
made more than once: 135f. and 143f.) and that it actually needs
backing up by several lines on the effects of wine (which are
conducive to love).   In addition, what he says about the res-
ults of drinking had already been said by many authors from
earliest times and would, of course, be well-known to anyone
who had ever had a few drinks himself, yet Ovid goes on at
length as if his pupil needed this information, and at 138 and
140 actually repeats in similar language the most trite obser-
vation of all (wine banishes unhappiness) as if this was an im-
portant new point that had to be underlined.

        The second half of the section (145ff.) entertains and
expands in another way.   It contains a useful tip, but one
that is, strictly speaking, beyond Ovid's brief (he is only
supposed to be explaining where to pick up women).   It seems
likely that here Ovid may be parodying passages in earlier did-
actic that contain hints and observations which are helpful but
not strictly to the point (cf. e.g. Virgil *Georgics* 1.305ff.,
advice about jobs to do in the winter, which is not really
relevant to that book's subject of crops, and *Georgics* 3.409ff.,
on the use of dogs for hunting, which has no connection with
herds, the subject of book 3).

135-136   positis...mensis: ablative absolute.   Tables were port-
    able.   vina: plural for singular or standing for the various
    types of wine (so too in 137).   petas: potential subjunctive.

        The hexameter looks like a (learned) reminiscence of
    Propertius 3.25.1 *risus eram positis inter convivia mensis.*

        The neuter aliquid is another unemotional term, but it
    also makes the pentameter humorously suggestive.

137-138   caloribus is plural for singular.   diluiturque: the *-que*
    would normally be attached to multo (see on 73-74).

        For the frequently remarked connection between wine and
    love cf. e.g. Euripides *Bacchae* 773, Ovid *Remedia* 805 *vina*

parant animum Veneri. For the extremely common idea that wine
drives out anxiety and sorrow, bringing happiness and laughter
(139), cf.e.g. Alcaeus 96.3-4D "for the son of Semele and Zeus
gave men care-banishing wine", Horace *Odes* 3.21.2.

cura...diluiturque mero: a verbal joke (the phrase
means literally: "care...is diluted by undiluted wine"). This
type of combination of contradictory terms is known as oxymoron.

This is a pleasingly light and musical couplet, opening
and closing with a word for wine.

139-140   pauper is used as a noun.   cornua: the horns are meta-
phorical here, denoting (bull-like) courage and defiance. abit:
singular because it agrees with its nearest subject.

The belief that wine gives a man defiance and bravery was
also common. Ovid seems to be imitating Horace *Odes* 3.21.18
(to a wine-jar) *addis cornua pauperi.* The reference to the pauper
here may be intended to suggest that everyone (including *even*
the poor man) is so affected, or Ovid may be making this remark
because he is advising the (conventionally poor) lover.

141-142   artes: "artificiality"(i.e. lack of naturalness). deo:
i.e. Bacchus, the god of wine.

It had long been established that wine encourages frank-
ness and reveals people's natural feelings: cf. e.g. Alcaeus
66D "wine, my dear boy, and truth" (i.e. *in vino veritas*),
Horace *Odes* 3.21.15f. *arcanum iocoso/consilium retegis Lyaeo.*

Note the order tunc...tum.../tum.../tunc in 139-141.

143-144   rapuere: for the form see on 131-132.   ignis in igne
fuit: ignis refers to the "fire" of love (cf. caloribus, 137)
and igne to wine's inflammatory effect (making emotions and
passions "flare up"), i.e. Venus (love) at a dinner-party has
inflamed an already inflammable situation.

With a humorous switch (similar to that in 133-134) Ovid
in the hexameter suddenly represents men as passive prey and
love as an emotional business.

The pentameter is a skilful line: it is neatly epi-
grammatical and contains balance, repetition, alliteration and
word-play. The latter half of the line cleverly adapts a
proverbial expression first found in Greek (cf. e.g. Plato *Laws*

666A).

145-146   hic: "in these circumstances".   ne crede: this form of
    prohibition was common in early and colloquial Latin, and in
    poetry.   fallaci...lucernae: the oil-lamp was the only source
    of light at the dinner-party, and, of course, artificial ill-
    umination often conceals faults that are revealed in the bright
    light of day.

          Ovid's helpful expert hint here with amusing abruptness
    reverts to the rational view of love (it is a matter of cool,
    careful selection).

          There is parody in tu (see on 47-48) and the use of *credo*
    (cf. especially Virgil *Georgics* 4.48 *altae neu crede paludi*).

          The pentameter is another epigrammatical line.   For the
    repeated *-que* see on 121-122.

          The predominantly spondaic nature of 145 adds a touch of
    (mock-) solemnity.

147-148   The reference here is to the famous judgement of Paris:
    Juno, Minerva and Venus were rivals for a golden apple inscribed
    "for the fairest", and Jupiter directed them to the Trojan
    prince Paris for a decision;   Venus, who offered Paris the most
    beautiful woman in the world (Helen) as a reward, was declared
    the winner (Paris' abduction of Helen was, of course, respons-
    ible for the Trojan War).   luce: (in view of nocte, 149) most
    probably temporal ablative ("in the daytime").   caeloque...
    aperto: local ablative (see on 11-12):   in prose *sub* would have
    been added.   dixit: indicative because the *cum* clause gives
    the date of the action in the main sentence (see on 59-60).

          This is a novel and ingenious use of the judgement of
    Paris.   The analogy from mythology adds variety and also
    parodies similar analogies in didactic poetry.   To drive home
    his point Ovid places important words in emphatic positions
    (luce and aperto in 147, nocte in 149 and diem in 152).

149-150   ignoscitur is an impersonal passive ("forgiveness is
    shown to...").   With quamlibet understand *puellam*.

          The cynical expert reappears in the pentameter.

          Ovid reverses his stance when he advises women in book
    3 of the *Ars* and points out the advantages for them of wine and

darkness at a dinner-party: *etsi turpis eris, formosa videbere*
potis,/et latebras vitiis nox dabit ipsa tuis (753f.).

151-152   *consule diem de* ("consult daylight about") means "judge
in daylight".   facie is singular for plural ("faces").

The idea of love as a matter of cold, rational selection
is here taken to its outrageous extreme as Ovid puts falling in
love on a par with financial transactions.

This is an elegant couplet to close the section (the rep-
etition, balance, chiasmus (in plural and singular forms) and
the pattern of alliteration and word-endings in 152).   The
elegance heightens the cheek.

153-158   After telling you where to find a girl I will now move
on to how to win her.   Men, give me your attention and support.

This is an amusing little section.   Apart from the joke
in 154 and the various minor instances of didactic parody noted
below, this whole passage, with its careful and logical trans-
ition, is a burlesque of the didactic recapitulation (cf. Luc-
retius 3.31ff., 5.55ff., especially Virgil *Georgics* 2.1ff. *hac-*
tenus arvorum cultus et sidera caeli:/nunc te, Bacche, canam...).
In addition, Ovid again suggests the importance of love and
again shows a clinical approach to love (particularly over the
winning of the girl, which is surely a matter of the heart
rather than a business calling for cool, calculating *artes*).
The fact that in these six lines only two variable feet are spon-
dees makes for an apt lightness.

153-154   unde and ubi introduce indirect questions depending on
praecipit.   legas and ponas are deliberative subjunctives in
these indirect questions.   For quod ames see on 19-20 and
133-134.   The pentameter refers to what Ovid has written so
far (in elegiac couplets):   Thalea, the Muse who inspires his
poem, stands here for the poem itself;   using an image from
chariot-driving, he depicts the progress of his poem so far as
a ride by Thalea in a chariot, and, since Ovid's "vehicle"
is the elegiac couplet (consisting of hexameter plus shorter
pentameter), rather comically he describes the chariot as having
one wheel smaller than the other.

The picture of the chariot bumping its way along is even

funnier because Ovid is here adapting the serious use of such
chariot-imagery in lofty poetry (see on 23-24).   For similar
jokes about the elegiac couplet see *Amores* 1.1.1ff. (Ovid writes
two (hexameter) lines of epic, when Cupid pinches a foot from
the second line, thereby leaving the poet with an elegiac coup-
let), 3.1.8 (the Muse Elegy has one foot shorter than the other).

The Muses were not strictly confined to individual genres
of poetry until quite late in antiquity, so that Thalea here
may simply be used for "Muse" in general, but Thaelea does appear
elsewhere (e.g. Statius *Silvae* 2.1.116) as the Muse of Comedy
in particular, and so Ovid may be alluding to the fact that the
Ars is humorous in both intent and execution.

155-156   The convoluted word-order makes this a rather difficult
couplet: quas sit capienda per artes (i.e. *per quas artes cap-
ienda sit*) is an indirect question depending on dicere;   the
subject of sit capienda is tibi quae placuit (i.e. *(ea) quae
tibi placuit)*; praecipuae...artis opus is (accusative) in
apposition to dicere and its indirect question.

capienda continues the hunting-imagery in ubi retia
ponas (153).

For the claim in the pentameter that the poet's task
is a demanding one cf. Virgil *Georgics* 1.40 *audacibus adnue coep-
tis*, 3.41 *tua, Maecenas, haud mollia iussa*, and see on 2.13-14.

157-158   With quisquis ubique understand *es* ("whoever (and) wher-
ever you are"), a not uncommon use of the singular when the
main verb is plural (advertite).   pollicitisque...meis here
must mean something like "the enterprise which I have just pro-
mised to undertake".   favens vulgus (a collective noun) is
in apposition to viri.

Again there is burlesque: for the hexameter cf. e.g.
Lucretius 1.50f., 4.912 (*tu mihi da tenuis auris animumque sag-
acem*), and for the pentameter cf. e.g. Lucretius 1.499, Virgil
Georgics 2.39, 44 (for the imperative of *adsum*), 4.2 *hanc etiam,
Maecenas, aspice partem.*

159-178   First of all, you must assure yourself that all women
can be caught.   A charming approach will never encounter res-
istance.   Girls, like men, enjoy a secret affair, and, in

fact, if we didn't proposition them, they would proposition us.
What's more, sexual desire in women is frantic and knows no
bounds, as is proved by the examples of Byblis and Myrrha.

Before telling his pupil how to win a girl, Ovid begins
with some preliminary advice. In essence he maintains that the
reader should be confident about approaching a girl, since girls
actually want a boyfriend. The tip is helpful, and in a lot
of cases the supporting observation is true enough, as many a
shy and nervous young man has realized in later life, but in
a truly outrageous fashion Ovid actually states that *all* women
can be won because *all* are willing, *all* enjoy having an affair
on the sly and *all* are mad about sex.   Even bearing in mind
Ovid's claim at 15-18 that he is thinking only of liaisons with
unmarried women (which by now most readers will have forgotten),
his remarks here are certainly not invariably correct. His
sweeping generalizations and exaggerations are urbanely cynical
and become more and more scandalous as the passage progresses.
The humour is increased by the frequent elegance and cleverness
of expression and by the fact that here Ovid, in his pose as the
sophisticated and experienced man of the world, gives us the
full professorial treatment with an argument that is dogmatic,
carefully ordered and backed up by various analogies and examples.
The section is partly to put the prospective lover in the corr-
ect (confident) frame of mind (going along with the fiction of
the *Ars* as genuine instruction), but its main intention is to
entertain and be provocative.

159-160   prima is adverbial.   cunctas is used as a noun here
    ("all women") and cunctas/posse capi is an accusative and infini-
    tive after fiducia. tu modo tende plagas: see on 261-262.

         Ovid begins his argument by succinctly stating his main
    proposition (his three "proofs" come in the following lines and
    are progressively longer).

         For tu see on 47-48.

         The emphatic positioning of important words in this coup-
    let (prima, cunctas, posse, capi and capies) and the allitera-
    tion make for greater forcefulness.

161-162   vere: from *ver*. prius is picked up by quam in 163

("sooner would...than..."). We have here what is known as an
adunaton (impossibility): a common way in Latin (and Greek) of
expressing the idea that A is very unlikely to happen is to say
that B, C and D, which are impossible, are more likely to come
about than A (cf. e.g. *Ex Ponto* 4.5.41ff., Horace *Odes* 1.33.7ff.).
taceant is common to volucres and cicadae. The subjunctive is
potential (so too det and in 163 repugnet). Maenalius: Arcad-
ian hunting-dogs were supposed to be one of the best breeds.
terga: plural for singular.

Ovid's first "proof" (*all* women are willing, if you app-
roach them correctly) occupies this couplet and the next.

The pentameter may contain a reminiscence of Lucretius
3.750f. (*effugeret canis Hyrcano de semine saepe/cornigeri
incursum cervi*), transferred to a frivolous context.

163-164 quam in 163 is postponed. iuveni seems to go with both
temptata (as dative of the agent) and repugnet. poteris...
volet: future tenses because Ovid is talking about a situa-
tion in the future.

blande is important: a charming approach is necessary
(and later Ovid will instruct his pupil on this approach). In
real life, of course, this is *not* invariably successful.

The pentameter is especially cynical: even women who
seem unavailable (through an air of aloofness, lack of interest
or respectability, or because they already have a boyfriend)
are really available. Cf. *Amores* 1.8.45f. *has quoque, quae
frontis rugas in vertice portant,/excute, de rugis crimina multa
cadent.*

The pentameter is a particularly clever line: it is
alliterative and epigrammatical, and great emphasis is given
to the all-important volet by the juxtaposition of the antith-
etical nolle and by its brevity and position at the end of the
line.

165-166 Note the compression in the hexameter (= *utque furtiva
venus grata viro est, sic furtiva venus grata puellae est*).
tectius: with more (i.e. better) concealment.

Ovid's second "proof" (165-170) is even more scurri-
lous than the first: *all* women in reality positively enjoy a

secret affair, and, in fact, if we men didn't take the initia-
tive, they would.

furtiva venus denotes an affair that is kept secret from
parents or the prying eyes of the public, or (more outrageous
still and probably uppermost in Ovid's mind) one that is con-
cealed from the girl's existing boyfriend.

The cynicism in the pentameter is similar to that in
164.

167-168   conveniat.../...aget: equivalent to a condition ("let
us males agree not to...the woman will soon..."). ante is the
temporal adverb. rogantis is used as a noun ("the asker") and
goes with partes (plural for singular).

The suggestion made in the hexameter conjures up an
amusingly improbable situation, but, Ovid claims, in this situa-
tion *all* women will demean themselves.   Note the emphatic posi-
tion of femina.

169-170   femina here stands for the female of the species.

To drive home the "truth" of his observation in the pre-
vious couplet, Ovid cites situations in which unnatural human
conventions do not operate.   Intentionally Ovid's point here
is hardly valid or flattering to women (they are not really like
animals).

For the analogies see on 37-38.

There is mischievous reminiscence of Virgil in mollibus
in pratis (cf. especially *Georgics* 2.384) and cornipedi...equo
(cf. *Aeneid* 6.591, 7.779).

admugit and adhinnit are onomatopoeic.

171-172   nobis: "us men" (cf. virilis in the pentameter).   In the
hexameter understand *est*.   legitimum finem: "a proper limit"
(but legitimum also contains the idea of "lawful", in contrast
to the loves of the mythical women below, which contravened the
laws of man and nature).

Ovid's third "proof" of his main proposition (171ff.)
is the most shocking of all: by nature *all* women are more lust-
ful than men, and their sexual desire is frantic and without
limit, so that they entertain monstrous passions (e.g. Byblis
and Myrrha).   The implication is that since women are so

maddened by desire that they are capable even of illicit passions,
the reader need have no fears of failure in starting an ordinary
harmless affair.

      The chauvinistic and dubious claim that sexual desire is
greater in women than in men is based on Propertius 3.19 (where
Myrrha (cf. 175ff.) and Pasiphae (cf. 179ff.) are also used as
examples to back up the argument).

173-174   Byblida is a Greek form of the accusative. quid ("why")
is postponed. vetito, which is here used as an adjective ("for-
bidden"), belongs inside the quae clause, and the phrase vetito...
fratris amore goes with arsit. fratris is objective genitive
("love for..."). Byblis conceived an ill-fated passion for her
own brother Caunus   In some accounts she subsequently committed
suicide, here apparently through remorse (est...fortiter ulta
nefas).

      The stories of Byblis and Myrrha are cited to back up
Ovid's assertion that women's sexual desire is wild and knows
no bounds (they are even capable of something as monstrous as
incest). It seems (deliberately) extreme and unfair to tar *all*
women with the same brush. Of course, it suits Ovid's point
to make Byblis (here) and Myrrha (below) themselves see the
evil of their ways and feel shame. The mythological examples,
as well as constituting a particularly scandalous use of the
expert's *doctrina*, are mock-didactic. The myths are also a
good example of Ovid's interest in unusual and grotesque stories
and his employment of them to add interest and variety to his
poetry.

175-176   Myrrha was desperately in love with her father Cinyras.
Her nurse out of pity for her state took her to Cinyras' bed
at night, pretending that it was not Myrrha but another young
woman, who loved him. Cinyras was deceived until one night
he brought in a lamp, eager to see the face of his new mis-
tress. When Myrrha was in this way discovered she had to flee
her father's murderous rage, and she wandered for several
months, until finally she was transformed into a myrrh-tree.
qua here is the relative adverb ("as").

      Note the suggestive juxtaposition and the black humour

in the aside in the hexameter.

There is great emphasis on constriction and conceal-
ment in the pentameter. The (bizarre) idea seems to be that
Myrrha was covered by the bark of the tree rather than trans-
formed.

The pentameter here, most of the previous pentameter and
the whole of the following couplet are not entirely relevant to
the point about female passion that Ovid is making. This in-
creasing expansiveness is leading up to and smoothing the path
for the lengthy digression on Pasiphae that follows at 179ff.
The growing emphasis on the strange and the grotesque in lines
173-178 performs the same function.

177-178   The subject of <u>fundit</u> is *illa* (to be supplied from <u>illius</u>).
<u>nomina</u> is plural for singular. Even after her transformation
Myrrha cried (out of shame), and her tears were identified with
myrrh, the sap exuded from the myrrh-tree, which was used as a
perfume.

The idea of people anointing themselves with a person's
tears is, of course, fantastic and peculiar.

179-220   Then there is always the story of Cretan Pasiphae, who
loved a white bull and was jealous of cows that might be attrac-
tive to him. In an attempt to win his love she gave him choice
fodder and accompanied the herds in all her regal finery. When-
ever she suspected that a cow had taken his eye, she had it put
to the yoke or sacrificed. Eventually she disguised herself
as a cow and seduced the bull. Such are the lengths to which
women are driven by their frantic sexual desire. So, you
should be confident of success in starting an affair with any
(or almost any) woman you want.

Continuing in his role as the expert carefully backing
up his observations with examples, Ovid now adds another story
to illustrate his third "proof" (sexual desire is greater and
more frantic in women: 171-172). He makes a progression
from incest to the more monstrous crime of bestiality, and
the length at which he tells the tale of Pasiphae means that
he is putting emphasis on the most shocking "proof" of all.
It is also outrageous of Ovid to go into this myth in such

detail and to treat it in such a flippant fashion.   Of course,
the message for the reader is similar to that in 173ff. (since
women are so maddened by desire that they are capable of such
monstrous passion and ludicrous behaviour, the reader should feel
rather superior and confident of success in starting an ordinary
natural affair).   There is a danger that this message might be
lost sight of (and Ovid himself seems to become carried away in
his narrative) - hence the careful underlining of the point in
the conclusion at 217ff.

Ovid with his interest in female psychology puts himself
in Pasiphae's position and wonders amusedly how she might have
felt and behaved in this bizarre situation.   The resultant
account is highly inventive and entertaining, it is carefully
and skilfully ordered (including a deliberate tease of the reader
in the opening lines),and it is also constantly enlivened by
Ovid's eye for detail, the intrusion of personal observations,
questions, exclamations, address, quotation of Pasiphae's words,
a short simile and Ovid's usual metrical and stylistic ingenuity.
In fact the length of Ovid's treatment of the myth means that
it amounts to a digression (and so mimics the digression in
didactic poetry: see on 59-92).   Indulging his interest in
the strange and the unusual, Ovid allows full play to his sense
of humour and his wit and seizes on another chance to show at
length his narrative skill and *doctrina*.

As well as mythological learning there is also literary
doctrina here, as Ovid takes for his model the treatment of
Pasiphae's story by Virgil in *Eclogue* 6.45-60.   Although there
are numerous reminiscences of Virgil, there are also several
minor variations and refinements.   So too Ovid produces a
much longer and more detailed version, and instead of the
sympathy, pathos and occasional delicate irony in the *Eclogue*,
we find amusement, comedy and black humour, as Ovid brings
out the incongruity and grotesqueness of the circumstances.
Similarly Ovid's account of the queen's jealousy of the cows
(203ff.) is an expansion of a mere hint of this idea in
Virgil (see on 185-186), while her attempts here to win the
bull's love (189ff.) represent an entirely novel addition.

179-180   armenti gloria is in apposition to candidus...taurus.

      The first four lines with their leisurely description of
the bull provide an innocuous and peaceful enough beginning.
At this point most readers would be wondering why Ovid is talk-
ing about a bull at all (after stories of incest), and, as
there were two mountains called Ida, they would not even be cer-
tain of the location.   If anything, they would incline (mis-
takenly) toward Troy rather than Crete, since nemorosae recalls
one of Homer's epithets (= "wooded") for Mount Ida near Troy
and vallibus recalls another (= "with many valleys"): cf. e.g.
Iliad 21.449.   Note also that the most recent detailed version
of the myth of Pasiphae (Virgil *Ecl.* 6.56) set the action near
Mount *Dicte* in Crete and that this was by no means the only
myth that involved a bull (see especially on 213-214).   Ovid
is teasing by disguising his true subject.

      Note the clarity of the picture here (especially the
contrast between the white bull and the dark background).

      Virgil also makes the bull white (cf. *Ecl.*6.46), but
in the next couplet Ovid adds a tiny black spot (perhaps also
part of the tease).

      For the word-order in the pentameter see on 83-84.

181-182   media inter cornua: "midway between his horns".   nigro
is here used as a noun ("black mark").   lactis: genitive of
description/quality (*lac* here denotes a milky-white colour).

      Ovid's eye for small detail adds vividness to his des-
cription, and again there is the contrast between white and
black.   For these contrasts cf. Virgil *Ecl.* 6.53f. (of the
bull) *ille latus niveum molli fultus hyacintho/ilice sub nigra
pallentis ruminat herbas.*

183-184   Cnosiades is the nominative plural of *Cnosias*.   opta-
runt is a contracted form of *optaverunt*.   tergo...suo: sing-
ular for plural.   sustinuisse: the perfect infinitive is often
used by the Augustan poets as an alternative for the present
infinitive, as here.

      The element of sexual desire (natural sexual desire)
is introduced.   After the description of the handsome bull in
the previous lines that progression is smooth enough, but at

the same time readers suddenly realize that the scene is in
fact set in Crete.   Before most can try to decide the implica-
tions of this and while they are still laughing at these lines
the next couplet is upon them.

When the pentameter is read we realize just how mis-
chievous is Ovid's use in the hexameter of -que...-que (see on
121-122) and the learned, lengthy and sonorous adjectives (as
well as the alliteration and rhyme throughout the couplet).
The epithets also add colour to the description and suggest
that the bull's fame had spread beyond Ida itself.

185-186   adultera tauri: the genitive denotes the partner in
    adultery ("adulteress with a bull").   invida is adverbial.

Ovid triumphantly introduces Pasiphae (first word in the
line), and now the reader realizes what the previous couplets
have been leading up to.   Here the poet succinctly summarizes
the whole amusing and grotesque situation.   The couplet acts
as a signpost and mentions the two main aspects of the myth that
Ovid will dwell on (185 = Pasiphae's attempts to win the bull's
love, picked up at 189ff.;   186 = her jealousy of cows, picked
up at 203ff.).

gaudebat is not without point: such was her madness
that Pasiphae actually delighted in her ludicrous attempts to
further her awful passion.

adultera tauri: the use of adultera in this situation
and the position of tauri make this an aptly startling, strange
and comic phrase.

Pasiphae's grotesque jealousy of the cows (much expanded
below) is based on the suggestion in Virgil *Ecl.* 6.55 and 60
that the bull prefers his natural mates and the merest hint in
60 that the queen is envious of them.

187-188   non hoc goes with Creta negare potest.   centum quae
    sustinet urbes (i.e. *quae centum urbes sustinet*) has Creta as
    its antecedent.   mendax: Cretans were proverbial liars.

This is a very funny couplet in several ways.   In nota
cano Ovid ironically suggests that the reader might not have
heard of the tale of Pasiphae (and so suspect that it was en-
tirely Ovid's invention), and in the rest of the couplet with

similar irony he claims that such a tall story is perfectly true.
The poet also pretends that he seriously feels that his remarks
in the last couplet need backing up like this before he can con-
tinue the narrative in more detail, that it is a matter of gen-
uine concern to him whether or not the reader believes the tale
at all and that his affirmations in this couplet really would
be likely to convince anyone of the veracity of the myth. Be-
cause the events of the story took place in Crete, Ovid takes
the opportunity of working in two further jokes: (i) a novel
twist to the proverbial mendacity of Cretans (here they would
be falsely denying a story instead of their usual practice of
making up false stories); (ii) a learned and clever reference
to Homer's epithet (= "hundred-citied": e.g. *Iliad* 2.649) for
Crete (here the number of cities underlines the multitude of
liars who cannot deny the story).   In addition, the rhythm,
forceful alliteration and ponderous assonance contribute to
the mock-solemnity.

> nota cano echoes Callimachus fragment 612 Pfeiffer
("I tell of nothing unattested").

189-190   prata here denotes not meadows but what grows in the
meadows.   fertur...subsecuisse: literally "she is said to
have cut...".

> Following the order announced at 185-186, Ovid resumes
first with an account of Pasiphae's efforts to win the bull's
love (lasting until line 202).

> The queen's amusing attempts to ingratiate herself by
giving the bull choice fodder (novas and tenerrima) may have
been suggested by Virgil *Ecl.* 6.59 (of the bull) *herba captum
viridi*.   It is odd enough for a woman to do this for a bull,
but it is particularly lowering for a queen to act like this
(a point brought out by ipsa in emphatic position and by inad-
sueta).

191-192   it: historic present.   In the following lines Ovid
again (see on 67-68) mixes historic presents with past tenses.
nec ituram cura moratur/coniugis: understand *eam* ("and care
for her husband (i.e. Minos) does not restrain her about to
go", i.e. restrain her from going).

The incongruity of a queen accompanying herds is followed
by the paradox of a woman deserting her husband for an animal
and preferring a mere bull to (regal, wealthy and stately) Minos.

193-194   quo tibi...sumere: the infinitive seems to be governed
by something (e.g. *libet*) to be understood (i.e. "what's the
use of...?").   ille tuus...adulter refers to the bull.

The incongruity of the situation in the previous couplet
is here expanded as we are given the ludicrous picture of Pasi-
phae in her royal finery among cows and bulls. Her attention to her
dress and (below) her hair in an attempt to make herself attrac-
tive to the bull is both ridiculous and grotesque (she is act-
ing as if the bull was a man - hence the pointed ille tuus...
adulter).

The address to Pasiphae has a parallel at Virgil *Ecl.*
6.47ff.   Here Ovid's air of superior incredulity adds greatly
to the humour.

195-196   quid tibi cum speculo: understand *est* (i.e. "what do
you want with a mirror...?").   quid in 196 means "why".
inepta is adverbial.

montana armenta petenti: cf. Virgil *Ecl.* 6.52 *a, virgo
infelix, tu nunc in montibus erras.*

The detail of the frequent alterations of the hair in
the mirror may have come from Callimachus *Hymn* 5.21f. ("But
Cypris (i.e. Venus) taking the shining bronze often altered
again and again the same lock").   The collocation totiens
positas fingis brings out Pasiphae's laughable fastidiousness.

197-198   cuperes is potential subjunctive.   fronti...tuae goes
with cuperes ("for your forehead").

The detail of the mirror in the previous couplet is
given a neat twist here (a mirror is not totally useless - it
does show you how ill-suited to the bull you really are).

The pentameter may have been suggested by Virgil *Ecl.*
6.51 (of the daughters of Proetus) *et saepe in levi quaesisset
cornua fronti.*

199-200   With placet understand *tibi*.   quaeratur is jussive
subjunctive.   virum...viro: Ovid is here cleverly playing
on the two different senses of *vir* ("husband" and "man").

Translate virum as "your man" and viro as "with a man" (i.e. not
an animal).   The ablative is instrumental.

The lines are rather spondaic for Ovid.   This suits the
pretence of seriousness and sternness that he maintains until
the end of the couplet (where he actually acquiesces to adultery,
only objecting to the queen's bizarre choice of partner).

This is an ingeniously constructed couplet with its con-
trast, repetition, chiasmus, juxtaposition and great emphasis given
to the pointed viro by its brevity and position.

201-202   nemus is singular for plural.   fertur: "goes".   Aonio...
deo: dative of the agent.   The reference is to Bacchus, who
was born at Thebes in Aonia (= Boeotia in Greece) and whose
mother was the Theban princess Semele.   Baccha: the female wor-
shippers of Bacchus, when inspired by the god, roved the coun-
tryside in wild ecstasy.   In the same way Pasiphae is frenzied
and goes off into the country.

In this couplet Ovid closes his account of the queen's
attempts to win the bull's love.   By again placing Pasiphae in
a rustic setting of trees and grass (cf. 189f.) and by echoing
fertur (190) at the same point in the pentameter here he provides
ring-structure.

in nemus et saltus: cf. Virgil *Ecl.* 6.56 *Dictaeae*
Nymphae, nemorum iam claudite saltus.

The pentameter mischievously contains a simile common
in loftier genres of poetry (e.g. Homer *Iliad* 22.460, Virgil
Aeneid 4.301ff.).   For the idea that Pasiphae is mentally dis-
turbed cf. Virgil *Ecl.* 6.47 *a, virgo infelix, quae te demen-*
tia cepit!

This is a musical couplet with its alliteration, frequent
assonance and internal rhyme.

203-204   domino...meo: women used *dominus* as a term of affection
for the man they loved.   Here it is applied to the bull that
Pasiphae loves.

Following the order announced at 185-186, Ovid now moves
on to the theme of Pasiphae's jealousy (203-212).   Note also
that there is a progression from her silly and harmless attempts
to seduce the bull to the more serious and harmful business of

her *invidia*.

      a̲: cf. Virgil *Ecl.* 6.47 and 52 (quoted above). There is
an ironical twist here to the sympathetic tone of the word in
Virgil.

      Comically the legendary queen Pasiphae's suspicions here
resemble those of a contemporary elegiac mistress (cf. e.g.
Amores 2.7.1ff.), with a bizarre and rather ludicrous change of
circumstances. Ovid also has her speak like a woman in elegy,
and he makes her (in a particularly grotesque fashion) apply to
a bull and a cow words normally used of a man and a woman (for
dominus cf. *Amores* 3.7.11; for *placeo* cf. line 26 above).
Virgil (*Ecl.* 6.55ff.) also quotes Pasiphae's words.

205-206   u̲t̲: "how". h̲e̲r̲b̲i̲s̲: plural for singular. s̲e̲...d̲e̲c̲e̲r̲e̲
p̲u̲t̲e̲t̲: "thinks it (i.e. frisking about) becomes her". s̲t̲u̲l̲t̲a̲
is here used as a noun ("the stupid cow").

      The humour is increased by the fact that the action of
the cow for which Pasiphae shows such contempt *would* quite probab-
ly be becoming to a cow and attractive to a bull.

207-208   i̲u̲s̲s̲i̲t̲: the (unexpressed) object is *vaccam* (the cow
mentioned in the previous lines), with which i̲m̲m̲e̲r̲i̲t̲a̲m̲ agrees.
i̲u̲g̲a̲ ̲c̲u̲r̲v̲a̲: plural for singular. Of course, Pasiphae sets
the cow to work under a yoke or (in the following lines) sac-
rifices it in order to punish it for attracting the bull (as
she jealously imagines) and to remove it as a rival to herself.

      The way in which Pasiphae suddenly remembers her royal
status and uses it to deal with this imagined rival is most
amusing. This is a variation on the manner in which a woman
in a position of greater power might treat a *human* rival (cf.
e.g. Propertius 3.15.13ff., 43f.).

      For i̲n̲g̲e̲n̲t̲i̲...d̲e̲ ̲g̲r̲e̲g̲e̲ cf. Virgil *Ecl.* 6.55 *in magno...*
grege.

209-210   a̲n̲t̲e̲ ̲a̲r̲a̲s̲ ̲c̲o̲m̲m̲e̲n̲t̲a̲q̲u̲e̲ ̲s̲a̲c̲r̲a̲ is odd Latin: literally "be-
fore the altar and a fabricated sacrifice", i.e. before the
altar *in* a fabricated sacrifice (Pasiphae was only pretending
to make a sacrifice to the gods - her real purpose was to kill
her rival).

      The element of black humour now appears (the pentameter

is especially grisly).

The application of *paelex* to cows here and in 211 re-
flects Pasiphae's point of view (see on 203-204).

211-212   'ite, placete meo': "(now) go (and) attract my lover!"
(i.e. "let's see how attractive he finds you now"). *Meus* is
used as a noun here and is rather similar to *dominus* above (see
on 203-204).

Unless one can believe Ovid capable of producing a pale,
boring repetition of the last couplet, there must be some sort
of climax here: paelicibus...caesis and ite, placete suggest
that Pasiphae's jealousy finally became so great that she slaugh-
tered whole groups of "rivals" en masse, while the quotation in
the pentameter of her unpleasantly gloating words also represents
a progression from the previous lines.

In this couplet Ovid completes his account of Pasiphae's
invidia. By again quoting Pasiphae (cf. 204) and by repeating
here *quotiens* (cf. 203), *placeo* (cf. 204) and *meus* (cf. 204) he
provides ring-structure.

Once more Ovid makes the queen speak like an elegiac mis-
tress (for *placeo* cf. 26, and for *meus* cf. Tibullus (?) 4.7.8).

213-214   Europen and Ion are Greek forms of the accusative. se
and fieri are common to both halves of the hexameter, and est
to both halves of the pentameter. quod has been postponed (in
prose it would precede the first altera). There is play on the
two different genders of *bos* in the pentameter. Jupiter loved
Io, but when Juno became suspicious he transformed Io into a cow
in an attempt to conceal the affair. Jupiter at another time
also changed himself into a bull and by appearing tame encouraged
Europa to mount his back; he then rushed with her into the sea
and carried her off to Crete, also, of course, seducing her.
Pasiphae wishes that she was a cow like Io so that she would
thus be attractive to the bull, and like Europa she would like
to be carried off by the bull and seduced.

With some apt *doctrina* Ovid makes a careful transition
prior to 215-216 and brings us back to the theme of Pasiphae's
sexual desire. In the pentameter the idea of seduction may be
brought out more fully by vecta (this Latin term for "ride",

like the English word, can also be used with reference to sexual
intercourse (cf. *Ars Amatoria* 3.777), and such a pun here would
be typical of Ovid).

This is an elegant couplet with its balance, its chias-
tically arranged references to Europa and Io and its repetitions.

215-216   The craftsman Daedalus made for Pasiphae a counterfeit
cow which was hollow; Pasiphae gratified her passion by climbing
into the fake cow and letting the bull mount her; she became
pregnant and gave birth to the Minotaur, which was half man and
half bull, clearly taking after its father.

Ovid saves the most monstrous and grotesque details of
all (her intercourse with the bull and the offspring of this un-
ion) to produce a fitting climax to the narrative. The refer-
ence to the bull and his pre-eminence in the herd (cf. 179ff.)
produces ring-structure within the whole digression on Pasiphae.

The lines are rather spondaic for Ovid, which gives them
a tone of (mock-) solemnity.

217-218   omnia...ista refers to the behaviour of Byblis, Myrrha and
Pasiphae (and of several other mythical females mentioned by
Ovid but not included in this selection).   feminea agrees with
libidine.   The subject of the pentameter is *feminea libido*
(understood from the hexameter).   With nostra (comparative ab-
lative) understand *libidine* ("than our (i.e. male) sexual des-
ire").   furoris is a partitive genitive.

This couplet reminds the reader of the reason for the
digression on Pasiphae and neatly rounds off Ovid's third "proof"
of his main proposition by repeating his assertion that all
women are mad about sex.   The claim that sexual desire is
greater and more frantic in women than in men directly recalls
171-172, and there are also verbal reminiscences (libidine cf.
libido 171, nostra cf. nobis 171, furoris cf. furiosa 171).

219-220   ne dubita: see on 145-146.   In the pentameter the
prose order would be: *vix erit e multis una quae tibi neget.*
multis is used as a noun here ("many women").   neget is sub-
junctive in a generic relative clause (denoting the sort or
type).

The final couplet carefully ties up this whole piece

of preliminary advice by repeating Ovid's scandalous main prop-
osition (note especially that cunctas here echoes cunctas in
159).   Vix is given emphasis by its position at the start of
the line.

There is parody in the hexameter: for ergo age cf.
Virgil *Georgics* 1.63 (*ergo* on its own is common in Lucretius),
and for ne dubita cf. Virgil *Georgics* 4.241f. *at suffire thymo
cerasque recidere inanis/quis dubitet?*   A cheekily epigram-
matical pentameter closes the section with a flourish.

221-252   Make your first approach to the girl by means of a letter.
This should contain flattery, the type of declarations that people
who are really in love make and earnest entreaties.   It should
also contain promises of presents.   If you actually give her
something, she will not lose financially by leaving you; get
her to bed first, and she will keep on going to bed with you
in the hope of making good her losses through the gifts that
you promise.   So send her a letter.   It should be eloquent,
but not ostentatiously so.   Be convincing and use everyday speech
and ingratiating language.

At last (nearly one hundred lines of further preliminary
comment have been omitted from this selection) we come to the
actual point of this part of the *Ars* (how to win over the girl),
and Ovid gives some shrewd advice as he now returns to actual
instruction.   The (to many people) tricky and perplexing busi-
ness of how to make the first approach, what to say and how
to express it causes the experienced Ovid no problems.   With-
out any doubt or hesitation he firmly recommends the use of a
letter and reduces the writing of this to a series of clear and
easy-to-follow general rules, giving full instructions supported
by discussion and examples.   Here again is the joke of Ovid in
his role as the clinical and knowledgeable expert, taking a dis-
passionate view of love.   In fact, not only does he reduce an
affair of the heart to a matter of calculating *artes* but he also
dispels totally any notions of romance or sentiment with an out-
rageous cynicism (he automatically assumes that all his pupils
will not be in love at all (223f.) but be mainly after sex, and
he nowhere even mentions the idea that any girl might fall in

love herself, but suggests that she is mainly interested in
gifts).   For the present Ovid takes the man's side in this
battle of wits (his support is reversed in book 3), and he gives
some opportunist (and diverting) tips tinged by his cynicism.

Also in line with Ovid's expert stance is the overall
neatness and precision of expression and structure.   Many of
his comments and observations (especially the more scandalous
ones) are epigrammatical and eminently quotable (in particular
228, 229, 230, 231, 233, 235, 237, 238, 249 and 250). So too the
section is skilfully ordered: his basic advice to send a letter,
repeated for emphasis and enclosing a description and discussion
of contents (221-242), is followed by remarks on the style of
the letter (243-252).

221-222   cera...rasis infusa tabellis: writing-tablets consisted
of two rectangular pieces of wood joined together by metal rings.
On the inside of each block of wood a smaller rectangular recess
was hollowed out, into which wax was poured to form the writing-
surface.   The edges of the blocks were higher than the writing-
surfaces, so that when the tablets were closed and bound toge-
ther the words inscribed on the wax were not smudged or rubbed
out.   vadum temptet: a nautical metaphor, continued in eat
and ferat (223).   The first approach to the girl is a tricky
business in which Ovid's pupil may reach an impasse.   So the
writing-tablets containing the reader's message (223f.) which
are to be sent to the girl on this mission are compared to a
ship with a cargo of flattery etc. (ferat) trying to make its
way through difficult shallows (where it may run aground).
primum (adverb) goes with eat.   conscia: "sharing knowledge
of" and so containing a declaration of. mentis: "intentions".

The only (brief) acknowledgement in this whole passage
of any possible difficulties in this first approach occurs in
vadum temptet (this confident tone, based on a cynical appraisal
of the female character, continues in the following section).

223-224   imitataque amantum/verba: the past participle of the
deponent here has a passive sense ("the imitated words of lovers",
i.e. an imitation of lovers' words).   This form of the present
participle (-um instead of -ium) is mainly poetic.   nec exiguas...

<u>adde preces</u> = *et adde non exiguas preces.*   <u>quisquis es</u>: i.e.
no matter how important, attractive etc. you are (or think you
are).

The three ingredients are all given emphasis by their
positions.   Ovid's recommendations here show insight into the
female mind in general.

This is a pleasantly light and musical couplet with its
dactyls, assonance and alliteration.

225-226   <u>Hectora</u>:   a Greek form of the accusative.   The (learned)
reference in the hexameter is to the episode (recounted at length
in Homer *Iliad* 24) in which the Greek hero Achilles is moved by
the entreaties of Priam, king of Troy, and returns to him the body
of his son Hector, whom Achilles had killed.

In case the reader thinks himself above employing entrea-
ties Ovid here carefully points out their effectiveness.   To
make his point better, he deliberately chooses rather extreme
examples of stubbornness (note the emphatic positions of <u>Achilles</u>
and <u>deus</u>), but the use of such serious and lofty parallels in
a non-serious and trivial context is also rather mischievous.
Of course, the analogies are mock-didactic.

227-228   <u>promittas facito</u>:   for the form of *facio* and the construc-
tion see on 103-104.   <u>quid enim promittere laedit</u>:   <u>quid</u> is an
internal (adverbial) accusative, and the infinitive is the sub-
ject of <u>laedit</u> ("what harm is there in promising?", i.e. promis-
ing (as opposed to giving) won't hurt you).   <u>pollicitis dives</u>:
ablative of respect ("rich in promises", not actually rich in
money).

For the parody in <u>facito</u> see on 97-98.

The psychology behind the recommendation to promise a lot
(of gifts: cf.231ff.) is dubious, unless one assumes with Ovid
that all girls really are mercenary.   In case his pupil jibs
at the idea of making such promises Ovid goes into further dis-
cussion.   He is quick to explain that he means just promise
(not actually give) presents, and he goes on in the following
lines to point out the effectiveness of this stratagem.

229-230   <u>tenet</u>:   "lasts", "holds on" (intransitive).   <u>semel est</u>
<u>si credita</u>:   i.e. *si semel credita est.*

The hexameter contains an astute enough observation (note
that <u>semel est si credita</u> means that the reader must be convin-
cing), and the pentameter is urbanely opportunist.

<u>231-232</u> <u>dederis</u> here and in 233 is future perfect. <u>ratione</u>:
"with good reason". <u>praeteritum tulerit perdideritque nihil</u>:
"she will have gained what is past and lost nothing" (i.e. she
will have taken your gift, which will then have become a thing
of the past, and she will not have been forced to give you any-
thing in return).

No-one can fault Ovid's logic here, but the coldly cal-
culating cynicism banishes all romance (so too below).

This is an amusingly light and pleasant-sounding couplet
with its dactyls and extensive alliteration and rhyme.

<u>233-234</u> <u>videare</u> (an alternative form for *videaris*) is jussive
subjunctive. The object of <u>daturus</u> is (*id*) <u>quod non dederis</u>.
In the analogy in the pentameter the unproductive field is the
equivalent of the reader and the field's owner the equivalent
of the girl: the idea is that similarly the girl will be tricked
into wasting time, care and effort on the reader in the (vain)
hope of getting something out of him and making a profit.

Again (cf. 229) we find the idea that the reader must be
convincing (<u>videare daturus</u>).

There is burlesque in the analogies in the pentameter
(and in the next couplet).

<u>235-236</u> <u>ne perdiderit, non cessat perdere</u>: "keeps on losing to
avoid being in the position of having lost" (the perfect sub-
junctive in the purpose clause denotes completion and finality).
The idea in this couplet is that like the gambler the girl will
go on staking unsuccessfully what she has to give (cf. 238) in
the hope of recouping her losses: she will continue giving her
favours with no return in the (vain) expectation of getting
enough money out of the reader to make her the winner in the end.

Again Ovid shows psychological insight (this time in a
non-amatory context), and the personification in 236 is partic-
ularly expressive and vivid in its attribution of power to the
dice themselves.

The hexameter is a skilful line with its alliteration,

anaphora and rather paradoxical repetition of *perdo*.

237-238   hoc and hic (attracted into the gender of labor) are pros-
pective: "this is the task, this the struggle - to copulate
without giving a present first".   dederit: for the tense see
on 235-236.   The subject (and of dedit and dabit) is "she".
quae: (i.e. *ea quae*) is neuter accusative plural (" to avoid
being in the position of having given for nothing what she has
given, she will go on giving").   Of course, *dare* here is used
in an erotic sense.

          The hexameter quotes Virgil *Aeneid* 6.129 (in a solemn
speech the Sibyl advises Aeneas, who is to descend into the
Underworld, that the way down there is easy, but the return is
very difficult) *sed revocare gradum superasque evadere ad auras,/
hoc opus, hic labor est*.   Here the Sibyl's words are applied
to getting a girl into bed without the inducement of a gift,
and the suggestion is that this too is a very difficult task,
an epic struggle.

          The comment in the pentameter is cynically calculating
and opportunist, but expressed with amusing and disarming neat-
ness (the thought, the compression and the triple repetition
are all extremely ingenious).

239-240   eat.../...temptet iter picks up the nautical metaphor
at 221-222.   animos: plural for singular, referring to the girl's
feelings.   prima is adverbial.

          After giving his pupil a glimpse of the success to be
had using his method and concluding his remarks on the effect-
iveness of promises, Ovid triumphantly returns to his basic
advice to use a letter for the initial approach (repeating it
for emphasis here and backing it up in 241-242 with an example).

          For ergo see on 219-220.

241-242   Cydippen: a Greek form of the accusative.   The purpose
of this couplet is to illustrate the effectiveness of writing
in the matter of getting a girl.   The reference is to the
story of Acontius and Cydippe: Acontius scratched on an apple
the words "I swear by Diana to marry Acontius" and rolled it
in front of Cydippe, who picked it up out of curiosity and read
the inscription; as the Greeks and Romans read aloud, she

thereby bound herself to marry him by an oath.   littera cannot,
of course, strictly mean "letter", although Ovid is playing on
that sense of the word (it was a sort of letter).   littera
here probably denotes a short piece of writing (translate: "a
line").   pomo is ablative of instrument.   inscia is adverb-
ial ("unwittingly", "unawares").

The learned poet shows ingenuity in lighting on the story
of Cydippe for use as an example here (cf. his use of the judge-
ment of Paris at 147-148).   The mythological analogy again
represents a burlesque of didactic poetry.

243-244   bonas artes: "the liberal arts" (here especially the
study of language, literature and rhetoric, which make a man
an accomplished speaker and writer, but the term also included
music and mathematics).   trepidos belongs inside the ut clause.
tueare is an alternative form for tuearis.

This is a grave couplet in both thought and expression.
Note especially that the use of the imperative of disco here is
in the formal didactic manner (cf. Virgil Georgics 2.35, 3.414)
and the phrase Romana iuventus is taken from the early epic poet
Ennius (e.g. Annals 537V).

245-246   quam.../tam: translate the pentameter first ("a girl
will...just as much as...").   The hexameter refers to the two
main uses of oratory (in politics, addressing the people or
the senate, and in law-cases).   lectusque senatus: the sen-
ate's membership was revised by the Censors and (three times
during his principate) by Augustus.   dabit...manus: "will
hold out her hands" (in submission), i.e. "will surrender".

The tone of solemnity is continued in the hexameter but
suddenly dispelled in the pentameter, as Ovid reveals that in
the previous couplet he was in fact being flippant, suggests
an outrageous use of the bonas artes and puts winning over a
girl on a par with political and forensic oratory.   Again
Ovid is poking fun at Roman conventions.

247-248   in fronte = "outwardly", "ostentatiously".   voces
("language") is plural for singular.   molesta: "affected".

Ovid's advice here displays common sense: to show off
with too clever and affected a style would probably bore and

irritate the girl (cf. 250), and it would also suggest lack of
sincerity (cf. 251).   As a former accomplished student of rhe-
toric himself, Ovid may also be alluding to current rhetorical
controversy (especially over the simpler "Attic" and the more
florid "Asiatic" styles of oratory) in his advice to avoid affec-
ted (248) and unusual (251) terms.   The cheeky implication
would be that such considerations are just as important in writ-
ing love-letters as in oratory (cf. 245f.).

249-250   mentis: the genitive is often found with verbs and ad-
jectives denoting fulness or emptiness (inops).   saepe...fuit:
i.e. *littera saepe fuit valens causa odii.*   littera: if the
word here means "letter", then we would have to assume that Ovid
means a letter of the wrong sort (i.e. ostentatiously clever
and affected).   This seems rather a lot to supply. *Litterae*
(plural) can mean "erudition", a sense which fits admirably here.
Probably Ovid is making use of the poetic licence of putting
the singular for the plural (especially since *litterae* will not
scan in elegiac verse) and littera here means "erudition".

Note the air of wisdom and experience to the remark in
the pentameter.

251-252   praesens belongs inside the ut clause.   videare: for
the form see on 233-234.

Again Ovid's common sense is evident, and again he
stresses the need to be convincing (credibilis; so too every-
day speech and ingratiating language will seem natural and sin-
cere, and so have greater impact on the girl).

253-270   If she returns your letter unread, keep on sending letters
in the hope that she will read one: continual pressure over a
period of time inevitably has an effect.   If she reads your
letter and won't write back, don't force her: carry on writing,
and she will come around.   She may send a harsh reply asking
you not to bother her: this is only a pretence, and if you per-
severe you will be successful.

Picking up the previous section, Ovid follows the situa-
tion through with professorial thoroughness.   He anticipates
all likely adverse reactions to the letter on the part of the
girl (of course, advice of this type is unnecessary if she

openly shows a favourable reaction), and with care and precis-
ion he lists them in descending order of actual severity accom-
panied by discussion and comments.   The expert's confident
tone continues, based on his disgraceful proposition that all
girls can be caught (159-220), and again his cynicism and gen-
eralizations greatly add to the humour.   The whole is made
still more entertaining by a virtuoso display of metrical and
stylistic skills.

        Yet there is even more to the lines than this. They are
also a good example of Ovid's *doctrina*.   He has in mind a pass-
age of Tibullus (1.4.15-20) where the god Priapus gives advice
on how to be successful in a love-affair.   Ovid similarly recom-
mends perseverance in the face of initial reluctance and backs
up his advice with a series of trite examples presented as if
they represented new information of importance.   But Ovid's
version is far from a pale repetition (in fact, he seems to be
trying to improve on Tibullus): it is much longer, more spec-
ific and more detailed, the language is his own, the expres-
sion is even cleverer and his examples (and their implications)
are different (apart from the effect of water on rock) and
more numerous.

253-254   lecturam spera: i.e. *spera eam scriptum lecturam esse*
    ("hope that she will read a letter").

        The many spondees in this couplet suit the gravity of
the situation and the persevering effort required.

255-256   tempore: "in time".   The parallels in these and the
    following lines are intended to show that if Ovid's pupil
similarly applies continual pressure over a period of time
he will be successful.

        In the previous couplet Ovid had mentioned the most un-
favourable and dispiriting reaction of all to the reader's
letter.   To back up his advice to persevere and to encourage
his pupil in these most difficult and trying circumstances
Ovid pretends to feel the need to cite not just one or two but
several parallels.   None of Ovid's examples here is new (in
fact, many of them are very old), and here again we have the
joke of Ovid driving home his point as though it was important

new information.   Of course, the analogies are also mock-did-
actic.   However, Ovid is aware of the danger of monotony and
does his best to avoid it (the implications in each couplet are
not exactly the same, care is taken over the structure of the
list, there is variety in the subject-matter, the expression is
neatly epigrammatical throughout, and Ovid's metrical and sty-
listic skills are very much in evidence).

The idea in this couplet seems to be that in time an
unyielding girl too will similarly be tamed and submit.   Ovid's
point is made clearer by the fact that *difficilis* is also app-
lied to stubbornly resisting girls (e.g. Horace *Odes* 3.10.11).

As the poet begins to cite his arguments the tone becomes
more optimistic and light-hearted, and the metre aptly becomes
much more dactylic.   There is also balance, (emphatic) anaphora,
alliteration and internal rhyme.

257-258   interit adsidua vomer aduncus humo: "the curved plough-
share is worn away by continual (contact with the) earth".
adsidua...humo is ablative of cause, like adsiduo...usu.

The implication seems to be that (like the ring and the
ploughshare) the girl's hard and unfeeling nature will be worn
down by continual pressure (*ferreus* is also applied to hard-
hearted girls who resist advances: e.g. *Heroides* 17.136f.).
There is variety in the change here from plurals to singulars
and from animate to inanimate.

The hexameter is a golden line, and there is also balance,
(emphatic) repetition and frequent assonance and alliteration.

259-260   magis goes with durum, and est is common to both parts
of the hexameter.   In 260 Ovid is thinking of rocks worn away
by constant contact with water (in the form of drips, streams,
rivers, the sea etc.).

Ovid's point in this couplet is apparently that even
the most hard and insensitive nature will be worn down by the
gentle (but continual) pressure of merely sending letters
(*durus* is also used of the woman who resists a man: e.g.
Propertius 1.1.10).   The question in the hexameter, the pres-
ence of only one example and the change from man-made objects
to natural substances add variety.

This skilful couplet contains much contrast and repetition.

261-262 Penelopen: a Greek form of the accusative. Penelope,
wife of the Greek hero Odysseus, who spent twenty years fighting
at Troy and making his way home again, remained faithful to him
during his absence and refused the offers of her many suitors.
persta modo: "just persevere!" (virtually equivalent to a conditional). With capta (both times) understand *esse*. It took
the Greeks ten years to capture Troy (sero), but it was captured
none the less (tamen).

Ovid here includes a line that contains no analogy,
while in the pentameter he cites a (learned) mythological parallel for a change. The repetition of tempore (cf. 255f.) neatly
rounds off the list,and the extreme nature of the examples and
the great impudence of the remarks here provide a fitting climax.

The implication in the previous lines was that continual
pressure is always effective. This is a cheeky enough generalization itself, but in the hexameter here Ovid is explicit and
specific. He states that with perseverance the reader will win
over the most difficult and forbidding of prospects - even a
woman who persistently refuses and stubbornly remains faithful
(note the positions of Penelopen and vinces). Of course, the
urbane cynicism in his reference here to the legendary Penelope
is truly scandalous (cf. *Amores* 1.8.47f. *Penelope iuvenum vires
temptabat in arcu;/ qui latus argueret corneus arcus erat*) and
leads one to conclude that even a married woman could be won
over in time (although Ovid is supposed to be concerned only with
unmarried women).

The pentameter is also mischievous with its use of such
a serious and lofty parallel in a non-serious and trivial situation: even as difficult a city to take as Troy was taken eventually, and in the same way the "capture" of the girl may prove
an epic struggle, but, if Ovid's pupil shows heroic endurance,
he will be successful in the end (for *capio* used of the capture
of a woman cf. e.g. line 155).

263-264 legerit et nolit rescribere: "suppose she has read (your
letter) and is unwilling to reply" (the subjunctives here are

used in a concessive sense).   modo: "just".   blanditias...
tuas is the object of legat.   fac legat: for the construction
see on 103-104.

      In these circumstances the sophisticated expert calls for
a civilized restraint and (again) patience.   The advice in the
pentameter seems shrewd enough (although, of course, such a tac-
tic would not be successful inevitably).

      For tu see on 47-48.

      This is an elegant couplet with its pointed repetitions,
assonance and internal rhyme.

265-266   quae (i.e. *ea quae*) is feminine nominative singular.
legisse: perfect infinitive for present infinitive (see on 183-
184).   lectis: "to what she has read".   per numeros veniunt
ista gradusque suos: "those things come about by their own
degrees and stages".

      Again Ovid's urbane cynicism is to the fore (in the general-
ization in 265).

      The hexameter is a clever line: *volo* is repeated with
point, rescribere echoes rescribere in 263, and legisse picks
up the two instances of *lego* in the previous couplet and is it-
self picked up in lectis.

267-268   roget: subjunctive in a generic relative clause (see on
219-220).   se obviously refers to the writer of the letter
(grammatically it should refer to the letter itself, strictly
speaking).

      At first sight this looks like the worst possible reaction
of all by the girl (but the next couplet shows that the exper-
ienced Ovid is not fooled).

269-270   (*id*) quod rogat illa is the object of timet.   (*id*)
quod non rogat may be the object of optat or of instes (i.e. "she
desires what she does not ask for, namely that you should press
on" or "she desires that you should press on with what she does
not ask for").   insequere: second person singular imperative
of the deponent *insequor*.

      Ovid's cynicism in this section is at its worst in these
paradoxes.   Exactly why the girl should be supposed to be pre-
tending is not clear (her intention could be to test the reader

or to keep up a semblance of respectability, or she could fear
discovery or be acting simply out of cruelty), but, whatever
the circumstances, Ovid is certain that this is merely a pre-
tence.

      This is a very ingenious couplet: it contains some neat
epigrams, contrast, repetition and assonance.

271-286 Meanwhile, if she goes out in a litter, approach her and
signal unobtrusively; if she takes a leisurely stroll, show
her your interest by doing a lot of strolling yourself nearby
and brushing against her; if she goes to the theatre, stay there
as long as she does, giving her admiring glances and frequent
signs.

      Ovid's cynicism now disappears, but the professorial tho-
roughness continues as he follows the situation through even
further and again recommends perseverance (in the form of addi-
tional pressure during the period of correspondence). This
section of purely practical advice (for the parody in this see
on 93-120) shows ingenuity in thought and expression.   There
is also good psychology.   The reader is advised to show his
interest in the woman and make his intentions plain to her on
numerous occasions.   The personal appearances would reinforce
the more impersonal letter, heightening its effectiveness and
ensuring that it could not be ignored or forgotten.   Ovid also
stresses the need for subtlety and concealment from others here.
Although he does not explain his reasons, the advice seems judi-
cious: this is all part of a smooth and gradual build-up, and
at this stage it might well irritate or embarrass the girl if
other people knew what the reader was up to, and there might also
be a danger then of a report or gossip reaching any parents or
boyfriend in the background.

271-272 toro here refers to a litter.

273-274 verbis: i.e. *verbis tuis*.   offerat auris (= *aures*):
    "intrude ears", i.e. "listen to".   qua is the relative adverb.
    callidus: adjective for adverb.   abde: the object is *verba*
    (understood from verbis in the hexameter).

      For ambiguis...notis see on 95-96.

275-276 vacuis: "idle", "at leisure".   illi: dative of the

agent.   socias tu quoque iunge moras: "you too must share friendly
delays", i.e. "be friendly and waste some time with her yourself".

277-278   facito: for the form and the construction see on 103-104
(all four subjunctives in this couplet depend on facito). terga:
plural for singular, referring to the girl's back.

The couplet contains a useful expert hint: the varia-
tion in position and speed would enable Ovid's pupil to loiter
for a long period of time showing the girl his keenness on her
without attracting the attention of others.

For facito see on 97-98.

279-280   de mediis: "in the middle", "in between" (of the pillars
that separate the reader from the girl).   lateri continuasse
latus: "to brush your side against her side".   continuasse
(a contracted form of *continuavisse*) is another example of per-
fect infinitive for present infinitive.

There is another helpful tip here: brushing against the
woman (apart from being pleasurable in itself) would be an un-
obtrusive sign of the reader's interest (it would seem acci-
dental to anyone who actually noticed it).

281-282   quod spectes: quod has a vague antecedent ("some-
thing"), which is not expressed in the Latin and which forms
the object of adferet.   spectes is subjunctive in a final
relative clause.

The advice in the pentameter is that what the reader
should look at is the girl's face (rather than the performance
on stage) - again, of course, to make clear to her his inclina-
tions.

There is verbal play (speciosa, spectes and in 283 res-
picias) in this musical couplet.

283-284   respicias: "look back at" (because of the segregation
of the sexes in the theatre: see on 67-68).   This subjunctive
and the other two in the couplet (mirere = *mireris* and loquare =
loquaris) depend on licebit.   A subordinate subjunctive
(normally without *ut*) is a common alternative to the infinitive
with *licet*.

This seems a useful suggestion: because of the large
crowd nobody except the girl herself could be sure of the ob-
ject of these admiring gazes and signals.

285-286   surges...sedebis: future indicatives with imperative
force (cf. "you *shall* sit" in English).   dominae...tuae goes
with arbitrio.   tempora: plural for singular.

      Again in the large crowd only the woman would realize
the point of the reader's actions in 285 (to show her that he
had only come to the theatre because she had).

      In 286 the positive injunction to waste time (especially
in such a trivial pursuit) would not have pleased Roman tradi-
tionalists, who had strict views on the proper use of time (cf.
Amores 1.15.1ff.).

      In this skilfully constructed couplet the hexameter
contains balance, contrast, repetition and juxtaposition, while
the epigrammatical pentameter contains alliteration and internal
rhyme.

287-304   But don't use curling-tongs or depilatories. Casual
good looks suit men.   Look how successful Theseus, Hippolytus
and Adonis were.   Aim at cleanliness and tidiness of person
and dress in every respect.   Only promiscuous women and homo-
sexuals go further than that.

      Now that the reader is to place himself under personal
scrutiny, his appearance is important, and the thorough Ovid
goes into this matter too.   Anticipating the possibility that
his pupil may go too far in an attempt to impress the girl, he
recommends instead a middle course (masculine, but clean and
neat), thereby showing a cultured but restrained sense of style
and incidentally giving us an interesting insight into con-
temporary standards of personal hygiene and grooming (Ovid's
advice coincides with typical civilized Roman views of the day).
The lines also represent a parody of passages in didactic works
on physical and sartorial requisites (cf. Hesiod *Works and Days*
536ff., Cato *De Agri Cultura* 59, Varro *Res Rusticae* 2.10.1ff.,
Oppian *Halieutica* 3.29ff.), and the implication is that such
considerations are just as important in love.   Ovid gives the
topic the expert's comprehensive treatment (literally from head
to toe), but carefully avoids boring his readers by ensuring
that there is variety in the list (e.g. the inclusion of mytho-
logical references, the type and number of details per couplet,

changes between commands and prohibitions). In the structure
of the lines Ovid shows an unobtrusive neatness similar to that
which he recommends: the section is framed by rejections of
excessive attentions (287f. and 303f.), and in between comes a
succinct statement of his basic advice (289), followed by care-
fully arranged examples of its effectiveness (289-292) and full
details of its practical application (293-302).

287-288   Some men did pay such attention to their appearance in
order to attract girls (cf. *Ars* 3.433ff.), but the use of cur-
ling-tongs (ferro) and depilatories (pumice) was generally con-
sidered effeminate (cf. 303-304).

         torquere (primarily = "curl") may also contain the mean-
ing "torture", reflecting Ovid's dislike of the violence done
to the hair (cf. *Amores* 1.14.24ff. (of his girlfriend's hair)
*heu, mala vexatae quanta tulere comae! / quam se praebuerant
ferro patienter et igni, / ut fieret torto nexilis orbe sinus!*
etc.).

289-290   Minoida: a Greek form of the accusative (from *Minois*).
Ariadne, daughter of king Minos, fell in love with the Athenian
hero Theseus when he came to Crete to be offered to the Mino-
taur. She gave him a sword to kill the Minotaur with and a
ball of thread to enable him to find his way out of the Labyrinth
again, and subsequently she sailed away with him (see 307ff.
below). a nulla tempora comptus acu: the use of *a(b)* with
the instrumental ablative is unusual and mainly poetic. The
perfect participle passive here has an active force, in imita-
tion of the Greek middle voice, which had a (generally) passive
form but an active (quasi-reflexive) sense (literally: "having
his temples adorned by no hair-pin"). This usage of the pass-
ive participle (and occasionally finite passive forms) is es-
pecially common in Augustan poetry.

         The (learned) mythological analogies here and in the
next couplet are mock-didactic. Again Ovid's ingenuity is
evident in lighting on these stories as illustrations of the
effectiveness of the attractions of forma...neglecta (cf.
on 241-242).

         In 290 Ovid conjures up briefly (if only to dispel it)

the comic picture of a manly, heroic figure of legend wearing hair-pins.

There is an expressive juxtaposition in the hexameter here (and in the following couplet). The mythological examples in this couplet and the next form a tricolon diminuendo, while male and female partners are arranged in order to produce a double chiasmus (Ariadne, Theseus, Hippolytus, Phaedra, Venus, Adonis).

291-292   Phaedra, wife of Theseus, fell in love with her stepson Hippolytus, who was fond of hunting and the outdoor life. Adonis, a handsome young hunter and shepherd (silvis aptus), was loved by Venus (cura deae).

deae is not simply allusive: Adonis' forma...neglecta attracted even a goddess.

293-294   munditie: the word denotes a clean, simple and restrained neatness. corpora: (plural for singular ("your body") or a real plural referring to male bodies in general) is the subject of both placeant and fuscentur. Campo refers to the Campus Martius, a favourite place for recreation. In both Greece and Rome it was considered proper for men to have a suntan, especially one acquired by means of healthy exercise. It was regarded as both boorish and ridiculous to have an ill-fitting or dirty toga (294), too large a shoe (296) or badly-cut hair (297).

Ovid recommends the traditional manly exercise on the Campus Martius simply as a means to attracting a girl.

295-296   For the significance of the daggers see on 71-72 (do not translate the words enclosed by the daggers). rubigine here refers to the deposit that collects on teeth which are not regularly cleaned and discolours them. natet is applied to the foot "swimming about" in a shoe that is too large.

rubigine, vagus and natet show the mocking distaste of a cultured man.

297-298   rigidos is probably proleptic (see on 2.287-288), referring to the bristliness and spikiness of the hair resulting from an inexpert haircut. barba: young men at this time favoured small, neatly-trimmed beards.

Again there is urbane mockery (in the collocation male
deformet rigidos).

299-300   nihil is here adverbial ("not at all").   sordibus is
plural for singular.

The recommendation about hair sprouting from the nos-
trils shows the expert's careful eye for detail.

There is much forceful alliteration in the hexameter.

301-302   naris (= *nares*) refers to the noses of other people
(especially girls).   virque paterque gregis: i.e. the he-
goat,notorious for its rank smell (here denoting the goatish
stink of B.O. : cf. Catullus 69.5f. *tibi fertur/valle sub alarum
trux habitare caper, Ars 3.193 quam paene admonui, ne trux
caper iret in alas*).

Again Ovid's superior derision is evident: note the
absurdly grandiose virque paterque gregis (the repeated -*que*
of high style (see on 121-122) and the lofty periphrasis for
a goat) with reference to the smell of armpits.

303-304   faciant depends on concede (for the omission of *ut* see
on 2.99-100).   male vir: the two words go together ("not prop-
erly a man", i.e. "an effeminate person").

Ovid's contempt for those who favoured a more dandified
appearance is clearly evident here.

male vir is a (learned) reminiscence of Catullus 16.13
male me marem putatis.

305-348   Lo, Bacchus summons me.   He helps lovers, being a lover
himself.   Remember how he turned up when Ariadne had been des-
erted by Theseus, carried her off and married her.   So, when
you are enjoying Bacchus' wine at a dinner-party in female com-
pany, pray to him to keep your head clear.

The section begins with the abrupt introduction of a
summons by Bacchus, who, it is claimed, is favourable to love.
At this point the reader cannot be sure why Bacchus should summon
Ovid or exactly how Bacchus is here supposed to help lovers, and
Ovid keeps the reader in suspense for some 38 lines, deliberately
teasing him after engaging his curiosity.   It is only at 345ff.
that Ovid reveals that Bacchus' summons means that it is now
time for the poet to talk about dinner-parties (which, it turns

out at 349ff., provide numerous opportunities for advancing an
affair) and that Bacchus is favourable to love in that he pro-
vides the gift of wine for such profitable dinner-parties and
can keep the lover clear-headed.

In between comes a lengthy passage on Ariadne to illus-
trate the statement that Bacchus himself is a lover, which rep-
resents a cheeky parody of the often rather free use of digres-
sions in didactic poetry.   Here too there is a tease, managed
with skill and subtlety: the account begins with an air of sup-
reme sympathy and sadness at Ariadne's plight (307-313), which
very effectively conceals Ovid's real attitude;   after gradu-
ally preparing the way with a few hints that he may not be so
serious after all (313f., 315), his levity surfaces fully
(317f.), and gaiety and humour dominate the remainder of the
piece right up to its happy ending.   Ovid's eye for detail
and his metrical and stylistic skills are used to good effect
throughout, and after the initial disguise the digression turns
out to be a lively, inventive and high-spirited passage, full
of action and incident.

But there is still more to the lines than this, and
again we find literary as well as mythological *doctrina*. As
far as we know, the most recent and famous account of Ariadne's
desertion was that of Catullus (in poem 64).   Ovid had al-
ready made one variation on Catullus' version in *Heroides* 10
(a pathetic letter from Ariadne to Theseus), and here he makes
another, by changing the approach and emphasis.   Initially
the present passage is reminiscent of Catullus 64 in tone and
details (307f. cf. 64.52ff.; 309f. cf. 64.56, 63ff.; 311f.
cf. 64.124ff.; 316 cf. 64.132f., 177ff.),but after this de-
ceptive start, which makes the reader think that the account
will be in the manner of Catullus, unexpectedly Ovid shows
amusement and plays up the comedy and gaiety (in contrast to
the sympathy, seriousness and sadness of Catullus 64).   So too
Ovid skims (comparatively) Ariadne's feelings and actions when
deserted by Theseus (on which Catullus dwells at length), allows
her only one and a half lines for her speech (which occupies 70
lines in Catullus) and almost totally ignores Theseus and the

background to the story (which play important parts in Catullus
64). Instead Ovid concentrates on the antics of Bacchus' fol-
lowers (these play a very minor role in Catullus' poem, and,
apart from the music, the details differ) and the meeting between
Ariadne and Bacchus that has such a happy ending (merely alluded
to in Catullus). Of course, the purpose of Ovid's version (to
show that Bacchus is a lover) is to a large extent responsible
for these variations in tone and emphasis, but they still do
represent innovations that give the story a fresh perspective
and a different savour.

305-306   Liber, originally an Italian god of vegetation, was
later identified with Bacchus. Bacchus was one of the patron
deities of poets (along with Apollo and the Muses). amantis =
amantes. flammae denotes the fire of love.

Ovid emphasizes the (as yet unspecified) help that Bacchus
gives lovers (the positions of adiuvat and favet).

307-308   Cnosis is used as a noun here ("the girl from Cnossos",
i.e. Ariadne). qua: "where". Dia: the island (identified
with Naxos in the Aegean) on which Theseus abandoned Ariadne.
feritur: from *ferio*.

The digression has a dramatic and very sad opening. In
the hexameter detail after detail builds up a pitiful and moving
picture (note the collocation ignotis amens errabat). In the
pentameter brevis is something of an exaggeration (Naxos is, in
fact, the largest of the Cyclades): the word in conjunction
with aequoreis...aquis brings out Ariadne's desolation and help-
lessness (on a little island in the midst of the (vast) sea).

Ovid's account of Ariadne's adventures begins with a
very spondaic line, suggesting both sadness and the girl's slow
wandering. In this couplet and the next four and a half lines
there is also mournful assonance (of i, a and e).

309-310   utque erat e somno: "just as she was straight from sleep"
(i.e. having only just woken up). pedem...comas: accusatives
of respect. croceas: blond hair was the general rule among
gods, heroes and heroines.

The pathetic sight of Ariadne still half-asleep with her
attire in disarray brings out her vulnerability and defencelessness.

311-312   Thesea crudelem: Theseu is a Greek form of the accusa-
tive.   Her actual words (*"Theseu crudelis"*) are put into the
accusative after clamabat. imbre here denotes a downpour of
tears.

            This is a particularly moving couplet - Ariadne's
repeated cries and tears, the idea of loneliness and futility
in surdas...ad undas (since Theseus had sailed away, there were
only the waves to hear her shouts, and they were, of course,
unresponsive), the emphasis on injustice in crudelem and in-
digno (note the position) and the suggestion of vulnerable
youth and femininity in teneras.

            The hexameter contains sad spondees.

313-314   turpior: "less attractive".

            In the first part of 313 the pathos continues as
Ovid repeats for emphasis the detail of Ariadne's simultan-
eous cries and tears (note the juxtaposition and the echo of
clamabat in 311).   The remainder of the couplet comes as
something of a surprise (notice the way in which decebat is
delayed until the very end of the line for maximum effect and
the pentameter reinforces the observation).   The reader is
tempted to smile and suddenly begins to suspect that if Ovid
can pass such a comment on Ariadne's attractiveness at this
point he may not be so serious and sad after all (cf. 84).
This remark and the one in 315 also act as subtle pointers to
Bacchus' interest in Ariadne.

315-316   pectora: plural for singular.   perfidus ille refers
to Theseus, who had promised to marry Ariadne.

            Amid the air of sadness (the action in 315 and the
(vivid) quote in 316) there is again a hint that Ovid is not
so solemn and sorrowful (the unexpected,voluptuous and urbanely
appreciative superlative mollissima).

            The alliteration suggests the actual sound of the
breasts being beaten.

317-318   Cymbals and tambourines were instruments commonly played
by the followers of Bacchus (who were also renowned for their
ecstatic frenzy: adtonita...manu). manu is singular for plural.

            In the first part of the hexameter the repetition of

words from 316 represents Ariadne's actual moving repetition.
However, in the remainder of the couplet Ovid's levity surfaces
fully.   Most amusingly before Ariadne can launch into the long-
er speech (as in Catullus 64) that the reader is probably ex-
pecting and as soon as her question is out of her mouth here it
is answered - Bacchus' train makes a sudden and dramatic approach
and the educated reader is reminded at once of what will happen
to her (she will be carried off by Bacchus: see 335ff.).

       Again the sound of the Latin reproduces the actual noise
(of the instruments), while the dactyls in these and the follow-
ing lines bring out well the excitement and movement of the scene.

319-320   novissima verba: "her most recent words" (i.e. what she
had just been saying).   The pentameter means that in her faint
she went pale all over.

       The humour is heightened as Ariadne abruptly falls into
a melodramatic swoon, terrified by the noise of Bacchus' followers
(who represent no threat to her, actually turn out to be light-
hearted and comic and, in fact, are the prelude to a happy ending).

321-322   Mimallonides: nominative plural of *Mimallonis*. sparsis
in terga capillis: flowing, disordered hair (due to the head
being wildly flung back or tossed) was a characteristic of
Bacchantes.   leves Satyri: Satyrs were minor nature-deities
(human in form, but with goat's horns and feet) who attended
Bacchus (praevia turba dei).   leves may mean "nimble", "gay" or
"fickle" (alluding to their notorious promiscuity).

       These lines usher in a lively, gay and humorous little
scene, full of colourful detail and incident.

       In Mimallonides, an original variant on Mimallon, an
unusual term for a Bacchante found in Hellenistic authors (e.g.
Callimachus fragment 503 Pfeiffer),Ovid uses his *doctrina* to add
interest and a touch of the exotic.

323-324   Silenus was an old, lascivious, Satyr-like demigod, who
was also an attendant of Bacchus, and who was often depicted as
being so drunk that he needed an ass to carry him.   arte ("with
skill") is ironical.   iubas: plural for singular.

       This is a funny picture in itself, but the comedy is
well brought out by the nice detail of the sagging back of the

ass (collapsing under his weight), the emphatic position of <u>vix</u>
and the juxtaposition <u>pressas continet</u> (Silenus is grimly hang-
ing on for all his worth to keep his very precarious seat).

325-326 <u>Bacchae fugiuntque petuntque</u>: with <u>petuntque</u> understand
eum. These words are also part of the hexameter's *dum* clause
(a connecting-link such as *et* has been omitted). The actions
of the Bacchantes are intended to tease Silenus in his lustful
pursuit. The pentameter contains a second *dum* clause (with *dum*
postponed) - the main clause comes in 327. <u>quadrupedem</u> is used
as a noun (i.e the ass).

The humour takes a bawdy turn here (the amatory element
is also a subtle anticipation of the succeeding episode in the
digression).

For the use of *-que...-que* here see on 121-122.

This is a very ingenious couplet: it contains a tri-
colon crescendo, repetition, juxtaposition, chiasmus, contrast
and assonance (note especially that the rhythm and sound of
<u>fugiuntque petuntque</u> suggest well the Bacchantes rushing to and
fro).

327-328 <u>aurito...asello</u> goes with <u>delapsus</u> ("fallen from...").
<u>clamarunt</u>: a contracted form of *clamaverunt*. <u>pater</u> is here
simply an affectionate term.

The comedy reaches its height as this little scene ends
in broad farce.

Note the vivid quote in the pentameter.

This is another skilful couplet: there is contrast
between hexameter and pentameter, internal rhyme and allitera-
tion in 327 and (excited) repetition, alliteration and asson-
ance in 328.

329-330 <u>deus</u>: Bacchus. <u>quem summum</u>: "the top of which".
<u>uvis</u>: the canopy of grape-clusters is, of course, very apt in
the case of the god of wine. <u>tigribus adiunctis</u>: Bacchus
was supposed to have subjugated India and to have made a vic-
torious progress through the Orient, teaching men civilization
and the cultivation of the vine - hence he is often depicted in
a chariot drawn by tigers. <u>aurea</u>: as befits a god (cf.
Amores 1.2.42 (to Cupid) *ibis in auratis aureus ipse rotis*).

<u>lora dabat</u>:   "gave rein to" (i.e. gave them their head).

At this point Bacchus makes an impressive entrance in his
exotic chariot.   The effect is heightened by the contrast with
Silenus (Bacchus is sober, not drunk, and he rides correctly in
a splendid chariot, whereas Silenus could not even keep his
seat on his ass) and reinforced by the weighty spondees in 329.

<u>331-332</u>   The cleverly compressed (zeugmatic) hexameter means that
Ariadne went pale, forgot about Theseus and lost her voice.
<u>abiere</u> is an alternative form for *abierunt*.   <u>puellae</u> is the
dative found with verbs of depriving etc. (a sort of dative of
disadvantage).

Ariadne again behaves in an amusing fashion (Bacchus'
entrance is so impressive that once more she goes pale and is
terrified - this time by her benefactor, saviour and future hus-
band).

There is clever word-play in the hexameter (<u>Theseus</u>...
<u>abiere puellae</u>:   Theseus himself had already left the girl).

<u>333-334</u>   <u>ut steriles agitat quas ventus aristas</u>:   i.e. *ut steriles*
aristae quas ventus agitat (<u>quas</u> has been postponed, and the ante-
cedent has been incorporated into the relative clause).   The
ears of corn are probably described as <u>steriles</u> because they
have been scorched by over-exposure to the sun (and so they are
light and easily moved by the wind: cf. *Heroides* 5.111f.).

The humour continues: note especially the (vivid) detail
of her trembling (brought out by the many dactyls) and the double
simile (see on 51-52).   The main point of comparison in the two
similes is the trembling, but in addition corn and reeds are
rooted to the ground, like Ariadne (332).

<u>335-336</u>   <u>cura fidelior</u> is in apposition to the unexpressed personal
pronoun *ego*.

The god Bacchus turns out to be a fast worker and a smooth
operator.   Here, wasting no time, he launches into a short, well-
chosen speech of soothing and winning words.   In the hexameter
there is a jibe at Bacchus' predecessor (just in case any affec-
tion for him lingers) and a protestation of fidelity (in case
Ariadne should fear that she will be left in the lurch again).
In the pentameter Bacchus tries to calm her immediate fears,

introduces himself (thereby explaining the reason for his im-
pressive entrance) and not only promises to marry her but, antici-
pating no objections, holds out to her the positive certainty
of marriage (and marriage to a god at that).

Again there is graphic quotation.

337-338   munus...sidus/...Cressa Corona: each is (separately)
in apposition.   caelo is a local ablative (see on 11-12).
spectabere = *spectaberis*.   In most versions Bacchus took Ariadne
off to heaven as his wife and made her crown a constellation -
here Ariadne herself wearing her crown seems to be the constel-
lation (cf. *Heroides* 6.115f. *Bacchi coniunx redimita corona/
praeradiat stellis signa minora suis*).

Bacchus clinches the contract with a suitably superb and
miraculous wedding-present (again no objections on Ariadne's
part are envisaged).

This is an apt and clever use of *doctrina*.

Bacchus' words here have gravity and forcefulness (the
spondees in the hexameter, the emphatic juxtaposition caelum:
caelo (both in emphatic position), the alliteration and the tri-
colon crescendo).

339-340   (inposito cessit harena pede):   i.e. his feet made im-
pressions in the sand (pede is singular for plural).

Not wasting any more time on words and without waiting
for a reply, Bacchus acts.   The dismounting here represents a
thoughtful touch (again he is concerned that Ariadne should not
be afraid).

Note the vivid detail in the pentameter.

341-342   With implicitamque understand *illam* (from 339).   neque
enim = *non enim*.   valebat refers to Ariadne.

Having apparently calmed her fears somewhat, Bacchus now
masterfully carries Ariadne off in her dazed state before she
has time to react or resist.

The proverbial aside in 342 (cf. Livy 1.39.4 *evenit
facile, quod diis cordi esset*) is extremely funny (almost verg-
ing on blasphemy) in this context.

The dactyls in general and in particular the doubly
emphatic abstulit bring out well the quickness and suddenness

with which Ariadne is carried off.

343-344   'Hymenaee':   an exclamation commonly found in the refrains
chanted at marriages.   'Euhion, euhoe':   a cry of the followers
of Bacchus.

        With speed and effectiveness Bacchus gets his way (the
marriage takes place in the hexameter and its consummation in
the pentameter).

        The quotations in 343 make for greater vividness.

345-346   positi...munera Bacchi: munera is plural for singular,
and Bacchi stands for "wine" (although the literal meaning
(Bacchus) is also present, since wine is Bacchus' gift to men).
Translate: "Bacchus'gift of wine set before you".   in socii...
parte tori: "shares a couch with you" (at a dinner-party).

        Rounding off the section, here and in the following coup-
let Ovid (at last) explains his remarks in 305-306 (see on 305-
348).

        For ergo see on 219-220.

        The dactyls in this couplet and the next suit well the
light-hearted tone of the end of this section.

347-348   patrem: the word is often used as a term of respect for
gods. nocturnaque sacra: Bacchus' rites most often took place
at night.   precare: imperative of the deponent *precor*.

        There is *doctrina* in the unusual (originally Greek)
epithet *Nyctelius* (based on nyx, the Greek word for "night", be-
cause of Bacchus' nocturnal ceremonies).

349-370   A dinner-party provides opportunities for informing the
girl that you are attracted to her in a variety of covert ways
and for showing yourself to good advantage.

        Picking up from the end of the previous passage, Ovid
now moves on to a series of precepts.   The thorough expert is
still concerned with the additional pressure to be applied during
the period of correspondence (cf. 271ff.), and again the need
for perseverance and shrewd stealth is stressed.   But here the
sophisticated Ovid recommends a subtle and gentle progression.
At a dinner-party the incipient affair can be further advanced:
there the pupil can show the girl his interest in her more fre-
quently and more fully (taking advantage of the general confusion

of drinking, conversation, laughter etc. customary at such par-
ties), and in addition he can impress her with a display of his
good points.

Many of the details in these lines are also found in
earlier love-poetry, especially Ovid's own *Amores* 1.4, in which
he instructs his girlfriend on how to behave at a dinner-party
which she, her *vir* and Ovid are to attend (for a similar use by
the poet of one of his own earlier poems see on 93-120). How-
ever, Ovid makes significant variations on the motifs taken from
Amores 1.4 (see below), while the other unoriginal material, in
view of the very fact that it is inherited, suits well Ovid's
pose as the learned expert, and, presented as it is from a new
(didactic) angle, is still entertaining enough (particularly
for those who meet it here for the first time).

349-350 sentiat: subjunctive in a final relative clause.   The
reader is advised to lard his conversation liberally with hints,
ambiguous remarks etc. so that the girl, who is aware of his
interest, may get the point, but not other guests. Cf. Plautus
Asinaria 792 *neque ullum verbum faciat perplexabile.*

351-352 leves: "insubstantial" (because the words are traced
on the table-top in slender smears of wine: tenui...vino).
In the pentameter understand *esse*.

There is emphasis in the juxtaposition leves tenui
(i.e. so that the words will be scarcely visible to anybody
other than the girl, who (346) is sharing the reader's couch).
This detail is a careful expansion of *Amores* 1.4.20 (to his
girlfriend) *verba leges digitis, verba notata mero.* Cf. also
Heroides 17.87f. (Helen to Paris) *orbe quoque in mensae legi
sub nomine nostro,/quod deducta mero littera fecit, AMO.*

353-354 oculos: the girl's eyes.   ignem: (object of faten-
tibus) refers to the fire of love.

Again, as the woman is sharing the reader's couch,
the passionate and silent gaze should escape the notice of
others (especially amid the general confusion). Cf. *Heroides*
17.77f. (Helen to Paris of his behaviour at dinner) *cum modo
me spectas oculis, lascive, protervis,/quos vix instantes
lumina nostra ferunt.*

The juxtaposition <u>oculos oculis</u> suggests well the inter-
locking gaze of the reader and his girl.   The pentameter is in-
geniously epigrammatical (the juxtaposition of opposites <u>tacens</u>
<u>vocem</u>, the emphatic juxtaposition <u>vocem verbaque</u> and the force-
ful alliteration).

355-356   For <u>fac</u> with the subjunctive see on 103-104.   <u>bibet</u>:
future because Ovid is referring to a situation in the future (cf.
<u>libaverit</u> in 357 and <u>petes</u> in 358).   When drinking a toast it
was customary to pass the wine-cup around.   The reader is to
drink from the same part of the cup as the girl because her lips
will have touched it, and so by his action he can show her his
affection and his desire for similar contact with the girl her-
self (cf. the food touched by her in the following couplet).

     This is another shrewd hint: only the woman herself
would know from which precise part of the cup she drank and the
real reason why Ovid's pupil is so keen for the cup (most people,
if they even noticed, would assume that he was simply eager to
make the toast, or just have a drink).   The couplet is based
on *Amores* 1.4.31f. (to his girl) *quae tu reddideris, ego primus*
pocula sumam,/et, qua tu biberis, hac ego parte bibam. Ovid
seems to improve on himself a little here with <u>rapias</u> (which
suggests greater eagerness than *sumam* and so would be more
flattering to the girl).

357-358   <u>tibi</u>:   dative of the agent.   <u>manus</u> refers to the girl's
hand.

     The first piece of advice here shows a subtlety simi-
lar to that in the previous couplet, and in the pentameter Ovid
adds an ingenious tip (the brushing of hands, if actually spotted,
would look accidental).   Cf. *Amores* 1.4.33f. (of the girl's
vir) *si tibi forte dabit quod praegustaverit ipse,/reice libatos*
illius ore cibos (note the inversion and addition here).

     For <u>tu</u> see on 47-48.

359-360   <u>caveto</u> = *cave*. The couplet means that the reader should
not get drunk and engage in a quarrel or a fight.

     There is good psychology here: such behaviour would be
dangerous and unseemly at a dinner-party (and so it might well
put the woman off).   For the lover drunkenly brawling at a party

to his own disadvantage cf. e.g. Theocritus *Idyll* 14.

       For caveto see on 97-98.

361-362   With si vox est understand *tibi*, and with si mollia bracchia understand *tibi sunt*.   In ancient dancing movement of the arms was important, and so suppleness (mollia) was necessary.

       Again this is astute enough advice: the reader is told to make the most of his good points and to show them all, while the girl (for whom, of course, this display is really intended) is much more likely to be impressed by this than by drunken brawling.

       This injunction would have offended conservative Roman opinion of the day, which frowned on such public singing and dancing (cf. e.g. Cicero *In Catilinam* 2.23).

       This is an ingenious couplet. In the hexameter there is balance, repetition and internal rhyme, while in the pentameter there is alliteration and juxtaposition (with emphasis given to place by its brevity and position). There is also a tricolon crescendo and frequent assonance.

363-364   In the hexameter ut is postponed and ebrietas is common to both halves of the line.   titubet: the verb (literally "stagger") is applied humorously to a tongue apparently the worse for drink.   subdola: adjective for adverb.

       Ovid now makes an amusing twist to his advice in 359-360, suggesting a particularly crafty ruse (cf. *Heroides* 16. 247f. (Paris to Helen) *quin etiam, ut possem verbis petulantius uti,/non semel ebrietas est simulata mihi*).

       There is onomatopoeia in 364.

365-366   aequo: "than is proper" (ablative of comparison).

367-368   mensa...remota: see on 135-136. conviva: singular for plural. accessus: plural for singular. locumque denotes room for action ("an opening", "an opportunity").

       Logically and with professorial thoroughness Ovid now moves on to the end of the dinner-party.

       The spondees in the hexameter suggest the slowness of the departing guests.

369-370   leviterque: i.e. unobtrusively. admotus eunti:

<u>admotus</u> is used reflexively, and <u>eunti</u> refers to the girl ("app-
roaching her as she goes"). <u>velle</u>: imperative of *vello*.

Of course, such contact (as well as being pleasurable
in itself) would be a clear sign to the girl, but could hardly
be spotted by anyone else in the milling group.

This piece of advice is based on *Amores* 1.4.55f. (to
his girlfriend) *cum surges abitura domum, surgemus et omnes,/*
in medium turbae fac memor agmen eas:/ agmine. me invenies aut
invenieris in illo;/ quidquid ibi poteris tangere, tange, mei.
Here Ovid is more specific over the form of contact, and it is
the man who is to do the touching.

371-404   At this stage you should boldly start a conversation.
Play the lover credibly, flatter her and don't be hesitant
over making promises. Tears too are useful. You should add
some kisses, even if she pretends to struggle, and then take
the small step to intercourse.

In an increasingly outrageous passage the thorough
expert takes the reader further on, making two progressions,
of which one (to conversation) is gentle enough after the
build-up so far, but the other (to the start of the affair
proper) is more startling. Many people are hesitant and un-
sure about what type of thing they should say when they first
talk to a girl, but the experienced Ovid does not falter and
sees no problems. Here again he reduces a situation in which
one would expect sentiment to play a large part to a matter of
artes, producing a series of general guide-lines accompanied
by perceptive (and often cynical)discussion. His shrewd
precepts here largely repeat those given at 221ff. concerning
the contents of the letter, and the implication seems to be
that the conversation will reinforce the earlier advances and
the addition of the personal touch will prove irresistible.
In the final eight lines of the section Ovid advises his pupil
to move on directly to kisses and intercourse, cynically deny-
ing the seriousness of any struggle against kisses by the girl,
scandalously claiming that copulation is but a short step from
kisses and contemptuously dismissing any restraint on the man's
part as unsophisticated. Something that makes this advice
even more shocking is the fact that all this is supposed to take

place in the very first conversation.   Nowhere here does Ovid
talk about more than one chat or the need for perseverance.
With supreme impudence he envisages a single conversation doing
the trick and also incidentally assumes that the primary inter-
est of all his readers is sex.

371-372   iam: not as the party breaks up (there would hardly
be time or opportunity then for all that Ovid envisages in this
section) but "at this stage" (after preparing the way with the
opening gambits described in the previous 150 lines).   rustice
...Pudor: vocatives.   audentem: the participle is used
as a noun.

        The advice is sound: many young men are unsuccessful
with girls because of awkwardness and bashfulness, whereas the
bold approach generally goes down well.

        In the second half of the pentameter there is an adapta-
tion of the Roman proverb *fortes fortuna adiuvat* (probably
influenced by Tibullus'modification at 1.2.16 *fortes adiuvat
ipsa Venus*).   For *-que...-que* here see on 121-122.

373-374   nostras stands for *meas*.   fac tantum cupias...eris:
for the constructions see on 103-104 and 261-262 (on *persta
modo*).   With cupias understand *puellam*.

        Ovid here declines to tell the reader exactly what to
say or how to express himself, but in the following lines he
does go on to give the main guide-lines.   There is probably
parody here, as the didactic poet occasionally shows a similar
unwillingness to go into detail (e.g. Lucretius 5.1281-2).

375-376   tibi.../...tibi: datives of agent.   vulnera: see
on 123-124.   haec...fides = "belief in this" (that you are
in love).

        Cynicism (the automatic assumption that the pupil will
not really be in love) is combined with perceptive insight
(the great importance attributed to credibility here - note
the positions of haec and fides).

377-378   pessima sit: "though she be extremely ugly" or
"though her looks (forma) be very poor" (the subjunctive is
concessive).   nulli non = "to every woman".

        This couplet is tinged with urbane cynicism.   After
the solemn emphasis placed on the need for credibility

qualibet arte in the previous line the claim at the very start
of the hexameter here that this is easily achieved is rather
amusing.   In the remainder of the couplet the sophisticated
expert passes some satirical comments on female psychology in
a couple of neat epigrams.

　　　　Note the positioning of amanda, pessima and placet.

379-380　　nunc sit = "now you should" (est (with the infinitive)
is used in the sense of "it is permitted", "one may"). subestur:
third person singular of the present indicative passive of
subedo.

　　　　Again there is good psychology here.

　　　　The simile (which may be based on Callimachus *Palatine
Anthology* 12.139.3f. (also in an amatory context) "often a
quiet river unnoticed eats away at a wall from underneath")
is apt enough: the water also exerts a gentle and impercept-
ible pressure.

381-382　　faciem is an object of laudare.   Slender fingers and
small feet in women were much admired (cf. Catullus 43.1ff.
(to an ugly girl) *salve, nec minimo puella naso/nec bello pede
nec nigris ocellis/nec longis digitis...).*

　　　　The expert helpfully goes into details.

383-384　　castas is used as a noun here.   curae: predicative
dative.

　　　　This is another piece of perceptive insight. To under-
score the effectiveness of his advice in the previous lines,
Ovid is here implying that all females, even respectable types
and virgins (note the position of virginibus), are bothered
about their looks and susceptible to flattery.

　　　　The spondees seem mock-solemn.

385-386　　pollicito testes: "as witnesses to your promise" (in
apposition to quoslibet...deos).

　　　　This recommendation is based on Tibullus 1.4.21ff.
*nec iurare time: veneris periuria venti/inrita per terras et
freta summa ferunt./gratia magna Iovi: vetuit pater ipse
valere/iurasset cupide quidquid ineptus amor:/perque suas im-
pune sinit Dictynna sagittas/adfirmes, crines perque Minerva
suos.*

　　　　Ovid does not specify what the reader is to promise,

and his vagueness may well be intended to be all-embracing.
Promises of fidelity would be prudent enough, but promises of
gifts (as at 227ff.) would imply a degree of cynicism (i.e.
the assumption that all girls are mercenary).   In any case
the advice is coolly opportunist, since Ovid immediately makes
it clear that he does not expect his pupil to keep his word.

The point of the injunction in the pentameter is, of
course, to give the promise added credibility.   Although the
perjury of lovers (and Jupiter's approval of such perjury) was
proverbial (e.g. Tibullus 1.4.23-24), the blatant recommenda-
tion of such conduct may well have offended pious and moral
Romans of the old school (as may the frivolous and rather im-
pertinent reference to Jupiter in the following lines).

The frequent alliteration makes for greater force-
fulness.

387-388   amantum: for the form see on 223-224.   Aeolios...
Notos: Aeolus was the god who controlled the winds (see
Virgil *Aeneid* 1.50ff.).   *Noti* here stands for winds in general.
The image of winds carrying away words, promises etc. and
thereby invalidating them was common in antiquity (cf. e.g.
Tibullus 1.4.21-22, quoted on 385-386).

To justify his advice in the previous couplet, Ovid
points out that the king of the gods himself (Iuppiter in
emphatic position) condones lovers' perjury.

The hexameter is an eminently quotable line and con-
jures up a superb picture of the laughing god on high.

In the pentameter Aeolios...Notos looks like a cheeky
reminiscence of Virgil's *Aeoliis...procellis* (*Aeneid* 5.791).

389-390   The reference in this couplet is primarily to Jupi-
ter's affair with Io (see on 213-214).   Jupiter swore to Juno
that he had never touched Io and thereafter ruled that lovers'
oaths could be broken with impunity.   Styga: a Greek form
of the accusative.   Homer (*Iliad* 15.37-38) describes an oath
by the Styx as "the greatest and most awesome oath that the
blessed gods can take".   falsum: internal accusative (equiv-
alent to an adverb).

The position of per Styga brings out the magnitude of
the offence.

solebat looks like an impudent exaggeration (Jupiter's
perjury to Juno is attested only in the case of Io).

The spondees are mock-solemn.

391-392 fallentes: the participle is again used as a noun ("the
deceivers", with reference to girls, who are also the subject
of sunt, posuere and cadant). in laqueos...cadant: for hun-
ting-imagery see on 29-30. Ovid's point is that women try
to trap men with their promises (e.g. to be faithful, to go
to bed with them), so it is a fitting repayal if girls them-
selves are trapped by promises. posuere = *posuerunt*.

The cynicism and exaggeration are expressed with epi-
grammatical neatness.

393-394 lacrimis adamanta movebis: adamanta is a Greek form
of the accusative. Adamant was a mythical metal of extreme
hardness (the gates of Tartarus were made of adamant, to
prevent escape: Virgil *Aeneid* 6.552ff.). It came to sym-
bolize unfeelingness and inexorability, so that the implica-
tion is that if tears will move even adamant they will cer-
tainly move a girl's heart. There is nothing unmanly in the
behaviour recommended here, as the ancients wept freely.

This is another judicious tip, aimed at the tender
female heart.

For prosunt see on 117-118.

395-396 neque enim = *non enim*. uncta...manu: the hand is
to be smeared with a substance that will make the reader's
eyes water (e.g. raw onion).

This expert hint is especially calculating, but, of
course, it is also ingenious and entertaining.

397-398 sapiens is used as a noun here. misceat is poten-
tial subjunctive. licet: "although". *Oscula* is to be
supplied in both halves of the pentameter.

The admixture of kisses is a gentle enough pro-
gression, but to take them without the girl's consent seems
rather presumptuous. The cheek mounts rapidly in the fol-
lowing lines.

The pentameter is epigrammatical.

399-400 pugnando: "in fighting", "in the fight" (a gerund
in the (instrumental) ablative is occasionally used so vaguely

that it is virtually equivalent to a present participle, as
here).

The suggestion here that any girl who fights back will
be putting up merely a token resistance is impudently cynical.

The many spondees in this couplet make it seem as if
Ovid is being serious - until the second half of the penta-
meter.

401-402   Ovid's point is that if a man goes no further than
kisses (i.e. does not have intercourse with the girl), then
he deserves to be deprived of what he has been granted (kisses)
as well.   qui is postponed, and *(is) qui oscula sumpsit* is
the subject of sumit and erit.   haec quoque, quae data sunt
(i.e. *oscula*) is the object of perdere.

This is an outrageous couplet for a number of reasons
(the continued suggestion that resistance is token (the kisses
which were in 398 non data are now actually described as
data), the attitude towards kisses (merely a prelude to sex),
the recommendation that the reader should now move on at once
to make the woman have intercourse with him, the view that the
man who does not go further deserves to forfeit that pleasure
too, and the assumption that all his readers are mainly interes-
ted in sex).

403-404   I.e. think back: after you kissed a girl how far
were you from the fulfilment of your desires (i.e. inter-
course)?   If you didn't go further, you were not modest but
unsophisticated.   defuerat: for the tense see on 61-62.
ille ("such conduct", i.e. not going further) is attracted
into the gender of its nearest complement (cf. 237).

This couplet underlines the points of the last one,
with the addition of the suggestion that kisses lead directly
to intercourse (i.e. any girl who has been kissed by a man is
in reality ready to go to bed with him immediately) and the
statement that to hold back is merely the action of a man
sadly (note the ironical ei mihi) lacking in sophistication.

405-436   You may call such conduct "force", but girls like to
be forced like this.   Phoebe and her sister were abducted
by force but enjoyed it.   Achilles used force on Deidamia,
but she wanted it and actually tried to detain him when he

was leaving her to go off to the Trojan War.

In this passage Ovid anticipates an objection by his
pupil that the behaviour recommended in the foregoing lines
amounts to force and defends his advice there at length.
Although there is a degree of truth in his observations in
the opening couplets here (*some* girls (notably the elegiac
mistress) do put up a resistance that is merely token), his
remarks are again outrageous, as he indulges in cynical exagg-
erations and generalizations, and then actually proceeds to
back them up with mythological examples (in which, it seems,
he impudently alters the details so that they illustrate his
contentions).   The second of these examples is long enough to
qualify as a (mock-didactic) digression.   The story of
Achilles and Deidamia is used to make Ovid's point, but he is
just as interested in the comedy and incongruity of the situ-
ation.   He begins by teasing the reader (raising his expec-
tations of a humorous and scandalous treatment of the myth,
but then, tongue-in-cheek, deliberately holding back his levity
and the more interesting details; there may be a further tease
too: see on 431-432).   He also enjoys some protracted joking
at the expense of Achilles, the most famous and fearsome Greek
warrior of myth and epic poetry.   He ends with some flippancy
on the subject of Deidamia's forced coupling with Achilles and
by mocking the heroine.

As well as being funny, these lines are also skilful
and neat.   The poet's metrical and stylistic dexterity is
employed to excellent effect throughout, and careful attention
is paid to arrangement and structure too.   In the opening coup-
let he states the reader's possible objection and his own ans-
wer to it (= his basic premise); this is followed by two
arguments (positive and negative: 407-410) and two mythological
exempla (411ff.).   It is also noteworthy that the passage
consists of four groups of eight lines.   The first four coup-
lets (before the digression) naturally form a unit (note that
vim, vis and gratus in 411f. pick up 405 and so neatly round
off those lines), while in the digression 413-420 provide a
general introduction, 421-428 concern Achilles in disguise and
429-436 concentrate on Deidamia and the force used on her.

405-406   vim licet appelles: "you may call it 'force' " (refer-
ring to the conduct recommended in the previous lines).   For
the construction see on 283-284.   invitae is adjective for
adverb, going with dedisse (perfect infinitive for present).
With (id) quod iuvat (the object of dedisse) understand *dedisse*
or *dare* ("what it pleases them to give").   Ovid's point is
that women actually enjoy intercourse, but often insist on a
show of unwillingness.

The outrageousness here is heightened by the positions
of grata and the generalizing puellis and by the pointed repe-
tition of *vis*.

The cynical expert is to the fore in the paradoxical
and epigrammatical pentameter.

407-408   veneris subita violata rapina: i.e. suddenly forced
to have intercourse.   inprobitas muneris instar habet: i.e.
the woman enjoys herself so much that she regards the man's
shameless conduct as an act of kindness.

The phrase veneris subita violata rapina seems a rather
solemn periphrasis and suggests that Ovid is being serious -
until gaudet and the rest of 408.

There is impudence in the placement of the generalizing
quaecumque, the doubly emphatic gaudet and the juxtaposition
inprobitas muneris.

The dactyls convey an appropriate air of gaiety.

409-410   quae stands for *ea quae*.   non goes with tacta ("un-
touched").   ut: "although".

Great point is given to the cynical tristis erit by its
position at the end of the couplet and the juxtaposed gaudia.

In these lines we find aptly sad spondees.

411-412   Castor and Pollux (the Dioscuri) carried off by force
Phoebe and her sister Hilaira, who were already engaged (to
Lynceus and Idas).

The knowledgeable expert actually backs up his argu-
ments by citing a learned and allusive mythological *exemplum*
(which also smooths the way for the much longer example that
follows).   This reaction by the sisters does not seem to be
attested elsewhere: Ovid here may well be taking an audacious
liberty with the myth to make it illustrate his point (cf.

431-432, 2.279-282).

     The spondees here seem mock-solemn.

413-414   The words in the pentameter form the subject, *est* is
to be understood in the hexameter and <u>fabula</u> etc. is the com-
plement.   In 414 there is a striking example of a participle
in agreement with a noun doing the work of a noun-phrase (lit-
erally "the girl from Scyros (sexually) joined with the man
from Thessaly", i.e. "the coupling of the girl from Scyros
with the man from Thessaly").   Cf. *post urbem conditam* ("since
the foundation of the city").   <u>Scyrias</u>: Deidamia lived on
Scyros (an island in the Aegean).   <u>Haemonio</u>: Achilles came
from Thessaly.

     Note the allusive *doctrina*.

     After Ovid's scandalous and funny remarks in the last
eight lines the story announced here (especially the words <u>non</u>
<u>indigna referri</u> and <u>iuncta</u>) would have raised the expectations
of the reader (who would have been acquainted with the main de-
tails of the myth and so would have been immediately aware of
the extensive possibilities of outrageous humour in Ovid's
treatment and keen to see his handling of the actual coupling).

     The pentameter is ingenious: the words are arranged
after the pattern of the golden line, there are two expressive
juxtapositions and there is an intricate pattern of word-
endings.

415-416   For the judgement of Paris (at the foot of Mount Ida
near Troy) and Venus' fatal reward see on 147-148.   <u>praemia</u>:
plural for singular.   <u>digna</u> agrees with <u>dea</u>.   <u>duas</u> refers
to the two goddesses who were Venus' rivals.

     In this couplet and the following two Ovid takes his
time over giving the background, relating perfectly well-known
facts (so well-known that he hardly bothers to use names) from
the most famous of myths in unnecessary and at times rather
repetitious detail.   Such an introduction is hardly vital and
could have been effected in a single line.   Ovid is teasing
the reader: after whetting his appetite in the last couplet
he is intentionally delaying the more interesting and humorous
parts of the story.

417-418   <u>nurus</u> and <u>Graiaque...uxor</u> refer to the Spartan Helen.

<u>Priamum</u>:   Priam was, of course, the father of Paris. <u>diverso</u>
<u>...orbe</u>:   i.e. from Europe.

  As part of Ovid's tease the pentameter virtually repeats
the hexameter.

419-420 <u>iurabant omnes in laesi verba mariti</u>: "all (the Greeks)
were swearing loyalty to the wronged husband" (i.e. Menelaus).
<u>publica causa</u>: "a national cause".

  Again the pentameter seems rather redundant after the
hexameter.

  The spondees emphasize the gravity of the situation.

421-422 <u>turpe</u> (qualified by <u>nisi...tribuisset</u>) is in apposition
to the rest of the sentence (<u>Achilles/...erat</u>), <u>virum</u> here
denotes "manhood" and <u>dissimulatus erat</u> is a passive with middle
force (see on 289-290): "Achilles had concealed his manhood
with long clothes, (which would have been) a disgrace, had he
not done this as a concession to his mother's entreaties".
Achilles' mother (Thetis) knew that her son would die if he
took part in the Trojan War, and so she begged him to hide on
Scyros in female dress working at household tasks among the
king's daughters.

  Especially in view of the behaviour of all the rest of
the Greeks in the previous couplet, Achilles' conduct might
have seemed truly disgraceful (note the position of <u>turpe</u>).
The raising of this point, the careful defence of Achilles on
the grounds of *pietas* and the matter-of-fact description of
his appearance keep the tone serious enough.

423-424 <u>Aeacide</u> is vocative. Achilles was the grandson of
Aeacus. <u>tua munera</u>: "your business". <u>alia Palladis arte</u>:
Pallas Athene (Minerva), as well as being the inventress of
wool-working, was also a goddess of war. <u>petes</u>: the future
has imperative force (see on 285-286).

  At last the long-awaited humour surfaces (but the details
of the coupling are still held back). In these and the follow-
ing lines Ovid's tone of superior dismay and bewilderment (be-
cause he knows how Achilles will conduct himself in the Trojan
War) adds greatly to the fun, as he breaks in to put a series
of incredulous questions to Achilles and to remonstrate firmly
with him. The comic incongruity of the situation is well

brought out here by the dignified epic title *Aeacides* (cf. e.g.
Homer *Iliad* 2.860, Virgil *Aeneid* 1.99) and the position of
lanae.

Appropriately the metre becomes more dactylic here and
in the following lines generally.   Note also the forceful allit-
eration and repetition of quid in this couplet and the next.

425-426   quid tibi cum: "what are you doing with...?" (see on
195-196).   pensa: the *pensum* was the amount of wool to be
spun in a day.   quid ("why") in 426 is postponed.   cadet Hector:
see on 225-226.

Again the incongruity is underlined (the juxtaposition
calathis? clipeo (both words emphatically positioned), the
placement of pensa and the allusion in qua cadet Hector).

Ovid makes much of Achilles' hands here and in the next
couplet.   This is because any epic warrior's hands were most
important in fighting and the deeds performed by Achilles'
hands (given the famous epithet "man-slaying" by Homer: e.g.
Iliad 18.317) were especially renowned.   Hence Ovid pretends
to be baffled at the use to which they are put here.

427-428   succinctos operoso stamine fusos: in spinning fibres
were drawn out from a loose ball of wool and spirally twisted,
and the thread so produced was wound upon the spindle.
Operosus here means "produced with much effort".   Pelias
hasta: Achilles' long, heavy spear, made from an ash on Mount
Pelion (in Thessaly), which no other Greek could manage to
brandish.

Achilles' bizarre conduct at present is brought out
this time by the position of fusos, the reference to the
famous 'Pelian spear' (cf. Homer *Iliad* 19.387ff., 20.277) and
the epic flavour of *quassare hastam* (cf. Virgil *Aeneid* 12.93f. ;
perhaps a reminiscence of Homer *Iliad* 16.142f., 19.389f.).

The spondees are mock-solemn.

429-430   virgo regalis: Deidamia, daughter of king Lycomedes.
stupro: she became by Achilles the mother of Neoptolemus
(also called Pyrrhus).

The pentameter with its abrupt bald statement of Dei-
damia's rude awakening is very funny.   Here at last Ovid comes
to the coupling.

431-432   sed...tamen: "but...all the same".

       After the hexameter, which underlines the point that
Deidamia was forced (the position of viribus, the addition of
quidem and the parenthesis), the pentameter comes as an
amusing surprise.   If, as appears to be the case from the few
surviving accounts of this story, Ovid was the first to attri-
bute this use of force to Achilles, we have here another in-
stance (cf. 411-412) of an audacious alteration of a myth to
make it fit Ovid's point, and ancient readers will have been
kept unsure of the relevance of the digression until now.

       There is pointed repetition and vigorous alliteration
in 432.

433-434   nam is postponed.

       The absurd inconsistency attributed to Deidamia here
(if she had really been forced against her will) makes Ovid's
point.

435-436   vis ubi nunc illa est? : i.e. why do you no longer com-
plain about his use of force? quid: "why".

       Again Ovid breaks in to address one of the characters
of the story in order to increase the humour.   There is mis-
chievous mockery in his questions (especially the position of
vis and the detail in blanda), and the rhythm is deliciously
mock-solemn.

437-454   Women are bashful about starting things but enjoy sex
when the man takes the initiative.   So you cannot expect them
to do the propositioning.   That is your job - their job is
to say Yes.   Ask, and you should be successful (even Jupiter
had to do that).   You may, however, find that your entreaties
make her arrogantly scornful - if so, reduce the pressure.
Sometimes too, with difficult propositions, you have to pretend
that it is friendship that you are after.

       Having dealt with the possibility of (pretended) resis-
tance, Ovid in the first half of this section (437-446) now
moves on to the normal and proper state of affairs (as he sees
it).   Here the cynicism and generalizations continue, as
Ovid, picking up from the story of Deidamia, claims that women
are eager for sex but want the male to make the first move,
so that the reader stands a good chance of success if he takes

the lead by propositioning the girl.   Other jokes are worked
in too, and it should also be noticed that copulation still
seems to be envisaged as taking place at the end of the very
first conversation.   In the second half of the section he be-
comes more realistic and admits that there may be serious prob-
lems and that his pupil may not achieve success in his initial
chat.   However, the relegation of these difficulties to the
end suggests that the expert views them as rather outside pos-
sibilities, and, nothing daunted, he is immediately ready
with resourceful solutions.

437-438   quaedam: neuter accusative plural, object of coepisse
(and to be understood in 438 as the object of pati).   priorem:
adjective for adverb.   The accusative and infinitive depends on
pudor est (literally: "there is shame to...").   What is upper-
most in Ovid's mind in this couplet is that a woman is too
embarrassed to take the initiative over sexual intercourse.

For scilicet see on 91-92.

With regard to human affairs in general this remark
seems fair enough at first sight, but when applied specifically
to women and their sexual relations it takes on a cynical edge
(it is not really true that all girls enjoy (or even consent
to) intercourse, if the man makes the first move).

439-440   si quis (referring to iuveni) is postponed in 440 (trans-
late: "if any young man waits...then he...").   prior is
again used adverbially (and in 441).   roget: rogo here and
below is used in the explicit sexual sense of "proposition"
(cf. Amores 1.8.43 casta est quam nemo rogavit).

a is ironical.

The suggestion that the woman might ask first is delib-
erately absurd, and the couplet conjures up a comic picture
of a vain young man waiting to be propositioned.

441-442   comiter: i.e. saying Yes and without resistance.

In the pentameter Ovid gives his view of how the woman
should behave and rather amusingly defines her duty as ready
acceptance.

This is a skilful couplet: there is contrast with and
pointed echoes from the previous line, as well as repetition,
alliteration, internal rhyme and balance.

443-444 potiare (= *potiaris*): "gain her submission" (*potior*
    may take the ablative or the accusative, so understand *illa* or
    illam). da...tui: i.e. by propositioning her you are taking
    the first step (principium) towards the fulfilment of your
    desire and providing her with good reason/an excuse (causam)
    for granting it.

      Ovid is here pointing out why the girl should give in
when asked.   Once more there is urbane cynicism (she is just
waiting to be propositioned, and merely being asked gives her
a pretext/good enough grounds for going to bed with you).

      The hexameter contains two neat epigrams.

445-446 heroidas: a Greek form of the accusative (plural),from
    herois.   Jupiter's conquests among heroines were countless (Io,
    Europa, Danae, Semele, Alcmena, Callisto, Maia, Electra etc.,
    etc.).   corrupit: "seduced".   The implication is that if
    even Jupiter (the king of the gods and the most acceptable lover
    imaginable) had to take the initiative like this, then so does
    Ovid's pupil.

      This is an entertaining addition: it parodies the my-
thological analogy of didactic, it is an intentionally grandiose
parallel, the reference to Jupiter is rather frivolous (note
the position of Iuppiter and the point to magnum = "great
though he is"), the application of supplex to Jupiter is funny
(people normally made supplications to *him*) and the pentameter
suggests a humorously absurd picture.   The conventional would
probably not have appreciated such frivolity at Jupiter's ex-
pense.

447-448 The reader's pressing entreaties may produce a scorn-
    ful arrogance in the girl instead.

449-450 (*id*) quod refugit, like (*id*) quod instat, refers es-
    pecially to men.   odere = *oderunt*.   tui: objective geni-
    tive ("for you").

      As an expert in his subject, Ovid is acquainted with
and bases his advice on a relevant piece of proverbial wisdom
(449; cf. e.g. Theocritus *Idyll* 6.17 "she flees when one
loves and pursues when one does not love").

      This ingenious couplet contains repetition of *quod* and
instare, a chiasmus (including juxtaposition) in 449 and

alliteration in 450.

451-452   roganti: dative of the agent.   Either the participle
is used as a noun or *tibi* is to be supplied.

Ovid now moves on to even more difficult propositions,
but in their case too he envisages no real problems.   His ad-
vice is to be more subtle and indirect.

453-454   *Dare verba* (with the dative) means "to give (empty)
words to", i.e. deceive, take in.   qui = *is qui.*

The expert has good grounds for his advice in the prev-
ious couplet - personal observation (for the parody in this and
in vidi see on 55-56).   The *tetrica puella* here is an example
of a difficult proposition, and the implication is that if the
reader follows Ovid's recommendation, he too could get even a
tetrica puella into bed.

Note the patterns of word-endings (and the alliteration).

455-470   One final point.   Women vary greatly in personality and
experience.   This means that you have to adapt your methods
accordingly and be extremely versatile.   Failure to do so will
prove fatal.

At this stage Ovid has completed the second part of his
programme (winning the girl), but here he adds a word of cau-
tion, apparently as an afterthought.   Again he is more realis-
tic (in admitting difficulties and the possibility of failure),
but again the knowledgeable Ovid is immediately ready with the
solution.   Playing to the full his role as the wise expert
and didactic poet, he subjoins some perceptive enough obser-
vations and astute advice presented with mischievous humour.

455-456   excipe: "catch" (for the hunting-imagery (picked up
below) see on 29-30).

There is a neat epigram in the pentameter.

457-458   eadem: feminine nominative singular.   hic is the ad-
verb.   Ovid's point is that soils yield different produce
and so call for different types of cultivation, just as girls
have different characters that call for different approaches.

The comparison of women to different varieties of soil
is certainly clinical, and to many women it may seem offensive.

The analogy from nature is mock-didactic, and the

humour is heightened by the fact that Ovid has Virgil's
Georgics in particular in mind here: cf. 1.54ff. *hic segetes,
illic veniunt felicius uvae,/ arborei fetus alibi, atque in-
iussa virescunt/ gramina* and 2.109 *nec vero terrae ferre omnes
omnia possunt* (the joke lies in the new context, which is triv-
ial and frivolous, and in the use of Virgilian didactic as
illustrative material in Ovid's didactic poem).

This is the first of several comparisons in this section.
It may be felt that Ovid is overdoing things, but in fact he
is stressing with deliberate pedantry his remarks about variety
and versatility, while his examples are different and have subtle
point.

459-460   in ore figurae: "facial looks". qui = *is qui*. aptus
erit: "will adapt himself to".

Again the expert produces a phrase with a wise pro-
verbial ring to it (459; cf. e.g. Terence *Phormio* 454 *quot
homines tot sententiae: suo' quoique mos*).

461-462   utque and Proteus go together ("and, like Proteus, he
will...").   Proteus was a sea-god who could alter his form at
will.   The sensible lover should, like him, change into water,
a lion, a tree and a boar at different times (an amusing (meta-
phorical) way of saying "be versatile").

The Proteus-like transformations here look like an
abridged version by the learned poet of Homer *Odyssey* 4.456ff.
(of Proteus) "first he turned into a fine-maned lion, then
into a snake, a leopard and a huge boar; he turned into run-
ning water and into a tree with lofty foliage".

463-464   Different methods are necessary to catch different fish,
just as (465) differing approaches are needed for women of
varying age (and experience).   pisces and capiuntur are com-
mon to both halves of the hexameter, and *pisces* (accusative)
is understood with hos. ab: see on 289-290.   cava:
either "concave" (i.e. bulging) or "full of holes" (i.e. with
mesh).   retia: "drag-nets" (as opposed to the *iaculum* =
casting-net).

The analogy is mock-didactic and compares love to a
(conventionally) more worthwhile and serious occupation. The
example here is especially apt because imagery from fishing

was quite often applied to love (see on 29-30), but again one
suspects that many women might find it offensive.

465-466 longius: "from quite far away" or "from further away"
(than a younger one). anus is a noun but is here used as a
feminine adjective. The implication in the pentameter is that
similarly the older and more experienced woman will see the
reader's "trap" more easily.

Ovid is here making a new shrewd point: one must take
into account a woman's age (and experience) too.

The expert again produces a line with a proverbial flav-
our to it in 466 (cf. e.g. *Ex Ponto* 2.7.9f.), and again the anal-
ogy is mock-didactic and particularly apt (see on 29-30).

467-468 videare = *videaris*. The verb in the main clause is in-
dicative. The subjunctive is used here to show that the sit-
uation in the *si* clause is "improbable but possible" (North &
Hillard *Latin Prose Composition*). rudi and pudenti are used
as nouns.

Ovid produces some concrete examples to back up his ad-
vice and in these too shows perceptiveness.

miserae is probably ironical.

469-470 fit ut: "it comes about that". quae = *ea quae*.
honesto and inferioris are used as nouns.

Paul Turner's translation may well catch a sly nuance
in honesto ("a wonderful chap like you").

471-472 This couplet announces that Ovid has completed part of
his task (how to find the girl and how to win her) and at this
stage he will pause (472, i.e. end the book here) before going
on to the remainder of his enterprise (how to keep the girl).
nostras...rates may be genuine plurals (see on 2.5-6), in
which case ancora iacta is singular for plural, but are most
probably plural for singular (= *meam ratem* or perhaps (see on
2.5-6) *nostram ratem*).

Ovid rounds off the first book with a couplet that con-
tains extensive parody of (especially Virgilian) didactic. For
pars superat cf. Virgil *Georgics* 3.286 *hoc satis armentis:
superat pars altera curae*. For *labor* of the didactic poet's
work cf. e.g. *Georgics* 4.116 (quoted below). Virgil at the
end of *his* second book had also called for a pause before

continuing (*Georgics* 2.541f. *sed nos immensum spatiis confecimus aequor,/et iam tempus equum fumantia solvere colla*). In place of Virgil's chariot-image Ovid here has a ship (or ships). As the application of such nautical imagery to the poem's progress had a long ancestry and was especially common in solemn genres, it is cheeky of Ovid to employ it here of the *Ars*. He may have particularly in mind the similar use of such imagery in didactic (e.g. *Georgics* 4.116f. *extremo ni iam sub fine laborum/vela traham et terris festinem advertere proram*).

BOOK II

1-18   At this stage my advice has caught a girl for the de-
   lighted,appreciative reader.   But we are far from finished
   yet.   I still have to instruct you on how to keep the girl,
   something which also needs technique.   This is a major enter-
   prise for me, since retaining love is a very difficult accom-
   plishment.

         In this careful introduction to the third part of his
   programme Ovid opens with a flourish that sets the tone for
   the rest of the book.   His cheeky and clever humour is once
   more much in evidence, especially in the way in which he resumes
   and in fact plays to the full his role as the didactic poet
   and learned expert.   So this whole section represents a bur-
   lesque of the recapitulation in didactic (especially that
   found at the start of books: cf. e.g. Lucretius 5.55ff.,
   Virgil *Georgics* 2.1ff.), and he also parodies the behaviour
   of the didactic author when approaching a particularly diffi-
   cult part of his work.   So too in emphasizing the need for
   technique in keeping the girl he makes it clear that he will
   be (again) making a clinical, rational approach to a matter in
   which one would expect feeling and sentiment to play a leading
   part.

1-2   dicite is addressed to Ovid's readers.   'io Paean' :
   a cry (here of triumphant joy) addressed to Apollo, who may
   be relevant here as the god of poetry (who   has inspired the
   poem which has ensured the reader's success so far) or in his
   (occasional) role as a god of hunting (cf. Sophocles *Oedipus
   at Colonus* 1091 "Apollo the hunter").   The imagery in 2 means
   that the "traps" taught by Ovid are in imagination supposed to
   have "caught" for the reader the "prey" (the woman) he wanted
   (see on 1.29-30).

         It seems irreverent and perhaps even irreligious of
   Ovid to tell his reader to give the solemn cry "io Paean" simply
   because he is supposed to have caught a girl.

3-4   palma: the wreath or branch of palm awarded to the
   victor. praelata agrees with carmina.   Ascraeo Maeonioque seni:
   i.e. the poetry of Hesiod (see on 1.11-12) and Homer (here
   supposed to be born in Maeonia, a part of Lydia in Asia Minor).

         Ovid's pupil might be supposed to value the *Ars* so far

because of the help it has given him over finding and catching
a girl.   It would be presumptuous enough for Ovid himself to
claim that, but it is positively outrageous of him to assert
confidently that the reader rates the first book alone of his
flippant and trivial poetry above all the work of Hesiod (the
founder of the didactic genre) and Homer (the earliest sur-
viving and (in the opinion of many) finest poet of antiquity).
Ovid is suggesting the importance of love and of his own advice
on that subject.

Note the allusive *doctrina* in the reference to his two
predecessors (there may also be literary learning, since
Ascraeo...seni looks like a reminiscence of Virgil *Eclogue*
6.70).

5-6   pinus here means "ship".   quem peto: the antecedent
is portus.   In the nautical imagery the idea may be that Ovid
is the helmsman in a ship shared by himself and the reader
or that he is in his own ship leading the way for the reader
in his.   In any case Ovid is guiding his pupil and together
they still have to make much progress before they reach their
ultimate goal (i.e. they have to get through the business of
how to keep the girl before they are finished).

For the ship-imagery see on 1.471-472.   The detail of
the fellow-traveller may have come from Virgil *Georgics* 2.39ff.
tuque ades inceptumque una decurre laborem,/...Maecenas,
pelagoque volans da vela patenti./...ades et primi lege litoris
oram.

7-8   me vate: ablative absolute (= "thanks to my poem").
For vate see on 1.13-14.

arte...arte: a pun is probably intended (*ars* and the
Ars).

9-10   Ovid means that it is just as hard to keep a girl you
have won as to win her: luck plays a part in winning her,
but keeping her will be a work of skill alone.   quam: "than".
parta: neuter accusative plural ("things that have been
gained").   illic ("in the former") refers to quaerere, and hoc
("the latter") refers to parta tueri.

The hexameter has a wise proverbial ring (cf. e.g.
Demosthenes *Olynthiac* 1.23 "it often seems harder to maintain

prosperity than to acquire it").

11-12   puer et Cytherea: Venus (the Greek island Cythera was
a famous centre of her worship) and her son Amor.   nunc Erato:
understand *mihi fave*.   nomen Amoris habes: Ovid connects
the name of the Muse Erato with "Eros", the Greek name for Amor –
hence his invocation of her in particular.

          Ovid here parodies the renewed call for inspiration (es-
pecially at difficult points) in didactic (cf. e.g. Virgil
Georgics 3.294, 4.6f., Manilius 3.1ff.) and the invocation of
Erato because of her name's erotic connotations at Apollonius
Rhodius *Argonautica* 3.1-5.

13-14   quas...artes (i.e. *per quas artes Amor remanere possit*)
is an indirect question depending on dicere.   tam...puer is
in apposition to Amor.   The thought here is clever and none-
too-serious.   Ovid says that Amor wanders widely over the
vast world because people all over the world fall in love, which
is, of course, caused by Amor visiting them and shooting arrows
into them etc.   Because of this tendency to globe-trot Ovid
maintains that it is difficult to keep Amor in one spot and
stop him from leaving (by which he means here that it is hard
to make love remain in the girl).

          For magna paro (he stresses the difficulty of his task
below too) see on 1.155-156 and cf. in particular Virgil *Geor-
gics* 3.289f. *nec sum animi dubius, verbis ea vincere magnum/
quam sit,* Manilius 3.1 *in nova surgentem maioraque viribus
ausum.*   Note the position of magna.

          This is the fourth time that Ovid has used the word
ars so far (cf. 8, 10): he is emphasizing the importance of
technique for keeping the girl.

15-16   avolet: subjunctive in a final relative clause. Again
there is humour in the thought: the fact that Amor is nimble
(levis) and can fly is also supposed to make it hard to detain
him (i.e. make love remain in the girl).

          The rhythm in 15 is very apt.

17-18   In the hexameter the reference is to the famous crafts-
man and inventor Daedalus, who made wings out of feathers and
wax and (together with his son Icarus) flew away from Crete,
where the king (Minos) was trying to detain him.   (Icarus,

of course, flew too close to the sun, so that the wax melted
and he fell to his death in the sea.) The implication in the
couplet is that if even a powerful king found it hard to res-
train a mere mortal with wings, then *Ovid* will find it very
difficult indeed to check a winged *god*.

Note the ingenious and flippant *doctrina*.

19-26 Recourse to withcraft is mistaken. Magic does not
have the power to preserve love, and in fact it can prove harm-
ful.

Before actually giving instructions on how to keep the
girl the thorough Ovid treats of another *ars* which the reader
might try instead, and by disposing of it he underlines the
importance of and need for both amatory technique and his own
advice. This is a learned little section in general, and
especially noteworthy is the way in which the expert demon-
strates that his knowledge also extends to another field
which has a bearing on his own. There may well be parody in
these lines too, which would give them especial point (did-
actic authors sometimes criticized and attacked rival methods,
systems and theories: cf. e.g. Lucretius 1.635ff., Varro
Res Rusticae 1.18, 1.19).

19-20 si quis would more normally precede Haemonias. Hae-
monias: Thessaly was particularly renowned as a land of
magic and magicians. In the pentameter the reference is
to hippomanes, a small black growth on the head of a new-
born foal, which was a notorious love-charm.

Haemonias...artes: as opposed to Ovid's own *artes*.

The pentameter contains a learned reminiscence of
Virgil *Aeneid* 4.515f. *quaeritur et nascentis equi de fronte
revulsus/et matri praereptus amor.*

21-22 Medeides herbae: Medeides is the nominative plural
of *Medeis*. The herbs of Medea (the most famous and skilled
witch in the ancient world) were supremely effective.
Marsa: the Marsi (a people of central Italy) were the
most notable and powerful local magicians. magicis...
sonis: as well as using recognizable words, magicians inclu-
ded in their incantations indistinct mutterings and animal-
like howls, and in love-magic they also used the rhombus

(bullroarer), which emitted a buzzing sound when whirled around
(cf. Theocritus *Idyll* 2).

Again there is literary learning: nenia Marsa is taken
from Horace *Epode* 17.29 *caputque Marsa dissilire nenia*.

The pentameter may well be onomatopoeic.

23-24   tenuisset is common to both halves of 23. *Phasias* (here
used as a noun) denotes Medea (the Phasis was a river in her
native land of Colchis), who fell in love with and married Jason
(son of Aeson), only to be supplanted later by another woman.
Aesoniden is a Greek form of the accusative.   Circe was another
famous witch.   On his return from Troy the Greek hero Ulysses
(Odysseus) stopped off on her island (Aeaea) and stayed with
her for a year, but finally left her to continue his journey
back to his wife and home.

Note the expert and entertaining *doctrina* here and in
particular the way in which it cleverly turns the reference to
Medea in the previous couplet.

25-26   profuerint: both the present and (as here) perfect tenses
of the subjunctive are used with potential force, referring to
the future.   pallentia: "that produce pallor" (the pallor of
sickness). puellis goes with data.   vimque furoris habent:
the emperor Caligula and the poet Lucretius, for instance,
were supposed to have been driven mad by love-potions.

For profuerint see on 1.117-118.

27-62   To be loved, you must be lovable.   Good looks alone
are not enough for this - you need a good mind as well.   Physi-
cal qualities are much less enduring than mental ones too.
So cultivate your mind, paying great attention to intellectual
accomplishments.   The effectiveness of intelligence in love
is illustrated by Ulysses, who was not handsome but through
his eloquence and quick wits made goddesses such as Calypso
love him desperately.

The opening of this section is serious enough as Ovid
finally begins his precepts on how to keep the girl with some
sound advice, but his sense of fun is not held in check for
long.   Ulysses is introduced, to show the usefulness of in-
tellectual qualities, but the number of lines devoted to him
(41-60) means that they constitute a short digression.   This

learned passage (combining the Ulysses and Calypso story from
Homer's *Odyssey* with the Rhesus story from his *Iliad*) makes
use of Ulysses' legendary intelligence in an ingenious way and
also in a frivolous way (here again Ovid employs an Homeric
hero for a trivial purpose in his flippant poem). But there
is more to the digression than that. In it Ovid does make his
point by stating and showing that Ulysses was intelligent and
that his intelligence inspired great love, but it is particu-
larly noticeable that the hero's speech is suddenly interrupted
before he can tell in full the tale which he had begun and
that the whole digression ends abruptly and unexpectedly with
an air of incompleteness. So too a whole eight lines on his
diagram (49-56) is excessive if the purpose is simply to show
Ulysses' ingenuity (and to lead up to *nomina quanta* in 60).
The reason for all of this is that Ovid is again teasing the
reader. After being told by way of introduction that Uly-
sses did not even have good looks but that he was eloquent
(41), the reader, realizing that he is in a digression, begins
to suspect at 45ff. that the main function of the passage will
be to provide an example of this eloquence to back up Ovid's
point, and when Ulysses actually begins to speak at 51 this
suspicion seems likely to be confirmed. At this stage, since
it has been announced that the story will be about Rhesus
(an exciting short episode that would lend itself well to a
digression) and that it will be told from Ulysses' point of
view, the educated reader, knowing Ovid's powers of descrip-
tion and invention, has hopes for a substantial narrative
and an interesting new treatment. However, after eight
lines on the various details in Ulysses' diagram, which are
so numerous that we feel that the narrative is surely immi-
nent, Ovid frustrates us by surprisingly and ingeniously
cutting short the hero and terminating the whole digression
(57-62). Thus, although Ovid does make his point in the di-
gression, he does not do so as fully as or in the way that
one would expect, and so at the same time he manages to play
a trick on the reader.

27-28   sit procul omne nefas makes the transition from the
previous section. esto: for the form see on 1.97-98.

quod ("a thing which") refers to amabilis esto.

The second half of the hexameter is as true as it is
neatly epigrammatical.   The remark in the pentameter is acute
too.   Note that the attack on the efficacy of good looks here
and below also underlines the need for *ars* in general and for
Ovid's *Ars* in particular.

For esto see on 1.97-98.

29-30   With te...relictum understand *esse*.   mirere = *mireris*.
mirere looks like a sly dig.

31-32   quantumque...minor: "and it diminishes, the nearer it
approaches old age".   spatio carpitur ipsa suo: "it is
eroded by its own span of life".

The rapid passing of beauty (due to old age) was re-
marked upon extremely frequently in Greek and Latin literature.
Here again the expert is employing a relevant piece of pro-
verbial wisdom.   Note also that it is here used in a novel way
in an amatory context (usually it was cited to persuade the
boy or mistress to give in to the lover before he/she grew
old and despised or as a part of an exhortation to enjoy life
while one could: cf. e.g. *Palatine Anthology* 12.29, Tibullus
1.8.41ff., Ovid *Ars* 3.59ff.).

33-34   Ovid's point is that his pupil's beauty (like that of
violets and lilies) will not last for ever, and when it is gone
what remains of his looks will be unattractive (like the rose-
bush that has lost its roses).   riget...spina relicta: i.e.
hard thorns are left behind.   amissa...rosa is an ablative
absolute.

The analogies are mock-didactic.   The use of flowers
as an illustration in this context was also proverbial (cf.
e.g. Theocritus *Idyll* 23.28ff., Tibullus 1.4.29 *quam cito
purpureos deperdit terra colores*).

This is a subtly musical couplet.

35-36   formose is used as a noun here.   arent is subjunctive
in a final relative clause.

37-38   iam...formae: "now build up a mind to last and add it
to your good looks" (molire is imperative and duret is sub-
junctive in a final relative clause).   ille refers to animum.

extremos...rogos is probably a reminiscence of

Propertius 1.19.2 (*nec moror extremo debita fata rogo*).

39-40   nec levis = *et magna*.   ingenuas...artes: see on l.
243-244.   cura sit governs the infinitives.   linguas...duas:
i.e. Latin and Greek.

The cultured and sophisticated Ovid advises his pupil
to acquire similar culture and sophistication.   This is yet
another instance of good advice in this section, since such an
education would make the reader more impressive in most girls'
eyes (and in those of their acquaintances) and should mean
that he would be more interesting, have more depth and seldom
be short of conversation (in particular a mastery of Greek
would extend his reading and knowledge).

41-42   tamen picks up non formosus erat.   aequoreas...deas:
Circe (see on 23-24) and Calypso (see on 43-44).

Ulysses is a good example of the usefulness in love
of intellectual qualities because he did not even have good
looks, but even goddesses (note the plural and the position
of deas) fell desperately in love with him (torsit is a
strong word).

The couplet contains subtle sound-patterns.

43-44   properare: i.e. in his desire to leave.   Ulysses on
his return from the Trojan War was shipwrecked on the island
of Ogygia, the home of the goddess Calypso, who fell in love
with him and wanted him to marry her.   He refused, and she
detained him for seven years until finally Jupiter ordered her
to let him go.

This couplet illustrates clearly the love inspired in
Calypso by Ulysses (especially the forceful o quotiens).

45-46

In the pentameter we see that Ulysses' attractive
intellectual powers included ingenuity and versatility.
The hexameter probably makes the same point: she contin-
ually asked to hear about the story of Troy partly because
the man she loved had been involved, but also presumably
because she was not bored by the tale, thanks to Ulysses'
ability to tell it in different ways.

47-48   Odrysii...ducis: Rhesus, a Thracian king, went to
help the Trojans in the Trojan War, taking with him his
handsome horses (renowned for their size, speed and whiteness).

However, shortly after he arrived, Ulysses and Diomedes (an-
other Greek hero), who were on a night reconnaissance-mission,
found out about the horses from Dolon (see on 53-54) and
attacked the Thracians in their position at the far end of the
Trojan camp.   Rhesus and his twelve best men were killed, and
the horses were ridden off.   The story is told in detail by
Homer (*Iliad* 10).

pulchra accords with Homer's picture of Calypso (*Odyssey*
5.211ff.) but probably has further point (it brings out the
fact that the unhandsome Ulysses was attractive even to a
beautiful female).

Note the allusive *doctrina* in the pentameter.

49-50   quod rogat: the antecedent is opus ("the exploit that
she was asking about").

Ulysses' intelligence is further illustrated here (the
quick-witted way in which he employs the twig to produce a
diagram, which would make the story clearer and more vivid).

The sound in the hexameter is remarkable.

51-52   haec.../hic...haec: attracted into the gender and num-
ber of their complements.   tibi: dative of person judging
("in your eyes").   Simois: a river near Troy.

Ovid may be deliberately trying to intrigue the edu-
cated reader with the reference to Simois, since the river
plays no part in Homer's account of this exploit (all the
other details marked in the diagram by Ulysses are signif-
icant).

53-54   When Hector called for a volunteer, the Trojan Dolon
agreed to spy on the Greek camp by night if he could have as
his reward the famous horses of the Thessalian Achilles
(Haemonios...equos)   when they were captured.   On his way
to the Greek position he was caught by Ulysses and Diomedes,
who were on their reconnaissance-mission.   After he had
revealed to them details about the dispositions of the Trojans
and their allies (including Rhesus), he was put to death in
case he should try to make another such visit to the Greek
camp.   In 54 dum is postponed. vigil optat = "he was on
the watch, desiring...".

55-56   fuerant: see on 1.61-62.   hac: the adverb ("by
this route").

57-58   abstulit: indicative in an inverted *cum* clause (the
cum (in 57) is postponed).

Abruptly and unexpectedly Ulysses is cut short.

59-60   In the quotation vides is the main verb, perdiderint
undae nomina quanta is an indirect question depending on vides,
and quas...fidas tibi credis ituro is a relative clause whose
antecedent is undae.   Calypso is implying here that Ulysses
should hesitate to sail away and leave her in the belief that
the sea will be reliable (i.e. remain calm), because it is
actually treacherous and destructive (it may well destroy him,
as it has just destroyed the mighty names of his diagram on
the shore).   In fact when he left her Ulysses was shipwrecked
again (although he did survive).

This couplet is even more surprising than the last, as
Ovid has Calypso now suddenly break in to make an ingenious and
quick-witted point against Ulysses' departure (which again shows
her love for him).

61-62   fallaci: handsomeness is treacherous because it soon
fades, and so one cannot rely on it.   quisquis es: i.e. no
matter how handsome you are.   pluris is a partitive genitive
or a genitive of value (after aliquid).   corpore is an abla-
tive of comparison (after pluris).

In this the most unexpected couplet of all Ovid abruptly
terminates the digression and rounds off the section by re-it-
erating its main precept.   In addition to the joke of frus-
trating the reader's expectations of a narrative by Ulysses,
there is again great ingenuity (in the connection of thought):
the whole digression has illustrated the relative unimportance
of physical attractions and importance of mental qualities,
but note also that just as Calypso's point in the previous coup-
let was that Ulysses should hesitate to trust the unreliable
sea or it might well cause his downfall, so Ovid's point here
is that similarly the reader should hesitate to trust unreli-
able handsomeness or it might well cause his downfall (so
confide picks up fidas in 59).   Perhaps too the reader is
intended to reflect that Calypso's warning came true and so will
Ovid's.

For ergo age see on 1.219-220.

63-74   Kindness is particularly effective.   So avoid quarrels,
which are appropriate to married couples but not to lovers,
and say nice things to her instead, so that she will be glad
to see you.

Ovid continues with mental requirements in the lover,
here treating of a quality of character.   Again the expert
gives some sound advice, and again he combines it with a bit
of mischief (this time on the subject of marriage).   There
is humanity in Ovid's recommendation of civilized conduct here,
but, of course, there is an ulterior motive.

63-64   mentes: i.e. of girls.

Ovid's common sense is immediately to the fore.   Note
also that dextera (in emphatic position) highlights at the very
start the way in which he is again reducing emotions to an *ars*.

65-66   In the metaphor in the pentameter love is compared to
a tender creature (probably a child: cf. 151-152) that needs
the correct nourishment (dulcibus...verbis) if it is to stay
alive and thrive.

The expert's perceptiveness is especially evident in
the remark that love is something delicate and needs careful
and gentle treatment.

67-68   credant...agi: i.e. let them behave as though they
were forever arguing their case in a law-court (*res agere* =
causam agere = "conduct a case").

There is impudent humour here.   Ovid is satirical
about the married state (the frequency of quarrels, the (war-
like) "routs" and (by implication) the way in which partners
argue carefully and at length as though in court).   He is
also clearly making a distinction (continued in the following
lines) between love and marriage and implying that casual
affairs are more enjoyable.   Of course, although in Rome there
were arranged marriages, especially for considerations of
financial and political advancement, doubtless many couples
did not argue to such an extent and were in love with each
other.   The humour is heightened by the fact that Ovid him-
self was a married man.   Such remarks would not have gone
down well with the Establishment (Augustus in fact attempted
to promote marriage: cf. e.g. Suetonius *Divus Augustus* 34).

The skilful expression increases the cheek.

69-70   dos est uxoria lites: i.e. quarrels are what a woman
brings with her for her husband at marriage.

There is a continuation here of the impudence (particu-
larly in the epigrammatic dos est uxoria lites: note the posi-
tion of lites) and the shrewdness (the advice to the reader to
avoid arguments totally and the point that mistresses want to
hear something other than angry words from their lovers).

There seems to be an element of irony in the hexameter's
rhythm, and again the neatness heightens the insolence.

71-72   There is no law that makes you and your girlfriend go
to bed together (unlike husbands and wives, who, Ovid suggests,
only sleep together because they are married and so legally
obliged to do so); you do that because of love (therefore,
Ovid implies, the reader should behave not like a husband but
like someone in love).   in vobis: "in your case".

The hexameter is amusing in two ways (the mock-solemn
(notice the rhythm) affirmation that there is no law forcing
lovers to sleep with each other and the implication that it is
only because of the law that married couples do this).

There is a casual equation of the love-affair with sex
(yet again).

73-74   auremque: aurem is the object of iuvantia.

Once more there is good psychology here, particularly
in the stress on the need to make the girl positively pleased
to see the reader.

75-116   If she is not affectionate enough, persist, and she will
come around presently.   But don't force your attentions on her.
Instead be flattering and deferential by letting her attitudes
dictate yours, and show humility and loving devotion by volun-
tarily performing services for her, even letting her demand
such offices and eagerly carrying out her bidding.

At this juncture Ovid moves on to a possible problem
in the business of keeping the girl (an insufficient show of
affection on her part).   This problem warrants such detailed
handling because the circumstances clearly suggest that love
in the woman is not very strong and so may soon die out.
To combat this the poet (again undaunted) is immediately
ready with astute recommendations that once more reduce
emotion to a matter of calculating ploys.   The point of Ovid's

advice here is that the reader should try to make the girl
better disposed to him and strengthen love in her by flattering
and showing deference to her views and by making her believe
that his love and devotion are so great that he is ready and
eager to do anything at all for her, unasked or asked. The
thorough expert gives this serious situation an appropriately
full treatment, including numerous practical suggestions (which
show that a determined and concerted onslaught is necessary)
along with analogies and argument (in an attempt to overcome
any reluctance through laziness, timidity or pride on the read-
er's part to accept this important advice). This is a lengthy
section, but Ovid is careful to achieve variety and interest
in a number of ways. The passage is also in general more
serious than usual, but humour does surface after a while, and
the lines also contain much that staid, conservative Roman opin-
ion would have found impertinent, irreverent and offensive.

In fact, Ovid is here recommending the humility con-
ventionally shown by the literary (especially elegiac) lover,
and when he wrote this section he probably had particularly
in mind Tibullus 1.4.39-56, where the same precept is urged by
an expert in love, and similar results are claimed (there
are a few verbal similarities too: e.g. 76 cf. 1.4.53 *tunc
tibi mitis erit*, 77 cf. 1.4.40 *cedas: obsequio plurima vin-
cet amor*, 105 cf. 1.4.41f. *neu comes ire neges, quamvis via
longa paretur/et Canis arenti torreat arva siti*). However,
Ovid's handling is much longer and more detailed, the examples
of obsequiousness which he suggests are different and more
numerous, and he adds argument and analogies.

75-76   Ovid is here envisaging a situation in which the girl
does not show enough affection by sleeping with the reader as
readily or often as he would like.   satis is probably common
to blanda and comis.   perfer: "put up with" ("it", "the
situation").

The expert is confident from the start.

The placement of the two imperatives in perfer et obdura
is significant. This phrase is also found at *Amores* 3.11.7
and probably came from Catullus 8.11 (*sed obstinata mente per-
fer, obdura*). Here it is given a clever new twist, since
Ovid is recommending persistence in continuing the affair not

in ending it (as in Catullus and the *Amores* passage).

77-78   cede repugnanti: understand *illi* ("give in to her when
          she resists").   partes: the antecedent, incorporated into the
          relative clause.   agas: subjunctive after fac (see on 1.103-
          104).   In the pentameter Ovid means that his pupil should take
          his cue from his girlfriend and let her reactions positively
          dictate to him how he should react himself (examples are given
          in the following lines).

               Forcing unwanted attentions on a girl (even if you have
          started an affair with her) is not a good idea really, and Ovid
          has a more subtle and indirect course of action to suggest in-
          stead.

               Note the paradox and juxtaposition in the epigrammatic
          cedendo victor abibis.   For the military imagery see on 1.19-20
          and cf. 107ff. and especially 295ff. below.

               In the hexameter Ovid makes his point strongly by met-
          rical and stylistic means.

79-80   arguet: arguito : understand *si* before arguet ("if
          she criticizes (something), you must (also) criticize it").
          The construction is the same in riserit: adride in 81.   For
          the form arguito (and probato) see on 1.97-98.   dicet:
          "affirms".

               The purpose of the reactions recommended here and in
          the next couplet is to win over the girl by thus flattering
          her taste and sensitivity and showing deference.   The number
          of examples underlines the point that the reader is to take
          his cue from her in every reaction.

               For the imperative forms in 79 see on 1.97-98.

               The particularly skilful expression in this couplet
          makes for emphasis, interest and variety.

81-82   memento: "be sure to".   imponat...tuis: i.e. your
          face should show only the same expressions as hers.

               This time Ovid covers only two situations (laughing
          and crying).   This variety in the number of details per
          couplet is present throughout the section.

               The technical skill is still very evident in the hexa-
          meter.

83-84   distenta suis umbracula virgis: (literally) "the
          parasol stretched out on its rods".   Holding the parasol

and making a way in the crowd (84) were slaves' tasks - hence
ipse. qua is the adverb ("where").

Ovid now moves on to list various services that the
reader should perform for the woman (widening his pupil's
attack and adding variety to the section).   There is now a
progression in deference: the offices are thoughtful, gallant
and mostly servile (and so are intended to persuade the girl
that the reader is so much in love with her and so devoted to
her that he is ready and willing to do anything for her, even
to act as her humble slave).   The number of services listed
here clearly suggests that he should be obsequious like this
as often as possible.   There is emphasis in the anaphora.

It is worth noting that although love as a form of
slavery was an old literary theme Ovid's positive injunction
to free men to demean themselves by acting as slaves would still
no doubt have been offensive to serious, conservative Romans.

85-86   dubita: because the reader is here again told to
perform the function of a slave.   tereti: the adjective
seems to refer to the elongated shape of the couch.   scamnum:
the stool is apparently to help the girl get up on the couch.
         For nec dubita see on 1.219-220.

87-88   algenti agrees with dominae.   sinu = *sinu tuo*.
         This is an especially good detail.   This minor ser-
vice should be highly appreciated by the girl and in its own
way would show extreme devotion.   Note too that the reader is
strongly urged to do this often (saepe in emphatic position).
         saepe etiam is commonly found in Virgil's *Georgics*
(e.g. 1.84).

89-90   Holding the mirror was the duty of a (female) slave.
         There is emphasis in the pointed repetition and in the
placement of ingenua.   This would be a particularly degrading
action for Ovid's pupil in view of the sex of the slave who
would normally perform it.

91-92   Hercules is referred to here.   He was the son of Jupi-
ter and a mortal woman (Alcmene) and was consequently much
disliked by Jupiter's wife Juno (= noverca, Hercules' step-
mother), who was responsible for various monsters that Her-
cules had to fight during his life (especially while performing
the Twelve Labours).   When his life came to an end the hero

was rewarded with immortality and a place in heaven (meruit
caelum) because of his courageous exploits.   fatigata...noverca
is an ablative absolute.   qui has been postponed (it would
normally be placed immediately after ille).   quod prior ipse
tulit: prior is adjective for adverb.   One of Hercules'
Labours was to fetch the golden apples of the Hesperides. He
asked Atlas, the Titan who supported the heavens on his shoulders,
to get the apples for him, and while Atlas was gone Hercules
himself took over his burden.   Ovid will shortly advise even
greater obsequiousness.   To forestall any reluctance on the
reader's part, in this couplet and the next two he points out
how even the manly, high-born and famous hero Hercules obeyed
a mistress and acted as her slave in the same way as the
reader is to.

       To underline Ovid's point the couplet brings out Her-
cules' heroic achievements and deification (note also the rhythm
here, which appropriately changes in the following lines).
However, the learned analogy parodies didactic, and Ovid employs
the supreme hero of Greek mythology (who by now had divine
status) for a trivial purpose in his *Ars* and (in the following
lines) shows him in an amusing and very undignified situation.

93-94   Hercules at one time became the slave of Omphale,
       queen of Lydia.   Originally this was said to have taken place
       on the advice of the Delphic oracle, but later authors (e.g.
       Propertius 3.11.17ff.), like Ovid here, maintained that Her-
       cules acted as Omphale's slave and performed the most menial
       of tasks to please her because he was in love with her.
       Ioniacas here may be used loosely for "Lydian", or Ovid may
       be thinking of Ionian slave-girls.   lanas...rudes: i.e. un-
       worked fleeces.

       This is a rather bizarre picture of Hercules (who nor-
mally performed great, manly and glorious deeds) engaged on
the trivial tasks of a female slave, but it does show just
how far he was prepared to go in subservience to his mistress.

95-96   Tirynthius: Hercules was said in some accounts to
       have been born and brought up at Tiryns, and later he was based
       there while serving king Eurystheus (who sent him on the Twelve
       Labours).   i nunc et... : i.e. I dare you to... quod = *id quod*

       The solemn periphrasis Tirynthius heros is reminiscent

of Virgil's *Tirynthius* (*Aeneid* 7.662, 8.228).

Note the bantering tone in 96.

For dubita see on 1.219-220.

97-98   iussus: the participle has a conditional force here ("if
told to..."). iussa...hora: ablative of comparison. nec
nisi serus abi: i.e. don't leave until it is late (Ovid may
mean stay with her until late or keep waiting for her until
late if she does not turn up).

At this point Ovid moves on to ways of showing even
greater love and humble devotion (previously he had recommended
voluntary offices by his pupil; from now on he is to let her
demand such service, if she wants to, and treat him as though
he were her slave, carrying out her bidding with a gratifying
eagerness and alacrity). Of course, any reluctance on the
reader's part here could be interpreted as due to a lack of
love, and most people enjoy getting their own way (especially
those who make such demands). Remember too that in the situ-
ation with which Ovid is dealing here love in the girl is al-
ready weak (see on 75-116).

Turning up early and remaining until late would show
especial eagerness and devotion. Note also that the reader
is advised to do this invariably (semper and nec nisi).

99-100   occurras aliquo tibi dixerit: "suppose that she has
told you to hurry to meet (her) somewhere" (the future per-
fect here and the futures in 101 and 103 refer to situations
that may arise in the future). The omission of the conjunc-
tion *ut* in indirect commands is common in colloquial Latin and
in poetry. Apparently in the last couplet the reader had
been given due warning in advance of the meeting, but in this
one he receives a sudden summons to meet her quickly.

By picking up occurras with curre Ovid is making the
point that his pupil is to do exactly as he is told.

101-102 epulis perfuncta: "after a dinner-party". pro
servo: it would be a slave's duty to escort her home and
light the way with a torch (there was no street-lighting).

To be on call even at night (nocte and tunc quoque
emphatic by position) would show an ever-ready devotion. In
addition, the reader will not even have been at the party with
the girl.

103-104   dicet venias: for the omission of *ut* see on 99-100.
   si rota defuerit: "if you have no carriage" (rota here is an
   instance of synecdoche = part standing for whole).

       Ovid's pupil is to make himself available even outside
Rome (rure in emphatic position) and to undertake a long jour-
ney even on foot.

       Note the epigrammatic Amor odit inertes.

       For tu see on 1.47-48.

105-106   grave...tempus: "the oppressive season" (referring to
mid-summer).   sitiensque Canicula: "and the parching Dog-
star" (Sirius).   In Mediterranean countries mid-summer begins
with the rising of this star in July, and in Classical authors
the star itself is represented as a source of intense heat.
per iactas...nives: "through falls of snow" (going with can-
dida facta).

       The contrasting extremes here make the point that no
weather-conditions at all are to slow down the reader (it is
not even contemplated that they might make him abandon his
journey or refuse to set out in the first place).

107-108   In the hexameter Ovid means that being a lover, like be-
ing a soldier, is no occupation for the lazy (because of the
hardships mentioned in the following lines, which are a normal
part of love).   signa: (military) "standards".   It was a
supreme disgrace to lose the standards to the enemy in defeat,
so that here Ovid means that if the lover is to avoid an ig-
nominious defeat at the hands of his enemies (e.g. be ousted
by a rival) he must not be faint-hearted (but endure the dangers
involved in love, as described in the following lines).   In
case the reader feels that the actions recommended in the pre-
vious lines are too strenuous and perilous for him, Ovid in
this couplet and the following two points out that such hard
work and perils are standard features of love in general and
are vital for success in it (so he had better become resolved
to them now or give up altogether).

       Here again Ovid puts love on a par with a profession
that was traditionally more serious and worthy.   Although
the comparison of love to warfare was a long-established theme,
Ovid's levity (especially the claim here that lovers too have
to be energetic and brave and the suggestion in the following

lines that they endure labours and dangers similar to those of
the soldier) would have annoyed conservative Romans (and the
Establishment).

109-110   For some of the many occasions on which the lover has
to endure these dangers and hardships see on 111-112.   mollibus
his castris: *castra* here means (military) "service", "war-
fare" and refers to love.   The adjective *mollis* may mean "soft",
"easy" and be used ironically, or, as it is often applied to
love and to things/people connected with love (e.g. 66,255),
it may mean little more than "amatory".   inest: agrees in
number with its nearest subject.

           For labor see on 1.19-20.

111-112   In the pentameter Ovid will be thinking especially of
the lover spending the night on the ground outside his mis-
tress' door when locked out by her (a very common occurrence
in love-poetry).   The lover endures the downpour mentioned
in 111 in this situation and also when spying on rivals, keep-
ing a nocturnal rendezvous with his girl or returning from it
etc.

           Note the emphatic placement and repetition.

113-114   Cynthius is used as a noun here and denotes Apollo
(Cynthus was a mountain on Delos, the Greek island on which
the god was born).   The reference here is to the story (fer-
tur) that Apollo acted as the slave of Admetus, king of Pherae
in Greece, tending his cattle.   Originally Jupiter was sup-
posed to have ordered Apollo to do this as punishment for
killing the Cyclopes, but Ovid is here following a later ver-
sion of the story in which the god acted as Admetus' slave
because he was in love with him.   The point that the poet is
making in this and the following couplet is that the reader
should not consider humility in love unbecoming if even a
handsome, refined and august god became slave to a mortal
through love and undertook menial duties in degrading circum-
stances.

           At 113-116 Ovid rounds off the section by once more
attempting to undermine any reluctance on his pupil's part
to be obsequious towards his unaffectionate mistress,
driving home this important piece of advice and defending
it by means of a further (and a supreme) example.

In this mock-didactic analogy the poet irreverently shows
a god (notice the position of Cynthius) in an undignified situa-
tion and uses him for a lightweight purpose in his *Ars*.

There is literary as well as mythological *doctrina* here:
the example is taken from Tibullus 2.3.11ff., where Apollo's
slavery to Admetus is similarly cited as justification for slav-
ery to a mistress (cf. especially 11 *pavit et Admeti tauros
formosus Apollo* and 28 (addressed to the god) *nempe Amor in parva
te iubet esse casa).*

The juxtaposition in the hexameter is most expressive.

115-116   quod = *id quod*.   In 116 quisquis is postponed from the
start of the line.

There is bantering in the question.

117-132   Make her think that you are astounded by her beauty. Praise
her clothes in particular, but commend her hair-style too and mar-
vel at her arms and voice when shown off.   But do make sure that
she does not realize that you are only pretending.

This little section contains some dazzling displays of
Ovid's metrical and stylistic skills, and the overall structure is
neat (an enunciation of the basic precept in the first couplet is
followed by examples of its application, and the section is rounded
off with a word of caution, while by bringing to the surface again
the fact that the reader will be only pretending at 129ff. (cf.118)
Ovid ensures ring-structure).   There is also some excellent psychol-
ogy here.   By following the poet's advice the reader would greatly
flatter his mistress (in an area that is extremely important to the
vast majority of women) and would make her think that he was infat-
uated with her.   In addition, the number and variety of Ovid's rec-
ommendations imply a full and comprehensive attack (suggesting that
praise should be forthcoming in all circumstances and should cover
as many aspects as possible), and Ovid works in for good measure
several astute tips on the actual wording of the pupil's remarks.
The poet's final caution about not giving oneself away is also very
sound.   This section is not without humour too, as one realizes
from the start that this never-failing effusive praise is in reality
only a crafty, calculating ploy.

117-118   te...attonitum...esse: accusative and infinitive governed
by putet (which is subjunctive after fac).   cuicumque refers to

<u>te</u> (= "whoever you are, to whom...").

attonitum is a strong word placed deliberately at the start of the line.

In <u>putet</u> ("think" rather than "realize") Ovid shows that he is automatically assuming that the reader will not actually be *attonitus* (the reason for this seems to be that the girl may have some faults anyway, and, no matter how good-looking she is, Ovid does not imagine that his pupil will be really infatuated but expects that he will keep his wits about him and be coolly calculating).

119-120 <u>Tyriis</u>: "a dress dyed with Tyrian purple" (the neuter plural of the adjective is used as a noun and, like <u>Tyrios...</u> <u>amictus</u>, is an instance of plural for singular). Tyrian dye was one of the finest and most costly purple dyes. <u>laudabis</u>: see on 1.285-286. <u>Cois</u> and <u>Coa</u> mean "a dress of Coan silk" (see above on <u>Tyriis</u>). Such dresses were made of a very fine, transparent silk woven on the Greek island of Cos (the Classical equivalent of the see-through blouse).

The great stress on praising her clothes here and in the following lines shows insight into female psychology.

121-122 <u>aurata est</u>: understand *si* (so too with <u>astiterit</u> in 123). The reference is to a dress embroidered with gold.
<u>tibi</u>: dative of person judging. <u>gausapa</u>: plural for singular.
The hexameter suggests for the reader's use a clever complimentary twist.

123-124 <u>tunicata</u>: the tunic was an undergarment, usually with short sleeves and reaching a little below the knees - hence the remarks recommended by Ovid in the remainder of the couplet.
'<u>moves incendia</u>': "you're setting me on fire". <u>caveat frigora</u> depends on <u>roga</u> (for the omission of *ut* see on 99-100).

With the word <u>clama</u> (carefully positioned) Ovid advises a strong reaction, and in the following line the expert gives another ingenious tip (the plea, which is suggestive of thoughtful and unselfish concern).

For a change the expression in this couplet is not so ingenious.

125-126 <u>conpositum discrimen erit</u> = "if she has a carefully-arranged parting" (*si* is to be understood here and at the start of 126 too). <u>discrimina</u>: plural for singular. <u>igne</u> refers to heated curling-tongs.

The change to hair-styles here makes for variety and comprehensiveness (so too the switch to other attractive features in the next couplet).

127-128   In the hexameter understand *tuae puellae*, with which the participles agree.   <u>mirare</u> is imperative.   Note that here Ovid's pupil is to praise aspects of the girl's beauty revealed in the performances rather than the actual skill of the performances.   <u>bracchia</u>: see on 1.361-362. <u>et...habe</u>: i.e. be ready with words of complaint on the grounds that she has stopped (<u>desierit</u> is subjunctive because this is an alleged reason; <u>querentis</u> is used as a noun = "a complainer", "someone complaining").

<u>mirare</u> is a strong word.

There is a clever touch of flattery in the pentameter (he is to complain because he can no longer enjoy this display of her lovely arms and voice).

129-130   <u>tantum</u>: "only".   <u>ne...illis</u> depends on <u>efffice</u>.   <u>destrue</u>: spoil the effect, e.g. by grinning or wincing.

In these final four lines of the section the expert carefully (and quite rightly) emphasizes the need to take pains over not giving the game away (including the important detail of facial expression) and points out the disastrous consequences of discovery to reinforce his advice.

131-132   <u>deprensa</u> agrees with *ars* (to be supplied from the first half of the line).   <u>adfert...pudorem</u>: = "causes embarrassment" (in the man).

<u>si latet, ars prodest</u> is neatly epigrammatical.   For <u>prodest</u> see on 1.117-118.

The smooth, sophisticated expert shows a touch of sternness in <u>merito</u> (= and it serves you right for being so stupid and clumsy).

133-150   If she falls ill, bearing in mind the ample affection that your actions will produce in her, make a great show of loving concern and thoughtful kindness.   But draw the line at services that might make her dislike you, such as forbidding her food or giving her medicine - leave that to your rival.

The ingenuity and humour continue here.   Again the expert reduces sentiment to an *ars* and here comes up with yet another clever and effective way of making the woman believe

that she is deeply and truly loved.   The psychology throughout
is excellent, and the scope of the useful tips is wide (indicat-
ing that the reader has here a very good opportunity and should
exploit it amply, doing a great deal to convince the girl).
Amusingly Ovid assumes that these services actually need to be
recommended (they will not be done automatically, prompted by
any genuine affection) and advises that all this love, consid-
eration and anxiety be shown solely with a view to its profit-
able results (the strengthening of love in the girl, which will
ensure the continuation of the affair), thereby urging the
reader to take advantage of his mistress' vulnerable and rather
pitiful situation with an immorality as shameless as his own.
The humour reaches a climax in the crafty words of caution in
the final lines of the passage.

        The illness of one partner and the reactions of the
other are frequently mentioned in elegy (cf. e.g. Tibullus
1.5.9ff., Propertius 2.9.25ff., 2.28, Ovid *Amores* 2.13, 2.14).
Thus the poet once again cleverly utilizes an elegiac theme
and gives it a new (didactic) twist.

133-134   Understand *est* in the *cum* clause in 133.   aere non
   certo: "because of the changes of weather" (the ablative is
   causal, and non certo (= *incerto*) means "unsettled", "vari-
   able").   The Greeks and Romans often complained of the un-
   healthiness of autumn (Juvenal (4.56) calls it *letifer* =
   "death-bringing"), and in Italy fevers in particular were
   rife then.

135-136   valeat: the subjunctive may be potential or express a
   wish.   male firma: "unhealthy", "sick" (male here has the
   force of a negative).   quod has a vague antecedent, which is
   omitted, and introduces a final relative clause. By the agri-
   cultural metaphor in 136 Ovid means that his pupil by showing
   a lover's anxiety and kindness when the girl is ill will en-
   sure as his reward presently the enjoyment of the great affec-
   tion that he will cause her to feel by his actions (the reader
   will plant in her seeds of affection, which will grow, and
   presently he will reap them in abundance).   plena...falce is
   a rather curious phrase.   The adjective seems to mean "used
   with full force" and to refer to the full and vigorous use of
   the sickle necessary to reap such a large harvest (it is

probably easiest to be a little free in translation here and to
give the force of plena by using the phrase "in abundance").

The pentameter makes it clear from early on that all the
kindness and concern recommended is merely a ruse.

By using the agricultural imagery in 136 Ovid enables
himself to parody briefly Virgil's injunctions about the time
for sowing (here just before autumn!) and promises of an ample
harvest (cf. e.g. *Georgics* 1.49, 208ff.).

137-138   In the hexameter Ovid means that the reader should not
become impatient with the girl, who will be bad-tempered be-
cause of her illness.   morosi...morbi is an objective genitive
with fastidia ("impatience at...").   In 138 the advice is that
the reader should perform for her whatever services she will
permit.   (*ea*) quae sinet ipsa is the subject of fiant.

Ovid shows insight into the state of mind of invalids
here (their tendency towards peevishness, the resentment that
a show of impatience by others (especially loved ones) engen-
ders in them, their appreciation of thoughtful and concerned
acts of kindness and (alluded to in quae sinet ipsa) their
wish to retain some independence and/or not to be fussed).

perque tuas...manus is not without point (the reader
is to perform these services, rather than slaves or (cf. 150)
a rival).

139-140   In the first half of 139 understand *te*, with which
flentem agrees. nec taedeat oscula ferre: i.e. kiss her con-
tinually.   In the pentameter the idea seems to be that the
reader's tears are to be so abundant that when he kisses the
girl a plentiful amount will be transferred onto her lips and
into her mouth.   sicco...ore: ill people often have a dry
mouth.

videat is an important detail - the tears must be
noticed by the girl.   He also makes the point that there
should be a gratifyingly plentiful supply of comforting kisses
and anxious tears.

141-142   Understand *vove* with sed cuncta palam.   With quotiensque
libebit supply *illi* ("as often as it will prove agreeable to
her", i.e. often, but not too often, so as to irritate her).
referas: subjunctive in a final relative clause.   somnia
laeta: i.e. dreams of good omen suggesting that she will

recover.

The fact that the reader will be actually invoking the
aid of the gods and making numerous vows (multa is carefully
positioned) would suggest great concern on his part and would
allow him to cheer her by making it seem likely that (thanks
to him) she will have heaven on her side.   Note too the im-
portant specification sed cuncta palam.

As the significance of dreams seems to have been widely
accepted in the ancient world, the reader's report of somnia
laeta should also reassure the woman.   In addition, the bearer
of good news tends to rise in the recipient's affection anyway,
and the reader's dreams would suggest that his anxiety for his
mistress extends even to his unconscious.   There is also a
careful and judicious proviso in quotiensque libebit.

143-144   lustret and praeferat are subjunctives in a final rela-
tive clause.   anus: the antecedent, incorporated into the
relative clause.   The old woman is a witch, and the ceremony
referred to here is *lustratio* (purification).   The Romans
deified diseases, and *lustratio* was a sort of exorcism.   Sul-
phur and eggs were commonly believed to have purifying powers
and were often used in such rites.

This is an additional way of giving the girl hope.
So too in his apparent loving concern Ovid's pupil is to try
yet another cure and (presumably) actually pay for the witch's
services himself.

143 is a pleasantly musical line.

145-146   omnibus his refers to the recommendations of the pre-
vious couplets.   gratae: either "welcome" or, more likely
(because more calculating), "deserving of gratitude".
in tabulas...iter: "for many this route has provided a way into
(others') wills".   Ovid is here comparing his ruses to those of
"will-hunters" (*captatores*).   From the late Republic onwards
there were many rich men without children in Rome (especially
due to the decline of marriage), and so they were often culti-
vated by others who hoped thus to get themselves named in the
wills of these rich men (see Horace *Satires* 2.5 for a lengthy
attack on *captatores*).

There is parody in multis (see on 1.117-118) and in the
analogy (in which Ovid shamelessly and provocatively admits

the similarities between his methods and those of the immoral
and despised "will-hunter").

147-148   In 147 Ovid is advising the reader to avoid incurring his
mistress' dislike through his services (ab aegra is to be taken
with odium (not with quaeratur),   i.e. "dislike on the part of
the sick girl").   suus refers to blanda sedulitate ("let your
...have its limits").

The careful and thorough expert rounds off the section
with some entertaining words of caution, in case the reader be-
comes carried away and goes too far (modus is emphatically
placed).   Again there is perceptiveness (some *officia* may actually
arouse dislike).

149-150   With prohibe understand *illam*, and with porrige understand
illi.   amari pocula suci: i.e. medicines that have a bitter
taste.

In this very funny couplet Ovid gives examples of some of
the *officia* to be avoided and adds a cunning tailpiece (note the
position of rivalis).   The psychology here cannot be faulted, but
once more the morality can (Ovid's pupil is to be more concerned
with his own interests than with ensuring what is actually best
for his mistress).

151-178   While the affair is in its early stages, her love for
you needs strengthening, so visit her constantly.   When you are
quite confident that your absence will make her concerned, stop
seeing her, and she will be all the more affectionate when you
reappear.   But don't stop for long: in time love for someone
absent vanishes and is replaced by love for someone else, as is
proved by the case of Helen, who during her husband's absence
went to bed with their guest Paris.   That was entirely that fool
Menelaus' fault: he was mad to go off and leave the two of them
together like that; there she was, afraid to sleep in her empty
bed, and Menelaus had given them no alternative, being so ob-
liging.

Ovid here moves on to other ways of increasing affection
in the girl, and his insight and sense of fun are still much in
evidence.   His actual advice in the first part of the section
is consistently well thought out and amounts to a crafty manip-
ulation of the girl's feelings.   At 165ff. an example is in-
troduced to back up Ovid's observations which by its length

qualifies as a short digression.   The passage contains some
good examples of the poet's technical skills (often employed
with telling effect), but above all it contains a highly diver-
ting instance of *doctrina*.   With a truly disgraceful inversion
of morality the urbane and experienced man of the world totally
exonerates the adulterous pair and puts all the blame on the
wronged husband in a series of observations and arguments (main-
ly directed at Menelaus) which range from flippancy to irony,
cynicism, insolence and superior scorn, and which switch their
viewpoint and attack with stunning dexterity.   Needless to say,
Ovid's attitude and remarks here, which amount to a condonation
of adultery, would not have been appreciated by stern, moral
types (note in particular that the emperor took a strong official
line against adultery: see on 1.15-16).

151-152   In the metaphor in this couplet love is likened to a
young child (novus) aimlessly toddling around (errat), which
needs exercise (usu) and the correct nourishment (bene nutrieris)
to make it grow strong.   As becomes clear at 155ff., Ovid
means that while the girl's affection for his pupil has only
just come into being and is still unsure and without firm pur-
pose (i.e. when the affair is in its early stages), the reader
must strengthen it by constantly visiting the woman (seeing
her lover so often will allow her to exercise her feelings of
love again and again, and his presence will supply those feelings
with the sustenance they need to keep them alive and make them
grow).   nutrieris is future perfect indicative active, and its
object is *eum* (understood).

        The metaphor is ambitious and effective, and it works
especially well because Cupid was generally represented as a
young child.

153-154   quem...solebas: "the bull which you (now) fear you used
to stroke as a calf" (taurum, like arbore in 154, is the ante-
cedent incorporated into the relative clause).   Ovid's point
here is that the girl's love for the reader, which at the start
of the affair is rather frail and small (like the calf and the
twig), will (with the correct handling) grow into something large,
deep-rooted, stable and formidably strong (like the bull and the
tree).

        Note the analogies.

155-156   Understand *est* in the second half of 155.   The penta-
      meter is a difficult line (= *et dum eam capias, tu taedia nulla*
      fuge).   quam stands for *et eam* (referring to adsuetudine in 155)
      and is the object of capias in the dum clause.   tu, as the
      punctuation shows, goes with fuge, not with capias.   capias has the
      meaning "win", "achieve" and is in the subjunctive because the
      dum clause contains the idea of purpose.   taedia nulla fuge
      means "put up with any amount of trouble".

            In nil adsuetudine maius the expert is aptly applying a
      bit of proverbial knowledge (cf. e.g. Cicero *Tusculanae Dispu-*
      tationes 2.17.40 *consuetudinis magna vis est*).

            For tu see on 1.47-48.

157-158   exhibeat...tuos: i.e. let her see your face day and night.
            This important tip is forcefully expressed by means of
      emphatic positioning and repetition of individual words and the
      threefold statement of the basic point in the form of a tricolon
      crescendo.

159-160   maior: "quite strong".   With posse requiri understand *te*
      (forming an accusative and infinitive construction with fiducia).
      cum procul...eris: literally "when you will be likely to be a
      source of concern to her parted (from you)", i.e. when your
      absence is likely to cause her concern (supply *illi*, with which
      absenti agrees;   procul ("away", "apart") goes with absenti).

161-162   da requiem: understand *illi* (i.e. don't visit her).
      bene credita reddit: "well repays what has been entrusted to
      it" (i.e. the seed, which is often described as a deposit en-
      trusted to the earth).   Ovid means that a field that has been
      allowed to lie fallow yields a good crop when next sown.   In
      the same way, he suggests, letting the girlfriend "lie fallow"
      will prove profitable and produce good results (his pupil will
      reap an ample harvest of affection when he cultivates her
      again).   In the pentameter the implication is that just as
      the earth eagerly absorbs rain after a dry period, so the girl
      will be receptive and eagerly draw to her the reader when he
      turns up after a period of being deprived of him.

            Ovid's recommendation here mimics Virgil's advice to
      let fields lie fallow (*Georgics* 1.71f. *alternis idem tonsas*
      cessare novalis/ et segnem patiere situ durescere campum), and
      there is also burlesque, of course, in the analogies (which are

clinical and amusingly unflattering to women).

163-164   sed mora tuta brevis: *est* is to be supplied, and tuta
is the complement.   curae: "concern", "anxiety".   amor is
common to both halves of 164 (*absens amor* = love for someone
who is absent).

165-166   To back up Ovid's comments in the previous line this coup-
let introduces an example which shows that they apply even in
the case of married women.   The reference, of course, is to the
incident that caused the Trojan War.   The Trojan prince Paris
(hospitis) arrived at Sparta and was hospitably entertained by king
Menelaus and his wife Helen.   During Paris' visit Menelaus sailed
off to Crete, leaving Helen to entertain their guest.   Paris then
seduced her and carried her back to Troy.

        Ovid flippantly suggests that Paris' conduct was prompted
by a gentlemanly concern about Helen being alone and cold (sola,
tepido).   Note that no blame is attached to Paris (or Helen) here.

167-168   solus: i.e. without Helen.   Some connecting-link (such as
et) has been omitted at the start of 168.

        The humour is heightened here as Ovid, the urbane man of
the world, shows superior scorn and professes to be so astounded
by Menelaus' stupidity that he breaks in to put some incredulous
questions to him.

        The omission of the connecting-link suggests the poet's
impatience with Menelaus, and Ovid's words here seem to hiss con-
temptuously.

169-170   For furiose (vocative) see on 1.103-104 (on *studiose*).   The
metaphors bring out the lunacy of Menelaus' behaviour (to Ovid's
way of thinking) by representing Helen as helpless and tempting
prey (the doves and the sheep), Paris as its natural predator
(the hawk and the wolf) and Menelaus' action in going off and
leaving Helen with Paris as consigning this prey to the custody and
protection of its predator.

        As he remonstrates firmly with Menelaus here, the cynical
expert's scorn is even more apparent (the (amusingly) offensive
exaggeration in the metaphors and furiose, which is stronger
than stupor in 167).

        The pentameter contains a proverbial expression (cf.
e.g. Cicero *Philippics* 3.27 *o praeclarum custodem ovium, ut
aiunt, lupum!*).   The hexameter represents a novel and apt

variation on that expression (doves suggest Helen's beauty
and fair complexion and, as birds sacred to Venus and renowned
for their amorousness, also contain connotations of love).

The plural columbas and plenum bring out the tempting
nature of the prey, while timidas underlines its helplessness,
and the juxtaposition ovile lupo highlights the madness of the
action.   There is also effective emphatic positioning in these
lines.

171-172   nil is an internal accusative with an intransitive verb
(= "Helen does no wrong").   quod (both times) = *id quod*.
With quod tu understand *faceres*   (potential subjunctive, like
faceret).

Ovid here (and below) actually exonerates Helen and Paris,
and does so in no uncertain terms.

quod tu (*faceres*) is tactless and insolent in the extreme.

173-174   tempusque locumque: objects of dando (the gerund*ive* con-
struction is more usual in classical prose than a gerund gov-
erning an object like this).   After quid understand *fecit*
(i.e. "all the girl did was...").

Even more shocking is the twisted reasoning here, which
represents Menelaus as some sort of pimp and Helen first as
acting under duress and then as an obedient wife (note the im-
pudent positions of cogis and tuo).

175-176   faciat: deliberative subjunctive.   non rusticus: i.e.
Paris is no prude or coarse lout but an understanding gentleman
(who would not refuse Helen entry into his bed and who would
realize that her reason for entering it was merely fear of sleep-
ing alone).

Ovid pretends sympathy for Helen's "plight" (especially
the implication (in quid faciat?) that she could do nothing else
and the emphasis on the daunting prospect of sleeping in her
own bed in the juxtaposition in 176), and with similar flipp-
ancy he suggests that she slept with Paris because she was afraid
to be alone (picking up and reinforcing 165f.).

177-178   With viderit Atrides supply something like *haec*: "let
the son of Atreus (i.e. Menelaus) perceive/reflect upon these
points" (i.e. he should think on and realize that he is the
guilty party).   The perfect subjunctive here is jussive (its
use in a third person command is not common: most often it

is found in the second person (with *ne*) in prohibitions).
<u>Helenen</u> is a Greek form of the accusative.   <u>viri</u>: "of her
husband".

Ovid rounds off the digression by impudently implying
that Menelaus has not thought the matter out fully and on reflec-
tion would agree with the poet's judgement, by repeating for
emphasis his total exoneration of Helen (notice the position
of <u>solvo</u>) and by describing with cheeky irony Menelaus' action
in leaving Helen with Paris as being kind and obliging.

179-200   A woman's ferocity, when she discovers that she has a
rival, surpasses even that of wild animals at their fiercest.
Such an occurrence ends even stable relationships, so that
infidelity should be viewed with apprehensiveness. But that
does not mean that I restrict you to one mistress alone - have
other girls too, but be discreet about it.   Take the various
precautions I recommend, and, if nevertheless you are caught
out, steadfastly deny it.

Picking up from the digression at the end of the last
section, Ovid moves on to handle the topic of unfaithfulness,
and shows the same type of attitude.   Initially the passage
seems rather serious, as Ovid dilates on the gravity of the
situation when your mistress finds out that you have another
girlfriend too and gives the impression that his advice is to
avoid such infidelity altogether.   But this is all part of an
elaborate hoax, as we learn at 187ff., where Ovid suddenly re-
veals that he wouldn't think of making any such prohibition and
that all he meant was that his pupil should be careful to con-
ceal his extra affairs.   This is amusing and immoral enough;
however, not only does Ovid openly tell the reader to be un-
faithful but he actually goes on to instruct him on how to
avoid detection and what to do if he is nonetheless found out
(and makes a good job of it with his expert tips).

179-180   <u>tam</u> is correlative with <u>quam</u> in 183 ("but a tawny
boar is not as fierce...nor a lioness (181)...nor a tiny viper
(182)...as a woman is (183)...").   In the pentameter <u>cum</u> is
postponed.   <u>fulmineo...ore</u>:   i.e. with lightning-fast move-
ments of its tusks.   <u>canes</u>: (presumably) hunting-dogs which
have the boar at bay.

The examples here and in 181-182 are well-chosen, catching

some of the most savage of wild animals at their fiercest and
most angry moments.   The pentameter here conjures up a partic-
ularly vivid picture of the boar's ferocious fury in action (well
brought out by rhythm and sound).

181-182   The savage protectiveness of wild animals with young is
well-attested.   ignaro...laesa pede: i.e. stepped on unawares.

Note the variation in sex, shape, size and species in
this couplet and the previous one.   There is also an interesting
overall structure in the group of three examples.

183-184   socii deprensa paelice lecti: ablative absolute ("when
a rival to the bed she shares is detected", i.e. when she finds
out that she has a rival in her affair).   ardet: "she burns"
(with rage).

Ovid's claim is that a woman in these circumstances sur-
passes even the above examples of extreme anger and ferocity
and so becomes positively non-human in her passion.   The poet
is exaggerating here, but his basic point is sound enough and
the exaggeration is intended to underline the seriousness of
the matter and to press home the inadvisability of allowing such
a situation to arise.

185-186   hoc: "this occurrence" (i.e. the mistress' discovery
of a rival and her subsequent fury).   solvit and amores ("love-
affairs") are common to both halves of the hexameter.   crimina
...ista: "offences of that nature" (i.e. infidelity). timenda:
timeo here has the sense "view with apprehensiveness".   As
a deliberate trick Ovid makes it look as if he is saying that
infidelity should be avoided, but in the following lines he
makes it clear that what he meant here was not that the reader
should dismiss the idea of infidelity but that he should be
cautious and wary when being unfaithful.

There is great gravity and emphasis in both sound and
expression here.

187-188   nec: "but...not".   di melius = "heaven forbid!"
(some verb such as *ferant* is understood).   vix...potest: "a
married woman can hardly secure this" (i.e. restrict her man
to one woman (herself) alone).

This is an outrageous couplet (the sudden revelation
that Ovid does condone unfaithfulness after all and in fact con-
siders fidelity unthinkable in a love-affair and virtually

impossible in any case, the suggestion in censura that Ovid
with his lax and immoral advice is comparable to the *censor*
(a Roman magistrate whose duties included the superintendance
of public morals), the shocked di melius! (which some might
consider almost blasphemous in this context) and the cynicism
about the state of marriage).

189-190   ludite: "play around", "have your sport".   furto...
modesto: "by seemly concealment".   gloria...est: "no glory
is to be sought from one's own misdemeanour" (i.e. don't
boast about your infidelities).

          ludite (forming a brisk initial dactyl and given empha-
sis by its position) represents a positive injunction to be
unfaithful.   In the remainder of the hexameter Ovid finally
reveals his point (amusingly and immorally,all he means is that
the reader should avoid detection).

          Boasting would, of course, make the reader's exploits
more widely known and so heighten the possibility of a report
reaching his mistress.

191-192   dederis: see on 177-178.   cognosse (a contracted form
of *cognovisse*) belongs inside the quod clause.   possit: either
potential subjunctive or subjunctive in a generic relative
clause.   Such a gift would be, for instance, a distinctive pos-
session of the reader's or something given to him by another
girl.

          Ovid doubtless assumes that his pupil will not be open
about his affair with his extra girlfriend (especially after
189), but, whether he makes himself unavailable to callers while
enjoying a secret visit from her or disappears to go and meet
her himself, if this occurs at a regular time, it is more likely
to be noticed and arouse suspicion (on the part of either his
first mistress herself or someone who might inform her).

          The sound-patterns in 192 are remarkable.

193-194   sibi goes with notis.   omnis: "every woman".

          This is another shrewd tip: the mistress at some in-
opportune moment might go looking for the reader in this spot
or make a sentimental visit to it.

195-196   plus multae, quam sibi missa, legunt = *multae legunt plus
quam sibi missa*.   sibi missa ("things sent to them") refers
to messages sent to them.   Ovid's point is that the wax-tablets

on which any letter to his first mistress will be inscribed
by his pupil should be inspected beforehand, to make certain
that former love-letters to another girl have been completely
erased without leaving traces anywhere for the recipient of the
present letter to read.

      ipse is not without point: the reader must make sure by
means of a personal inspection and not leave this job to a slave.

      Note the humorous epigram in the pentameter.

197-198   quae...patebunt = *si acta, quae bene celaris, qua tamen*
patebunt (acta is the antecedent to quae bene celaris, celaris
is a contracted form of *celaveris* (future perfect indicative
active), qua means "by any chance" and tamen ("nevertheless")
picks up bene celaris). licet: "although".

      This is not bad advice: by following it Ovid's pupil
might just shake his mistress' confidence and incline her to
give him the benefit of the doubt, and he would also thereby
provide her with an excuse to disbelieve the obvious if she
loved him enough to want to do that and a means of saving face
if she decided to overlook his infidelity this one time.

      For tu see on 1.47-48.

199-200   nec has been postponed and belongs before solito (which
is an ablative of comparison). esto: for the form see on
1.97-98. haec...habent: "these things (i.e. these actions)
contain to a great degree signs of a guilty mind", i.e. such
behaviour is strongly suggestive of guilt (multum is the adverb).

      The psychology here is excellent.

      For esto see on 1.97-98.

201-216   I have just been telling you to conceal your infidelity.
Well, now I want you to reveal it. I am not being inconsistent:
ships do not always use the same wind on a voyage. Some women
do not like being treated kindly and their love fades in the
absence of a rival. So with that type, when they become apa-
thetic, rekindle their love by frightening them with a dis-
closure of your unfaithfulness.

      This section contains further remarks on the subject of
infidelity, and the immorality and levity concerning this seri-
ous and rather shocking situation persist - in fact this pas-
sage is even more disgraceful, in that here Ovid actually tells
his pupils to reveal their extra affairs. The humour is

increased by yet another hoax (whereby Ovid deliberately makes
it look as if he is contradicting his previous advice for sev-
eral lines at the start).   Similar structural cleverness is
evident in the overall arrangement of the poet's comments on
the whole topic of unfaithfulness on the man's part, as he
leaves this point to the end for maximum impact.   In addition,
Ovid here shows a penetrating insight into the mentality of
certain females, and once again we see his expert fullness of
knowledge and professorial thoroughness of treatment.

201-202   modo: "just now".   flecte iter: i.e. use another
tack.   For the nautical metaphor cf. 5-6.   Here Ovid is say-
ing that in order to reach his goal (keeping the girl) his
pupil should change direction and try another line of approach
(= do something different, i.e. reveal his secret infidelity
(detege furta) to his mistress).

         The couplet provides a highly startling and puzzling
opening to the section, as the poet seems to contradict totally
the advice he has just given and the points he has just made
at length in the previous lines by now recommending disclosure
of one's infidelity (apparently as a general rule in all cases).
The pointed contrast between hexameter and pentameter and the
verbal repetitions underline the apparent contradiction.

203-204   mea: "on my part".   impositos: "those placed in it"
(i.e. the passengers and/or crew).   panda refers to the
curved shape of the ship's keel.   Ovid's point in this and
the next couplet is deliberately unclear (to tease the reader).
He claims that he cannot be blamed for inconsistency (in reco-
mmending such a change of direction to the reader) because
sailing-ships do not always use the same wind on their voyages.
The logical basis of the claim and the precise point of the
analogy are at first sight rather mystifying.   It is only when
we read 207-208 that we realize that in fact Ovid means that
as the ship's captain on a voyage has to use the available
winds and may find a change of direction necessary to make his
destination, so the reader has to take into account prevailing
conditions and react accordingly to reach his goal (i.e. to
retain his girl he may actually have to reveal his infidelity,
showing her that she has a rival to rekindle her love, if she
is the type of woman in which love grows weak when it is not

threatened).

    Note the analogy.

205-206 Threicio: Thrace was a cold, wintry region to the
    north of Greece, and so in Greek the chill North Wind was of-
    ten called "Thracian" and described as having its home in
    Thrace (because it came from that direction).   The Romans took
    over the adjective, although in their case it was geographi-
    cally not so apt.   Borea is ablative.   currimus ("we skim along")
    is used of the rapid motion of those voyaging on a ship.

        The couplet seems a somewhat gratuitous expansion of
    non semper .../...vehit in 203f.(this is part of Ovid's trick
    as it continues to keep the reader in the dark).

        This is an elegant couplet in general, and the rhythm
    is particularly effective.

207-208 sunt...servit: "there are (women) whom timid kindness
    serves without giving pleasure", i.e. there are women who dis-
    like being treated respectfully with timid kindness.

        Here at last we realize that Ovid's injunction in 202
    was not meant as a general rule but applies only in the case
    of this type of woman and we see the purpose of his advice (to
    prevent their love from fading away), and now we also under-
    stand the logic behind his denial of inconsistency in 203 and
    (with a bit more thought) the point of the analogy in 203-206.

209-210 ut (picked up by sic in 213) introduces a simile that
    occupies this couplet and the next.   levis ("weak", "feeble")
    refers to the state of the fire after its strength has been
    used up gradually (by burning) and it has died down (absumptis
    paulatim viribus).   Before summo some connecting-link (such
    as et) has been omitted.

        This simile contains many points of comparison: (209f.)
    just as the fire gradually dies down when no attention is paid
    to it (no more fuel is added) and becomes feeble and is obscured
    (under the ashes), so with this type of woman their love gradu-
    ally fades when neglected by them (when they become apathetic
    and complacent: see on 213-214) and becomes weak and is less
    evident; (211f.) just as, when the powerful stimulus of sulphur
    is brought to bear, the fire blazes up again and regains its
    brightness, so, when such women are sharply goaded by the know-
    ledge that they have a rival, their love is rekindled and

becomes noticeable again.   The simile is particularly apt
because love was often described as a fire (cf. e.g. 1.144,
1.306).

211-212   extinctas...flammas/invenit: i.e. it bursts into flame
again (the subject here is ignis from 209).

213-214   ubi...torpent: "when hearts, torpid through inactiv-
ity and free from care, are sluggish", i.e. when girls are
apathetic, neglecting their feelings of love and not exercising
them, through complacency because they are not threatened by
a rival.

215-216   With timeat understand *illa* as subject.   mentem refers
to the girl's heart.

Ovid neatly concludes and rounds off the section by
repeating the injunction at its opening (202) and this time
making clear the purpose of this action (which picks up the
argumentation of the previous lines).

217-234   At this point Apollo suddenly appeared, making an impos-
ing spectacle.   He said: "Bring your pupils to my temple with
its world-famous inscription 'know thyself'.   To be an intelli-
gent lover you have to know yourself and make sure that you
show off your good points all the time."   Such was the advice
of the god, and, coming from his lips, it is absolutely reli-
able.

Ovid here leaves infidelity and moves on to a different
topic, introducing a new advisor on love.   This is a clever
and diverting section in many ways.   There is an elaborate
build-up with a series of red-herrings to engage the reader's
attention and interest, making him expect something of sig-
nificance and importance, but eventually it turns out that
Apollo has only some lightweight and rather self-evident
remarks to make on the subject of love.   Thus the god, who
appears solely as an advisor on casual affairs (and a not
very impressive advisor at that), and who shows an amusing
fondness for a levity and expression very similar to Ovid's
own, is placed in a trivial context and used in a flippant
fashion.   All of this would, naturally, have been offensive
to solemn, pious types and would not have charmed the Estab-
lishment (especially since Apollo seems to have been a
favourite god of the emperor's and was associated with him in

a variety of ways: see e.g. Propertius 4.6).

217-218   haec ego belongs inside the cum clause.   Apollo, patron
god of poetry and music and himself an accomplished poet and
musician, possessed an (appropriately magnificent) gilded
lyre.

     The section has an arresting and intriguing start.   The
entrance of Apollo is dramatic (his manifestation is sudden and
unexpected, its effect is heightened by the flourish of divine
music that accompanies it, and the god cuts an imposing figure).
In addition, one wonders what he is doing here at all, and the
educated reader would tend to think that the god's appearance
here will prove to be a serious and momentous event, probably
concerned with literary aspects of the Ars, when he remembers
similar interventions elsewhere by Apollo in Augustan poetry
(and in Callimachus Aetia frag. l), where he gives the poet
important advice on his powers and the themes appropriate to
them (cf. Virgil Eclogue 6.3ff., Propertius 3.3.13ff., Horace
Odes 4.15.1ff., and note that cum canerem may be a deliberate
echo of those words in Eclogue 6.3 and inauratae...lyrae may
be intended to recall aurata...lyra in Propertius 3.3.14).
The expectation is, in fact, never fulfilled.

     The rhythm is expressive.

219-220   Apollo carries a branch of laurel (understand erat in
the first half of 219) and has a laurel-wreath on his head be-
cause that tree was sacred to him.   vates...videndus is in
apposition to ille ("a poet worthy to be looked at", i.e.
Apollo with his gilded lyre, laurel and famous (long) hair
formed quite a spectacle).

     The god's impressiveness is further brought out here
by the emphasis on his divine trappings and by the phrase
vates...videndus (there is also solemnity in the sound and
in the stately term vates).   vates tends to reinforce sus-
picions that the god will have advice of a literary nature.

221-222   praeceptor Amoris: for Ovid as the teacher of Cupid
cf. 1.7-8.   mea templa: plural for singular, as we learn
in the next couplet.   The reference is to Apollo's temple
at Delphi (in Greece), on which the maxim mentioned in 223-
224 was inscribed.

     This couplet intrigues the reader still more: it makes

him wonder whether the advice will be literary after all, which
temples (templa appears to be a genuine plural at first sight)
Apollo is referring to, why Ovid's pupils should go to them
and why the god is so insistent (age and the sound in 222).

223-224 ubi is postponed. diversum fama celebrata per orbem:
the whole phrase (= world-famous) goes with littera (fama is
ablative, and celebrata is nominative, agreeing with littera).
diversum...orbem = all the different places in the world.
littera: "an inscription". cognosci...iubet: cognosci
belongs inside the quae clause, and quemque is the accusative
of *quisque*. The reference here is to the famous maxim "know
thyself" (i.e. be aware of your limitations, faults and quali-
ties).

    One puzzle is solved here (we see that the reference
in 222 was to Apollo's temple at Delphi), only to be replaced
by another (what exactly is the relevance of "know thyself"?).
The imposing solemnity here (the introduction of the revered,
wise maxim and the emphasis on its world-wide fame) makes the
reader imagine even more that Apollo will be giving deep and
weighty advice.

225-226 qui = *is qui* (so cui = *is cui* and qui = *is qui* in 227-
230 below). atque...suas: in the light of the following
lines the most probable translation is "and he will make
every activity conform with his powers", i.e. he will do what
shows off his good points all the time.

    Apart from making it clear that Apollo's advice in
fact concerns love, the hexameter is not particularly illum-
inating, and the expression in the pentameter is vague (opus,
vires and exiget are all ambiguous), so that the reader can-
not be sure about the god's point here and is thus kept in
the dark for yet another couplet.

227-228 spectetur ab illa: "let him be looked at with regard
to that" (illa picks up faciem), i.e. he should make a point
of displaying that quality. color denotes an attractive
skin-colouring, i.e. a healthy sun-tan (cf. 1.293).

    At last the point is revealed, as we see Apollo making
a scandalous application of the maxim in his own temple and
(after the great build-up in the previous lines) coming out with
a piece of advice which is hardly profound or of great import

but in fact lightweight and rather obvious (especially after
the very similar tip in passing at 1.361f.). The humour is
heightened by the fact that the whole perversion of "know
thyself" attributed to Apollo shows an ingenuity and levity
similar to Ovid's own and in these and the following lines,
where Phoebus gives the practical application of his precept,
he is made to sound exactly like Ovid himself (it is partic-
ularly irreverent of the poet to put such subject-matter and
stylistic tricks into the mouth of the god).

229-230   qui bibit arte probably refers to a connoisseur who
makes the whole business of drinking into an artistic per-
formance.

231-232   non sanus (= *insanus*) seems double-edged. Probably as
well as referring to the traditional inspired frenzy of poets
it also suggests that it would be crazy of a poet to read his
poems aloud like this.

          Phoebus concludes with an amusing caution (in case
Ovid's pupils are foolish enough to misapply their qualities
or not to realize that they possess skills which should not
be shown off at all). Again his remarks are obvious enough
and have been partly anticipated by Ovid. For 231 cf. 1.249.
As to 232, Ovid had already stated in a passage omitted from
these selections (*Ars* 2.274) *ei mihi, non multum carmen honoris
habet*. The pentameter is particularly funny in the mouth
of the god of poetry and has a satirical flavour (implying that
contemporary women are not impressed but actually bored by
poems).

233-234   certa...fides: i.e. anything Apollo says is abso-
lutely reliable (because of his oracular powers and wisdom).

          This is a fitting finale. Now that we know the
nature of Phoebus' advice we can see that it is reliable but
somewhat self-evident and unimpressive, so that the mock-
solemnity here (the emphatic placement, repetition and (in
234) juxtaposition) is even more impertinent. Note also
the mischievous use of the god's prophetic skill and sageness.

235-286   Let us return to business. What I am going to ask of
you now is extremely difficult to manage but vital for suc-
cess. You must patiently put up with a rival, turning a
blind eye and not interfering. If you catch them out, she

will only become brazen and they will actually carry on with
their affair, falling deeper in love.   When Vulcan discovered
that his wife Venus was being unfaithful with Mars he set
invisible nets around the bed and literally caught them in
the act.   But all that the fool achieved by that was to make
them more open about their liaison.   So don't you go trying
to trap your mistress and your rival.

     With an entertaining surprise here Ovid returns to the
topic of infidelity, but this time infidelity on the girl's
part (which renders the whole situation even more complex and
makes the relationship into something totally disgraceful,
with deception on both sides).   In handling this theme the
poet comes out with a series of jokes and impertinencies.
In the opening lines, where he gives his actual advice, this
is particularly evident in the cynicism, the generalizations
and the very low estimate of the morals of women.   That the
mistress will be promiscuous and immoral enough to take another
lover is considered by Ovid to be likely enough to merit dis-
cussion in the first place, and he actually recommends non-
interference and complaisance on the grounds that in these
circumstances detection, so far from making women feel ashamed
or end their illicit affairs, in fact makes them carry on
shamelessly.   Ovid then proceeds to back up his remarks with
a mythological example in which he audaciously emends the
details to make his point.

     This example is long enough to qualify as a digression,
and it is an unedifying and rather naughty tale of adultery
in high places in which the poet depicts with positive relish
deities behaving badly and totally losing their dignity.
The narrative is lively and funny, full of gusto and detail,
and given further interest and variety by asides, addresses,
quotation, exclamations and change of pace.   It has appeal
on a more intellectual level too, since it is based on the
version of the myth in Homer *Odyssey* 8.266-366, and it is
interesting to see what Ovid makes of the story and how he
achieves novelty.   In fact he selects and abbreviates to
produce a much shorter account and one in which the actual
events move more quickly, while he lingers (and even adds
details) over the more humorous aspects.   But the most impor-

tant difference is in the ending.   Homer concludes with
Mars and Venus (after they have been finally released from
Vulcan's nets) fleeing in embarrassment, and the wronged
husband recovers some of his dignity and his honour is satis-
fied thanks to his clever and successful trap.   Bearing this
in mind, the reader is puzzled all along as to the relevance
of the myth here (which he presumes is meant to illustrate
the point that one should *not* catch out lovers in this sit-
uation) until the final four lines of the digression (279-
282), where Ovid adds that as a result of being found out
Mars and Venus continued their liaison more openly, much to
Vulcan's chagrin.   By this unexpected and high-handed addi-
tion to his source Ovid makes the example in the end back up
his remarks about the dangers of interference; he also thus
alters the whole perspective of the story (Vulcan's ruse is now
actually counter-productive and the divine husband emerges as
a meddling fool) and implies that complaisance is the sen-
sible course in the case of infidelity in marriage too.

      Again the levity and sentiments to be found in this
whole section would have offended conservative Roman opinion
and the Establishment (note in particular that Augustus took
a serious official line on marriage and adultery: see on
67-68 and 1.15-16).

235-236   propiora: "nearer matters" (implying that the theme
of the previous passage was not of such close importance as
the topic that will now follow).   quisquis.../...feret =
the man who is a sensible lover will be successful (keep his
girl), and he will owe his success to my system (because Ovid
in the following lines will show why and in what way one
needs to be sensible).   e means "as a result of", "by means
of", and (*id*) quod petet (= "his end") is the object of feret
("he will gain").

      propiora is (rightly) rather dismissive of Apollo's
advice.

237-238   ardua molimur: ardua (neuter accusative plural) means
"difficult things" (of the tasks facing Ovid and the reader
mentioned in the following couplets).   nulla, nisi ardua,
virtus: understand *est* ("there is no excellence other than
difficult (excellence)", i.e excellence always involves

difficulty, it is never easy to attain a state of excellence
in anything).

What Ovid will ask his pupil to do is rather hard, but,
as he is only talking about a casual love-affair, he is
scarcely justified in making so much of the difficulty and toil
(note especially the emphatic positions and repetition).
For the parody in this and in the use of *labor* see on 1.19-20
and cf. also Virgil *Georgics* 2.256f. It is also impudent
to apply the remark nulla, nisi ardua, virtus with its prover-
bial ring (cf. e.g. Horace *Satires* 1.9.59f.) to amatory achieve-
ments.

239-240   habe: "endure". After stabit a connecting-link
(such as *et*) has been omitted.   eris magni victor in Arce
Iovis: i.e. you will win a glorious triumph (the reference
is to the Roman custom whereby a general celebrating a triumph,
after a procession through the city, ascended the Capitoline
Hill (Arce Iovis), entered Jupiter's temple there, dedicated
his insignia to the god and took part in a sacrifice to him).

The precept, when it comes, is startling, and the
forceful claim that it will bring success is challenging.
Conversely the implication is that if the reader does not do
this he will suffer a defeat (i.e. lose his mistress): cf.
249-250.

For the military imagery see on 107-108 (the use here
of the solemn, hallowed triumph is especially impertinent).

241-242   Understand *si* before innuet illa and scribet. Ovid
is here envisaging situations in which the reader's girl makes
signs and sends letters to another man.   For nods see on
1.95-96.   feras is jussive subjunctive.   quoque = *et quo*.
With libebit understand *illi ire*.

In effect Ovid is here saying that one should ignore
what is going on and not interfere (the point is expressed
forcefully and repeated for emphasis at 247).

243-244   faciam: deliberative subjunctive.   minor: "less
(than)" = "not equal (to)".

The suddenness and unexpectedness of this admission
make it very funny, and it also provides an amusing picture
of the expert lacking expertise (this joke is continued with
doctior in 245) and helpless to do anything about it because he

is simply not up to his own precepts. Again it emphasizes
just how difficult this task is.

      In the pentameter the sound produces an air of (mock-)
sadness.

245-246 non semel: i.e. more than once. In the pentameter
quo...conciliante is an ablative absolute and the sense of
the line is "through whose procurement other men/lovers come"
(to his mistress), i.e. who procures other lovers for his
mistress.

      For the citation of personal experience see on 1.55-
56.

      The description of his own inability to tolerate his
girl's immoral carryings-on as a vitium is bad enough, but the
suggestion in the pentameter is positively scandalous, im-
plying a very low estimate of female morality.

247-248 nescisse is a contracted form of *nescivisse*. fuit:
gnomic perfect (the tense is so used in general truths of
what has happened and is accustomed to happen). Use the
present tense in your English translation. sine: impera-
tive of *sino*. For the omission of *ut* in the following in-
direct command see on 99-100. ne...pudor: "lest shame (be)
conquered (and) flee from lips that have confessed", i.e. if
she has to confess she will lose all sense of shame.

      Ovid probably has in mind Virgil's use of the gnomic
perfect in the *Georgics* (e.g.1.287).

      The reasoning here is very cynical: Ovid claims that,
if a woman is found out and has to admit her guilt, she will
actually lose shame (rather than feeling shame). Of course,
it is only occasionally (in particularly bad cases) that this
situation does produce a mood of real brazenness and def-
iance.

249-250 prensis: "for (=in) people who have been caught".
in causa...sui: "both persist in the cause of (= that which
caused) their ruin", i.e. the reader's mistress and his rival
will persist in the illicit affair which caused their ruin.
Ovid's point in this couplet seems to be that when detected
guilty pairs feel a bond because of their shared misfortune
and continue their liaison, so that their love for each
other grows (which means, of course, that the reader will be

in great danger of losing the girl).

Again there is cynicism concerning women and a provocative generalization in the claim that, so far from being ashamed and trying to avoid each other (as many people, especially those with any decency, would), lovers in these circumstances actually feel drawn together and carry on.

251-252   The whole phrase in the pentameter is in apposition to fabula.

This couplet forms an apt introduction to the tone and emphasis of the whole digression. The rhythm and sound combine to give the hexameter an air of seriousness, which is immediately dispelled by the next line.   In the pentameter the juxtaposition amusingly suggests the actual connection between Mars and Venus (entangled together in Vulcan's nets), and Ovid by conjuring up this picture now ensures their loss of all dignity from the start.   For the use of *-que...-que* see on 1.121-122.

253-254   Mars pater: *pater* is often used as a term of respect for gods (cf. 1.347) but here may refer to the fact that Mars, as the father of Romulus (by Rhea Silvia/Ilia), was the progenitor of the Roman race.   Veneris: objective genitive ("(love) for Venus").   de: "from being a...".

In this couplet and the next Ovid lingers on aspects of the situation that appeal to him.   Here he makes two points not found in Homer's account (in 253 the great violence (insano and turbatus) of Mars' passion (which makes a diverting contrast with the dignified term *pater*) and in 254 the humorous incongruity of Mars' new role).   All of this, of course, shows Mars in an undignified light.

255-256   oranti (i.e. asking her to go to bed with him) agrees with Gradivo.   neque enim = *non enim*.   rustica: "prudish".

The very idea of the goddess of love being prudish or uncompliant is rather funny.   Again the point is not made in Homer.   There may also be joking word-play in mollior, since *mollis* is very often applied to love and to people/things connected with love (see on 109-110), and so no other goddess should be more deserving of the term than Venus.

257-258   lasciva here can have a variety of meanings and may be used adverbially ("jokingly" or "mischievously") or as a noun ("the joker" or "the mischievous goddess" or "the wanton").

Vulcan (_mariti_) was a cripple;   he was also a master-crafts-
man, often working with tools and at the furnace and anvil
(hence the hardness of the skin on his hands).

Ovid's powers of invention and his ability to give a
narrative life, vividness and humour are particularly evident in
this and the following couplet.   The couplets look like an
ingenious expansion of _Odyssey_ 8.308-311, where Vulcan complains
that Venus despises him because he is lame and gives her love to
Mars because he is handsome and sound of limb.   Of course, al-
though amusing, this is hardly very dignified conduct for a
goddess.

Note the ironic tone of disapproval in _a_.

259-260   _Marte palam_: "in Mars' presence", "in front of Mars".
simul: "at the same time" (i.e. as well as laughing at Vulcan).
est...imitata: probably with particular reference to his limp.
Before _decebat_ understand a connecting-link such as _et_ ("and
it suited (her)"). _multaque...fuit_: i.e. this gave her beauty
great added attraction.

This couplet shows the connoisseur's eye: beautiful
females are generally very attractive when they fool around.

261-262   _plena...erat_: i.e. they were very ashamed of their mis-
demeanour.

The detail of their shame (here given emphasis) is not
to be found in Homer's account.   The purpose of this addition
does not become clear until 279-280.

263-264   (_quis Solem fallere possit_?): since the Sun in his orbit
passed over the whole world and in his chariot on high was in
a position to see and hear everything, it was believed that no
deceit could escape him.   With _cognita_ understand _sunt_. _suae_
refers to _Vulcano_.

The action takes a step forward here.

265-266   _exempla_: plural for singular. _moves_: "you are setting".
ipsa refers to Venus.   In the pentameter _et_ means "too", _et_
tibi goes with _dare_ inside the _quod_ clause, and _si taceas_ also
belongs inside the _quod_ clause ("she has something which she
would be capable of giving you too, if you were to keep quiet",
i.e. in return for his silence Venus would go to bed with the
Sun too).

Again Ovid slows down the narrative to work in some humour,

and again he makes a clever addition to Homer's account, claiming
that the Sun did the wrong thing entirely and that what the god
should have done was ask for a bribe to keep silent, then pro-
poses a stint in bed with Venus as the bribe and implies that
the goddess would pay it.   The humour is increased by the sug-
gestiveness of the expression in the pentameter.

267-268   lectum circaque superque: in poetry prepositions often
come after their noun, as both do here.   lumina fallit opus: i.e.
his handiwork (the nets) was invisible.

      Events really start to progress now, and the reader's
expectations are heightened, as Ovid emphasizes the invisibility
(obscuros, lumina fallit opus) and completeness (lectum circa-
que superque) of Vulcan's trap.   Note also that the poet manages
to do this in only one couplet, so that the pace begins to pick
up.

269-270   Lemnon ("to Lemnos") is a Greek form of the accusative,
and, as Lemnos is a small island, a preposition would not be re-
quired even in prose.   Lemnos was Vulcan's favourite spot on
earth (Homer *Odyssey* 8.284), and he was friendly with the in-
habitants and had a workshop there.   veniunt ad foedus amantes:
"the lovers (i.e. Mars and Venus) come (to the bed) as agreed"
(ad here means "in accordance with").

      Here (and in the next couplet) Ovid greatly speeds up the
narrative by means of a series of short clauses tacked on without
connecting-links which skim details and so depict events as
rapidly successive.   Here this underlines the quickness with
which Mars and Venus went to bed and with which they were caught
in the trap.

      The nudity of the pair (not mentioned in Homer) really
brings out their undignified circumstances.

271-272   ille = Vulcan.   spectacula: plural for singular.
putant: "people reckon" (of course, as there were no mortal
witnesses, nobody can know for sure).

      The situation here becomes even more mortifying, and
Ovid highlights the humiliation of Mars and Venus.   The penta-
meter contains a (convincing and graphic) point not present in
Homer.

273-274   Both texisse and obposuisse depend on possunt.   denique:
"even".

Ovid slows his narrative again to linger gleefully on
the embarrassing position in which the divine couple find them-
selves. This detail (which looks like an expansion of Homer
Odyssey 8.298 "it was not possible for them to move or raise a
limb") contains a natural touch (the desire for concealment)
and paints a vivid and funny picture of these two deities with
their (red) faces and private parts exposed to general view.

275-276 hic: "at this point".   in me goes with vincula transfer.
oneri: predicative dative.

A further couplet is here added to crown the humour and
humiliation (the laughter of the unnamed god, the whole point
of his suggestion (with the all-important vincula transfer de-
layed), the application of the grand superlative fortissime to
Mars in these circumstances and the flippancy in si tibi sunt
oneri).

277-278 vix: i.e. with great reluctance.   precibus...tuis:
causal ablative.   Vulcan is the subject of resolvit. Thracen
and Paphon (also object of occupat) are Greek forms of the
accusative. Mars often resided in Thrace and was worshipped
by the warlike tribes there.   Paphos (on the island of Cyprus)
was a favourite haunt of Venus and she had a famous temple
there.

The narrative picks up speed again, and in the penta-
meter the sudden progression of events, the brevity and the ab-
sence of connecting-links amusingly suggests the rapidity with
which Mars and Venus departed.

279-280 tibi: dative of agent.   (*id*) quod ante tegebant is the
object of faciunt (for the reference see 261).

By way of a final joke in the digression this couplet and
the next come as a complete surprise. They represent an impu-
dent addition to Homer's version which at last reveals the point
of the digression and alters the whole perspective and impli-
cations of the story (see on 235-286).

liberius and abest are carefully positioned.

281-282 demens = "mad fool that you are".   stulte fecisse fat-
eris: "you admit to having acted stupidly" (*facio* is intran-
sitive here). ferunt: cf. putant (272). artis: "trick".

The final word in the digression cheekily dilates on
Vulcan's great stupidity (the strong term demens, the juxta-

position <u>demens stulte</u>, the claim that Vulcan himself often
admits his foolishness (note the position of <u>saepe</u>) and regrets
his trick).

283-284   <u>hoc vetiti vos este</u>: "be (in a state of having been)
warned off by this" (this is not a common use of the perfect
participle). The words are, of course, addressed to Ovid's
readers. Understand *vos* as the object of <u>vetat</u>.   <u>deprensa</u>
<u>Dione</u>: Dione was strictly Venus' mother, but (as here) the
name was also applied to Venus herself. The participle in
agreement with the noun here does the work of a noun-phrase (i.e.
"Dione detected" = "the detection of Dione"; see on 1.413-414).
<u>insidias illas...dare</u>: "to set that trap" (here, of course,
metaphorical and referring to an attempt to catch out the mis-
tress). <u>tulit</u>: "endured".

      Ovid triumphantly makes a smooth transition back to his
advice at the start of the section to round off and drive his
message home.

285-286   <u>laqueos disponite</u> is metaphorical. <u>excipite arcana</u>
<u>verba notata manu</u> = intercept secret correspondence (between
your mistress and another man). <u>arcana</u> agrees with <u>manu</u>.
      <u>laqueos disponite</u> echoes 268 and so is particularly pointed.

287-298   My task is completed: acknowledge my supreme achieve-
ment. Such superlative expertise deserves world-wide praise.
I have equipped you for the fray as Vulcan armed Achilles, so
go off and win, but remember to record your debt to Ovid.

      This passage represents a burlesque of the conclusion
found at the end of some didactic poems (cf. in particular
Virgil *Georgics* 4.559-566, where he similarly adds an epilogue
of several lines which (among other things) alludes to the
contents of the poem and gives the author's name). Now that
the course of instruction is finished, Ovid takes stock,
exaggerating his achievement and its due, and sends the reader
off in a confident frame of mind to put into practice what he
has been taught. The mixture of impudence, levity and clever-
ness provides an exuberant and apt close to the poem (the third
book was only added later, and originally the *Ars* consisted of
advice to men alone).

287-288   Wreaths or branches of palm and other wreaths were often
presented to victorious poets (Ovid claims a victory because he

has performed his task supremely well and no-one has produced
(or could produce) a better poem on the subject).   Ovid spec-
ifies myrtle-wreaths because of the amatory nature of his work
(myrtle was sacred to Venus).   odoratae is probably proleptic
(the adjective is not literally applicable at the present time,
but is used in anticipation: the garlands will make Ovid's hair
fragrant when they are put on; cf. 1.297).

finis adest operi may be intended to recall Virgil's
extremo...sub fine laborum (Georgics 4.116).

There is presumptuousness in the claim of pre-eminence here.

289-290   quantus (repeated in 291) is correlative with tantus
in 292.   Podalirius was a famous doctor with the Greek forces
in the Trojan War.   Aeacides: see on 1.423-424.   pectore:
pectus here may mean "wisdom" or "eloquence", since Nestor,
an aged Greek chieftain who fought against the Trojans, was re-
nowned for both these qualities.

In this couplet (and the next) we see an ingenious use
of doctrina as Ovid likens his expertise in love to the great
expertise of several ancient heroes in various other fields.
Thereby he shows supreme arrogance concerning the extent of
his own expertise.   It is also impertinent of him to compare
himself to these solemn, dignified figures of epic and mythol-
ogy (the use of Aeacides, an epic title (see on 1.423-424),
underlines the cheek) and to put love on a par with their occu-
pations.   The characters mentioned are all Greeks who took
part in the expedition against Troy, but there is probably
further point to these particular choices.   Note here that
Ovid too is skilled in dealing with disease and wounds (the dis-
ease and wounds of love), fights well (in love's battles) and
is wise/eloquent (concerning amatory matters).

291-292   Calchas was the wisest seer and chief prophet of the
Greeks at Troy.   extis: in divination the future was foretold
by examining the entrails of sacrificed animals with particu-
lar attention to their markings, size, colour and shape.   Tela-
monius: Ajax, the son of Telamon, who of the Greeks who fought
at Troy was second only to Achilles in bravery according to
Homer.   Automedon: see on 1.5-6.   With tantus amator ego
understand sum.

The fact that Ovid adds three more heroes to his list
here (and in Telamonius refers to Ajax by means of a patronymic,
which is a common feature of high style) increases the arro-
gance and impudence.

Again the figures chosen seem to have especial point,
since Ovid too is a kind of prophet (see on 1.9-10), fights
well (in love's battles) and controls love like a charioteer
(cf. 1.5-8).

293-294   me vatem celebrate: "praise me as a poet" (i.e. praise
me for my poem).

The poet underlines once more the greatness of his ex-
pertise and the importance of love, very forcefully demanding
extravagant praise as his due for his lightweight and frivo-
lous poem of amatory instruction.   Notice also the application
of the solemn, stately term *vates* to the composer of the *Ars*.

295-296   Vulcan made Achilles armour (a marvellous shield, breast-
plate, helmet and greaves described by Homer in book 18 of the
Iliad) which because it was impenetrable and light in weight
helped him to conquer his Trojan enemies.   Ovid here compares
his advice to this armour, suggesting that it will similarly
protect his pupils from hurt and help them to victory in their
warfare (i.e. thanks to it they will suffer no pain or set-
backs and be successful (see on 297-298) in love).   With
dederat understand *arma* as object.   Ovid seems to use the plu-
perfect here because the giving of the armour took place prior
to Achilles' victories.   vicit ut ille = *ut ille* (i.e. Achilles)
vicit.

There is a progression in presumptuousness and cheek
here: in elegant lines Ovid with irreverent flippancy com-
pares himself to the god Vulcan and the reader to the great hero
Achilles, suggesting that the love-affair will be an epic struggle
like the Trojan War, that in this struggle the *Ars* will prove
a great help to the reader (in fact as great an aid to him as
Vulcan's gift of armour was to Achilles) and that his poem is
wrought with similar skill and possesses such marvellous qual-
ities as one of the god Vulcan's most celebrated pieces of
handiwork.

<u>297-298</u>   Ovid here again describes the love-affair in terms of
a battle: the reader will be trying to conquer (<u>superarit</u>)
the girl (i.e. make her fall in love with him and go to bed
with him and keep things that way), and so the woman will be
his enemy (<u>Amazona</u>: the Amazons were a race of fierce and
barbaric female warriors); Ovid's advice (<u>meo...ferro</u>) will
constitute a useful weapon in this struggle and help his
pupils to victory; the victorious reader will win spoil (what
one strips from the defeated enemy, i.e. the girl's clothes),
and Ovid wants him to follow the common ancient practice of
adding an inscription to the spoil (which will acknowledge
the poet's help). <u>superarit</u> is a contracted form of *supera-
verit* (future perfect).

Ovid here continues with the idea of the affair as an
epic encounter (the Greeks fought the Amazons in the Trojan
War, and Achilles killed their leader Penthesileia), now des-
cribing his *Ars* as an offensive weapon as well (thereby rep-
resenting it as even more useful and helpful) and working in
two further jokes (the unflattering comparison of the girl
to an Amazon and the idea of spoil) which enable him to con-
clude triumphantly with a reference to himself and his impor-
tant contribution.

ABBREVIATIONS

abl. = ablative

acc. = accusative

adj. = adjective

advb. = adverb

conj. = conjunction

dat. = dative

defect. = defective

f. = feminine

gen. = genitive

imper. = imperative

indecl. = indeclinable

indic. = indicative

infin. = infinitive

interj. = interjection

interrog. = interrogative

intrans. = intransitive

m. = masculine

n. = neuter

nom. = nominative

pl. = plural

prep. = preposition

rel. = relative

subj. = subjunctive

trans. = transitive

voc. = vocative

1 = first conjugation

2 = second conjugation

4 = fourth conjugation

a (interj.) ah!, alas!
a, ab (+abl.) by, from, as a result of, on the part of, with regard to
abdo-dere-didi-ditum conceal, disguise
abeo-ire-i(v)i-itum go away, disappear, come off
absens-entis (adj.) absent
absum-esse afui be absent, be distant
absumo-ere-psi-ptum consume, use up
accedo-dere-ssi-ssum approach, advance, set in
accessus-us (m.) means of approach, access
accipio-ipere-epi-eptum accept, receive
accipiter-tris (m.) hawk
acer acris acre sharp, vehement, violent
acernus-a-um (made of) maple-wood
Achilles-is (m.) Achilles (a Greek hero)
actum-i (n.) deed, exploit, conduct
acus-us (f.) hair-pin
ad (+acc.) to, in accordance with
adamas-antis (m.) adamant
addo-ere-idi-itum add, put on (+dat.)
adeo-ire-(i)i -itum approach
adfero -rre attuli allatum bring, apply, apply to (+dat.)
adhinnio (4) whinny (to: + dat.)
adhuc still, yet
adimo-imere-emi-emptum take away, dispel
aditus-us (m.) opening, approach
adiungo-gere-xi-ctum yoke, harness
adiuvo-iuvare-iuvi-iutum help, assist
Admetus-i (m.) Admetus (king of Pherae)
admitto-ittere-isi-issum admit, give rein to, allow to speed
      (*admissus* = speeding)
admoveo-movere-movi-motum move near to (+dat.), apply
admugio-ire moo (to: +dat.)
Adonis-idis (m.) Adonis (a youth loved by Venus)
adrideo-dere-si-sum laugh in response
adsiduus-a-um continual
adstruo-ere-xi-ctum add, add to (+dat.)
adsuetudo-dinis (f.) habit, frequent association
adsum-esse-fui attend, be present (at), be favourable to,
      support (+dat.)
adtonitus-a-um see *attonitus*
adulter-eri (m.) adulterer, lover
adultera-ae (f.) adulteress
adulterium-ii (n.) adultery
aduncus-a-um curved
advena-ae (adj.) foreign
adventus-us (m.) approach, arrival
adverto-tere-ti-sum direct towards (*mentem advertere* = pay
      attention)
Aeacides-ae (m.) descendant of Aeacus (i.e. Achilles)
aeger-gra-grum sick
aemula-ae (f.) rival
Aeneas-eae (m.) Aeneas (Trojan hero and founder of the Roman
      race)
Aeolius-a-um belonging to Aeolus (god of winds)
aequo (1) level
aequor-oris (n.) sea, ocean
aequoreus-a-um of the sea, marine

aequum-i (n.) what is right/fair
aer aeris (m.) air, weather
aerius-a-um of the air, airborne
Aesonides-ae (m.) son of Aeson (i.e. Jason)
aestas-atis (f.) summer
aetas-atis (f.) age
aevum-i (n.) age, generation
ager agri (m.) field
agito (1) move, stir
agmen-inis (n.) group, body, column
agna-ae (f.) lamb
ago agere egi actum do, drive, act, conduct, play (*age* = come!)
aio ait (defect.) say
ala-ae (f.) wing
alea-ae (f.) gambling, die
algeo-gere-si be cold
aliquis-qua-quid someone, something
aliquo to some place, somewhere
aliquot (adj.) several, some
aliter in a different way
alius-a-um other, another
alo-ere-ui-tum nurture, nourish
alter-era-erum one, another
altum-i (n.) a high place
amabilis-is-e lovable, worthy to be loved
amans-antis (m.+f.) lover
amarus-a-um bitter, acrimonious
amator-oris (m.) lover
Amazon-onis (f.) an Amazon (female warrior)
ambiguus-a-um ambiguous
amens-entis (adj.) distraught
amica-ae (f.) mistress, girlfriend
amicitia-ae (f.) friendship
amictus-us (m.) clothing
amitto-ittere-isi-issum lose
amo (1) love
Amor-oris (m.) Love (the god Cupid)
amor-oris (m.) love, love-affair
amplexus-us (m.) embrace
ancora-ae (f.) anchor
anhelitus-us (m.) breath
animus-i (m.) mind, feeling, affection, intention
annus-i (m.) year, season (*anni* = old age)
ante (advb.) first, beforehand, formerly; (prep. +acc.) before,
     in front of
anulus-i (m.) ring
anus-us (f.) old woman (as adj. = old)
Aonius-a-um from Aonia (=Boeotia in Greece)
aper apri (m.) boar
aperio-ire-ui-tum open, reveal
apertus-a-um open, unclouded
apis-is (f.) bee
Apollo-inis (m.) Apollo (god of poetry, music and prophecy)
appello (1) call
aptus-a-um suitable, convenient; (+dat.) suited to, suitable
     for, efficient with
apud (+acc.) among

aqua-ae (f.) water, sea
aquila-ae (f.) eagle
ara-ae (f.) altar
aratrum-i (n.) plough
arbitrium-ii (n.) command, desire
arbor-oris (f.) tree
arcanus-a-um secret
ardeo-dere-si burn, burn with (+abl.)
arduus-a-um difficult
area-ae (f.) open space, field
arguo-uere-ui-utum criticize
aridus-a-um dry
arista-ae (f.) ear of corn
arma-orum (n.pl.) weapons, armour, warfare
armentum-i (n.) herd
aro (1) plough, wrinkle
ars artis (f.) technique, skill, expertise, art, artificiality,
       wile, occupation
artifex-icis (m.) expert
Arx Arcis (f.) the citadel on the Capitoline Hill
Ascra-ae (f.) Ascra (a village in Boeotia in Greece)
Ascraeus-a-um of Ascra
asellus-i (m.) ass, donkey
asperitas-atis (f.) harshness, acerbity
aspicio-icere-exi-ectum look, see
assisto-ere astiti stand (near), take up a posture
at but
atque and
attonitus-a-um thunderstruck, frenzied, stunned, spellbound
auceps-upis (m.) bird-catcher
auctor-oris (m.) source, agent, father
audeo-dere ausus sum dare, be bold
audio (4) hear
aufero-rre abstuli ablatum carry off, destroy
aura-ae (f.) air (often pl. in this sense)
auratus-a-um gilded
aureus-a-um golden
auris-is (f.) ear
auritus-a-um long-eared
aurum-i (n.) gold
aut or
autumnus-i (m.) autumn
avis-is (f.) bird
avolo (1) fly away

Baccha-ae (f.) Bacchante (worshipper of Bacchus)
Bacchus-i (m.) Bacchus (god of wine), wine
barba-ae (f.) beard
bellum-i (n.) war, battle, fighting
bene well, proficiently
bibo-ere bibi drink
bis twice
blaesus-a-um stammering
blande charmingly, persuasively
blanditia-ae (f.) flattery, blandishment
blandus-a-um flattering, ingratiating, coaxing, affectionate
bonum-i (n.) good point, blessing, gift

bonus-a-um good, noble
Boreas-cae (m.) Boreas, the north wind
bos bovis (f.) cow; (m.) bull
bracchium-ii (n.) arm
brevis-is-e short, small
Byblis-idos (f.) Byblis (a heroine)

cado-ere cecidi casum fall
caedes-is (f.) slaughter, blood
caedo-ere cecidi caesum kill, slaughter
caelestis-is-e of heaven, of the sky
caelestis-is (m.+f.) god, goddess
caelum-i (n.) heaven, sky
Caesar-aris (m.) Caesar, Augustus
caespes-itis (m.) turf, sod
calathus-i (m.) wool-basket
Calchas-antis (m.) Calchas (a famous prophet)
caleo-ere-ui be hot, be fired with (+abl.)
calficio-ficere-feci-factum warm
callidus-a-um cunning
calor-oris (m.) heat, fire of love
Calypso-us (f.) Calypso (a sea-goddess)
campus-i (m.) plain
Campus-i (m.) the Campus Martius
candidus-a-um white
caneo-ere-ui be white, be grey
Canicula-ae (f.) the Dog Star
canis-is (m.+f.) dog
canna-ae (f.) reed
cano-ere cecini cantum sing, recite, write of
canto (1) sing, praise
canus-a-um grey
capax-acis (adj.) capable of holding (+gen.)
capillus-i (m.) hair
capio-ere cepi captum catch, take, captivate, win (over), trap,
      achieve
captivus-a-um captive, caught
caput-itis (n.) head
careo-ere-ui-itum lack, be devoid of (+abl.)
carina-ae (f.) ship
carmen-minis (n.) poem, incantation
carpo-ere-si-tum erode, reduce, press on along
casa-ae (f.) hut, cottage
cassis-is (m.) net, trap
castra-orum (n.pl.) camp, warfare, military service
castus-a-um chaste
casus-us (m.) fall, chance, luck, event, disaster
catulus-i (m.) cub
causa-ae (f.) cause, (good) reason, excuse
cautus-a-um cautious
caveo-ere cavi cautum beware of, guard against, avoid
cavo (1) hollow out
cavus-a-um hollow, full of holes
Cecropius-a-um Athenian (Cecrops was an ancient king of Athens)
cedo-dere-ssi-ssum yield, give way to (+dat.)
celeber-bris-bre crowded
celebro (1) celebrate, discuss, make known
celo (1) conceal, hide

censura-ae (f.) control over morals
centum (indecl. adj.) hundred
cera-ae (f.) wax
certamen-inis (n.) contest
certus-a-um settled, regular, fixed, sure
cerva-ae (f.) hind, deer
cervus-i (m.) stag, deer
cesso (1) cease, stop
ceterus-a-um rest
cibus-i (m.) food
cicada-ae (f.) cricket
cinis-eris (m.) ashes
circa (+acc.) around
Circe-es (f.) Circe (a witch)
Circus-i (m.) the Circus (Maximus)
citus-a-um swift, quick
clamo (1) shout
clamor-oris (m.) shout
Clio-us (f.) Clio (a Muse)
clipeus-i (m.) shield
Cnosias-adis (f.adj.) from Cnossos (city in Crete)
Cnosis-idis (f.adj.) from Cnossos (city in Crete)
coeo-ire-ii-itum come together
coepi-isse-tum begin, start
coeptum-i (n.) undertaking, enterprise
cognosco-oscere-ovi-itum get to know, recognize (perfect =
        know)
cogo-ere coegi coactum force, compel
colligo-igere-egi-ectum pick up, acquire
collis-is (m.) hill, mountain
colo-ere-ui cultum cultivate, adorn
color-oris (m.) colour, complexion
columba-ae (f.) dove
columna-ae (f.) pillar
colus-i (m.) distaff
coma-ae (f.) hair, lock of hair
comes-itis (m.+f.) friend, partner, companion
comis-is-e obliging, affable
comiter pleasantly, obligingly
commentus-a-um fabricated
committo-ittere-isi-issum entrust (to: +dat.), commit (a crime)
commoditas-atis (f.) obligingness
commodum-i (n.) gratuity, fringe benefit, profit, reward
como-ere-psi-ptum adorn, arrange, settle
comperio-ire-i-tum find out
compono-onere-osui-ositum position, arrange, adjust
compos-otis (adj.) in possession of (+gen.)
conbibo-ere-i drink up
concedo-dere-ssi-ssum allow, permit
concieo-iere-ivi-itum set in motion, excite
concilio (1) procure
concubitus-us (m.) sexual intercourse
confido-dere-sus sum trust in (+dat.)
confiteor-fiteri-fessus sum admit, confess
coniunx-iugis (m.+f.) husband, wife
conloquium -ii(n.) conversation, chat
conpesco-ere-ui restrain

conpono see *compono*
conscius-a-um sharing knowledge of (+gen.)
consilium-ii (n.) advice
consisto-sistere-stiti halt, take up residence, remain
consuesco-escere-evi-etum become accustomed to (+dat.)
consuetus-a-um customary, ordinary
consulo-ere-ui-tum consult, refer to
consumo-ere-psi-ptum wear away
contendo-dere-di-tum draw tight
contineo-inere-inui-entum hold tightly, hold back
contingo-ingere-igi-actum befall, be granted to (+dat.)
continuo (1) join
convenio-enire-eni-entum fit, suit (+dat. or *ad*), meet
        (*convenit* = it is agreed, it is agreed by (+dat.)(also
        + *ut/ne*))
conviva-ae (m.+f.) guest
convivium-ii (n.) dinner-party
convoco (1) summon
copia-ae (f.) abundance, quantity
cornipes-edis (adj.) hooved
cornu-us (n.) horn
corona-ae (f.) crown
corpus-oris (n.) body
corrumpo-umpere-upi-uptum destroy, ruin, spoil, seduce
cortex-icis (m.) bark
Cous-a-um made of Coan silk (Cos = an island off the coast of
        Asia Minor)
credibilis-is-e credible, plausible
credo-ere-idi-itum believe (in), trust in, entrust (to) (also
        +dat.);   regard as
cresco-ere crevi cretum grow, ripen
Cressa-ae (f.adj.) Cretan
Creta-ae (f.) Crete (an island in the Mediterranean Sea)
crimen-inis (n.) charge, reproach, crime, misdemeanour
crinis-is (m.) hair
croceus-a-um saffron-coloured, yellow
crocum-i (n.) saffron perfume
crudelis-is-e cruel
cruentus-a-um bloody
crus cruris (n.) leg
cubo-are-ui-itum go to bed, be confined to bed, recline
culpa-ae (f.) misconduct
culpo (1) blame, find fault with
cultor-oris (m.) devoted friend, attendant
cultus-a-um smart, well-groomed
cum (conj.) when;   (prep. +abl.) with
cunctus-a-um all, every
cupidus-a-um eager, greedy, lecherous
cupio-ere-ivi-itum wish, desire, want
cur why
cura-ae (f.) care, anxiety, source of anxiety,loved one,
        eagerness
curro-ere cucurri cursum run, rush
currus-us (m.) chariot
curvus-a-um curved, curving
Cydippe-es (f.) Cydippe (a heroine)

Cydoneus-a-um from Cydonea (a city in Crete)
cymbalum-i (n.) cymbal
Cynthius-a-um of mount Cynthus (on the island of Delos)
Cytherea-eae (f.) the goddess of Cythera (i.e. Venus)

damnum-i (n.) loss, detriment, damage, ruin
Danai-um (m.pl.) the Greeks (descendants of king Danaus, the
     founder of the Greek city Argos)
de (+abl.) from, concerning
dea-ae (f.) goddess
debeo (2) ought
decet-ere-uit suit, become, be becoming
decido-ere-i fall down, fall
decipio-ipere-epi-eptum deceive
declamo (1) declaim, make a speech (to: +dat.)
decurro-rrere-rri-rsum have recourse (to)
deficio-icere-eci-ectum be lacking, fail
deformo (1) disfigure
delabor-bi-psus sum glide down, descend, fall from
delecto (1) please, delight
delitisco -iscere-ui hide onself, take shelter
demens-entis (adj.) mad
demitto-ittere-isi-issum let fall, allow to hang down
demo-ere-psi-ptum remove, remove from (+dat.)
denique even
dens dentis (m.) tooth
deprendo-dere-di-sum catch, captivate, detect
desilio-ire-ui jump down
desino-inere-ii-itum desist, finish
destruo-ere-xi-ctum destroy, ruin
desum-esse-fui be wanting, be lacking (to/for: +dat.)
detego-gere-xi-ctum reveal
detineo-inere-inui-entum detain, restrain
deus-i (m.) god
dexter-era-erum dexterous, skilful
dextra-ae (f.) right hand
Dia-ae (f.) Dia (an island in the Aegean Sea)
dico-cere-xi-ctum say, call, tell, affirm
dictum-i (n.) word
dies diei (m.+f.) day, daylight
differo-rre distuli dilatum postpone, put off
difficilis-is-e difficult, stubborn, unyielding
diffido-dere-sus sum have no trust, lack confidence in (+dat.)
digitus-i (m.) finger
dignus-a-um worthy, deserving
diluo-uere-ui-utum wash away, diminish
Dione-es (f.) Dione (mother of Venus), Venus
discedo-dere-ssi-ssum disperse, depart
discipulus-i (m.) pupil
disco-ere didici learn, find out
discrimen-inis (n.) parting
disertus-a-um skilful in speaking, eloquent
dispono-onere-osui-ositum distribute, lay out, arrange
dissimulanter dissemblingly
dissimulo (1) conceal, disguise
distendo-dere-di-tum outstretch
diversus-a-um different, distant

dives-itis (adj.) rich
do dare dedi datum give, grant, provide, place, hold out
     (*dare tergum* (+dat.) = flee before; *dare manus* =
     surrender)
doceo-ere-ui-tum teach
docilis-is-e ready to learn, attentive
doctus-a-um expert
doleo-ere-ui-itum be grieved at (+acc.+infin.)
Dolon-onis (m.) Dolon (a Trojan)
dolor-oris (m.) pain, distress
dolus-i (m.) trickery, cunning
domina-ae (f.) mistress, owner, queen (of goddesses)
dominus-i (m.) master, lord, owner
domus-us or *i* (f.) house, home
donec until, while
dono (1) give, present with (+abl.)
dos dotis (f.) gift, talent, dowry
dubito (1) doubt, hesitate, hesitate to (+infin.)
dubius-a-um doubtful
duco-cere-xi-ctum lead, lead along, bring
dulcis-is-e sweet, pleasant, affectionate
dum while, until
duo duae duo two
duro (1) endure, last
durus-a-um hard
dux ducis (m.) leader, chieftain, military commander

e, ex (+abl.) from, out of, as a result of, by means of
ebrietas-atis (f.) drunkenness
ebrius-a-um drunk
eburnus-a-um made of ivory
ecce (interj.) look!, behold!
edisco-ere edidici get to know thoroughly
effero-rre extuli elatum carry away, lift
efficio-icere-eci-ectum bring it about that (+ *ut/ne*)
effugio-ugere-ugi escape, avoid
ego mei I
eheu (interj.) alas!
ei (interj.) alas! (also *ei mihi*)
elicio-ere-ui-itum call forth, arouse
eligo-igere-egi-ectum choose, select
eloquium-ii (n.) eloquence
emineo-ere-ui protrude
en (interj.) look!, behold!
enim for
eo ire i(v)i itum go, travel, advance
epulae-arum (f.pl.) banquet, dinner-party
eques-itis (m.) horseman
equus-i (m.) horse
Erato (f.,nom. only occurs) Erato (a Muse)
ergo therefore, then
erro (1) wander
et and, also, even
etiam also, even
etsi even if
Euhion (interj.) Euhion (*Euhios* was a title of Bacchus)

euhoe (interj.) euhoe
Europe-es (f.) Europa (a heroine)
Eurus-i (m.) Eurus, east wind
ex see *e*
exanimis-is-e swooning
excido-ere-i faint, swoon
excipio-ipere-epi-eptum receive, greet, catch, intercept
excolo-olere-olui-ultum work, work at
excutio-tere-ssi-ssum shake off, brush off, expel
exemplum-i (n.) example, precedent
exhaurio-rire-si-stum carry through, complete
exhibeo (2) present, display
exigo-igere-egi-actum ask about; (+*ad*) make to conform with
exiguus-a-um scanty, meagre, small
exilio-ire-ui leap up
exoro (1) win over, persuade
expecto (1) wait
exploro (1) reconnoitre, investigate
exta-orum (n.pl.) entrails, guts
extinguo-guere-xi-ctum extinguish, put out
extremus-a-um final, occurring at the end
exulto-are-avi leap about, frisk
exuo-uere-ui-utum strip off, put aside

fabula-ae (f.) story, myth
facies-iei (f.) appearance, aspect, face, good looks
facilis-is-e easy, deft; ready for (+ad); (*in facili est* =
       it is easy)
facio-ere feci factum do, make, depict, act (imper.+subj.
       = see to it that; *facio ut* + subj. = bring it about
       that, ensure that)
facundia-ae (f.) eloquence
facundus-a-um eloquent
fallax-acis (adj.) deceptive, treacherous
fallo-ere fefelli falsum deceive, trick, escape the notice of
falsus-a-um false
falx falcis (f.) sickle
fama-ae (f.) report, renown
far farris (n.) wheat
fastidium-ii (n.) repugnance, impatience
fastus-us (m.) arrogance, pride
fateor-eri fassus sum confess, indicate
fatigo (1) weary, exhaust
fatum-i (n.) fate
faveo-ere favi fautum support, favour (+dat.)
femina-ae (f.) female, woman
femineus-a-um female
ferio-ire strike, beat
fero ferre tuli latum bear, bring, produce, carry, carry off,
       gain, say (*feror* = go)
ferreus-a-um iron
ferrum-i (n.) iron, sword
fertilis-is-e fertile, productive
ferula-ae (f.) stick
ferus-a-um fierce
festino (1) hurry, hasten

fictus-a-um sham, pretended
fidelis-is-e faithful
fides-ei (f.) faith, belief, credibility, reliability
fiducia-ae (f.) assurance, trust, confidence
fidus-a-um faithful, reliable
figura-ae (f.) features, looks
filia-ae (f.) daughter
filum-i (n.) string
fingo-ngere-nxi-ctum tidy, arrange, feign
finio (4) finish
finis-is (m.) end, limit
fio fieri happen, come about, become, be made, be done
firmus-a-um healthy, strong, stable
flamma-ae (f.) flame, fire (of love)
flecto-ctere-xi-xum bend, change, soften
fleo-ere-evi-etum cry
floreo-ere-ui bloom
flos floris (m.) flower
fluctus-us (m.) wave
foedus-eris (n.) agreement
forma-ae (f.) appearance, beauty, (good)looks
formica-ae (f.) ant
formosus-a-um handsome, pretty, lovely
fors fortis (f.) chance, luck
forsitan perhaps
fortassis perhaps
forte by chance, perhaps
fortis-is-e brave, valiant
fortiter bravely
fortuna-ae (f.) fortune, misfortune
forum-i (n.) forum, town-square
fragilis-is-e fragile, frail
frater fratris (m.) brother
frendo-ere fresum gnash
frenum-i (n.) harness, reins (also pl.)
frequens-entis (adj.) densely packed, crowded, constant, regular;
        (+abl.) abounding in, full of
frigidus-a-um cold
frigus-oris (n.) cold
frons frondis (f.) branch, leaf, foliage
frons frontis (f.) brow, forehead, front
frustra in vain
frutex-icis (m.) bush, shrub
fuga-ae (f.) flight
fugio-ere fugi (intrans.) flee, recede, vanish;   (trans.) flee from,
        shun, escape the notice of (+acc.)
fugo (1) rout
fulmineus-a-um lightning-swift
fulvus-a-um tawny
fundo-ere fudi fusum pour, shed
fungor-i functus sum perform (+abl.)
funis-is (m.) rope
furiosus-a-um wild, frantic, mad
furor-oris (m.) madness, frenzy
furtim stealthily, imperceptibly
furtivus-a-um stealthy, clandestine
furtum-i (n.) theft, secret love-affair, intrigue, concealment

fusco (1) darken, tan
fusus-i (m.) spindle

Gargara-orum (n.pl.) Gargara (mountain-peak or town near Troy)
gaudeo-dere gavisus sum rejoice, be glad (to: +infin.)
gaudium-ii (n.) joy, gladness
gausapum-i (n.) woolen cloak
geminus-a-um twin, a pair of
gena-ae (f.) cheek, eye
genialis-is-e connected with marriage, for marriage
genu-us (n.) knee
genus-eris (n.) race, type, class
gloria-ae (f.) glory, pride
Gradivus-i (m.) Gradivus (a title of Mars)
gradus-us (m.) step, tier, stage
Graius-a-um Greek
granifer-fera-ferum grain-bearing
gratia-ae (f.) attractiveness
gratis for nothing, without payment
gratus-a-um grateful, pleasing, agreeable, deserving of gratitude
gravis-is-e stern, august, oppressive
gremium-ii (n.) lap, bosom
grex gregis (m.) herd, flock
gutta-ae (f.) drop

habena-ae (f.) rein
habeo (2) have, have available, hold, contain, endure
hac by this route
hactenus so far
Haemonius-a-um Thessalian (a region in northern Greece)
hamus-i (m.) hook
harena-ae (f.) sand, shore
hasta-ae (f.) spear
Hector-oris (m.) Hector (a Trojan hero)
Helene-es (f.) Helen (wife of Menelaus)
herba-ae (f.) grass, herb
herois-idos (f.) heroine
heros-oos (m.) hero
hic haec hoc this, the latter; he, she, it
hic (advb.) here, at this juncture, in these circumstances
hiems-emis (f.) winter, storm
hinc from here
hio-are-avi be open
Hippolytus-i (m.) Hippolytus (son of Theseus)
hirsutus-a-um hairy, shaggy, rough
hirtus-a-um shaggy
homo-inis (m.) human being
honestus-a-um worthy, fine, handsome
hora-ae (f.) hour
horreo-ere-ui tremble, shiver
hospes-itis (m.) guest
humanus-a-um kindly, considerate
humus-i (f.) ground, earth
Hymenaeus-i (m.) wedding-refrain (voc. = an exclamation
      in the refrain)

iaceo (2) lie
iacio-ere ieci iactum throw, cast

iaculum-i (n.) casting-net
iam now, already, soon, at this stage
iamdudum immediately
Ida-ae (f.) Ida (mountain in Crete)
Idaeus-a-um of Ida
idem eadem idem the same
ignarus-a-um ignorant, unaware
ignis-is (m.) fire, fire of love
ignosco-oscere-ovi -otum forgive, pardon (+dat.)
ignotus-a-um unknown
Iliacus-a-um of Troy
ille illa illud that; he, she, it
illic there, in that
imago-inis (f.) semblance, imitation
imber-bris (m.) shower, downpour
imitor-ari-atus sum imitate, mimic
immeritus-a-um undeserving
impar-aris (adj.) uneven, unequal
imperium-ii (n.) command
impleo-ere-evi-etum fill, make pregnant
implico-are-ui-itum enfold, entangle
impono-onere-osui-ositum place on, place in, impose on
        (+dat.)
improbus-a-um immoral, shameless
in (+abl.) in, on, within, amid, at; (+acc.) into, to,
        on to, for
inadsuetus-a-um unaccustomed
inauratus-a-um gilded
incendium-ii (n.) fire
inceptum-i (n.) enterprise, attempt
incipio-ipere-epi-eptum begin, lead
inde from there, from this
indicium-ii (n.) disclosure, information
indignus-a-um undeserved, unworthy
induco-cere-xi-ctum bring on, exhibit
indulgentia-ae (f.) mildness, kindness
induo-uere-ui-utum put on, place on (+dat.)
ineptus-a-um silly
iners inertis (adj.) lazy, idle
inferior-ior-ius inferior, worse
infundo-undere-udi-usum pour on (+dat.)
ingemesco-escere-ui groan
ingenium-ii (n.) character, intellect
ingens-entis (adj.) huge, vast
ingenuus-a-um belonging to a free man, liberal, befitting a
        gentleman
ingrate without giving pleasure
inicio-icere-ieci-iectum put on (*manus inicere* (+dat.) = lay
        hands on)
iniquus-a-um unfriendly, resentful
inlectus-a-um unread
inmundus-a-um unclean, dirty
innumerus-a-um countless
innuo-ere-i nod, make signs
inops-opis (adj.) devoid of, deficient in (+gen.)
inpono see *impono*
inprobitas-atis (f.) shamelessness, audacity

inquam-quis-quit (defect.) say
inreligatus-a-um unbound
inritus-a-um invalid
insanus-a-um mad
inscius-a-um unaware, unwitting
inscribo-bere-psi-ptum write on (+dat.)
insequor-qui-cutus sum pursue, press on
insero-ere-ui-tum insert, introduce into (+dat.)
insidiae-arum (f.pl.) ambush, trap
insidiosus-a-um full of ambushes, dangerous
insigne-is (n.) sign, symbol, emblem
inspicio-icere-exi-ectum inspect, examine
instar (n.indecl.) the equivalent (*instar habere* (+gen.) = be
      the equivalent to)
instita-ae (f.) band (on the matron's stola), stola
insto-are-iti press, press on, press on with
insum-esse-fui be involved (in), be visible (in) (also +dat.)
inter (+acc.) between, among
interea meanwhile
intereo-ire-ii-itum perish, be destroyed
intro (1) enter
invenio-enire-eni-entum find, discover
invidus-a-um envious
invitus-a-um unwilling
io (interj.) ho!
Io (f., no gen.) Io (a heroine)
Ioniacus-a-um Ionian (an area in Asia Minor)
ipse-a-um himself, herself, itself
ira-ae (f.) anger, rage
iratus-a-um angry
iste-a-ud yours, that, of that type; he, she, it
ita so, thus, as follows
iter itineris (n.) journey, course, road, way
iterum again
iuba-ae (f.) mane
iubeo-ere iussi iussum order, enjoin, designate
iudex-icis (m.) judge, juror
iudicium-ii (n.) judgement, decision
iugum-i (n.) yoke
iungo-gere-xi-ctum join, join to (+dat.) share, unite
      sexually
Iuno Iunonis (f.) Juno (wife of Jupiter)
Iuppiter Iovis (m.) Jupiter (king of the gods)
iurgium-ii (n.) quarrel
iuro (1) swear
iussus - us (m.) bidding, command
iuvenca-ae (f.) heifer
iuvencus-i (m.) bullock
iuvenis-is (m.+f.) young man, young woman
iuventus-utis (f.) youth, young men
iuvo-are iuvi iutum please, delight, help

labellum-i (n.) lip
labes-is (f.) spot, blemish
labor-oris (m.) task, job, struggle, hardship
laboro (1) work (at), strive
lac lactis (n.) milk
lacrima-ae (f.) tear

lactans-antis (adj.) sucking
laedo-dere-si-sum harm, hurt, offend
laetus-a-um glad, happy, propitious
lana-ae (f.) wool
langueo-ere be feeble, lack vigour
languor-oris (m.) faintness, sickness
lanio (1) tear
laqueus-i (m.) noose, snare, trap
lascivus-a-um promiscuous, unruly, mischievous, joking
latebra-ae (f.) hiding-place
lateo-ere-ui be concealed, escape notice, hide
latus-eris (n.) side, flank
laudo (1) praise
laurus-us or *-i* (f.) laurel
laus laudis (f.) praise
laxus-a-um large, ill-fitting
lea leae (f.) lioness
lectica-ae (f.) litter
lectus-i (m.) couch, bed
legitimus-a-um lawful, proper
lego-ere legi lectum read (out), choose, select, review
Lemnos-i (f.) Lemnos (an island in the Aegean Sea)
leniter gently, mildly
lentesco-ere relax, become less intense
lentus-a-um slow, pliant
leo leonis (m.) lion
lepus-oris (m.) hare
levis-is-e swift, light, petty, shallow, gay,
       fickle, insubstantial, feeble
levitas-atis (f.) inconsistency
leviter quietly
lex legis (f.) law, control, rule, regulation
libellus-i (m.) little book, programme
Liber-eri (m.) Liber (a name for Bacchus)
libere freely, openly
libet-ere-uit or *-itum est* it is agreeable, it is pleasing
libido-inis (f.) lust, passion
libo (1) touch
licet-ere-uit or *-itum est* it is allowed (+infin. or subj.);
       (virtually a conj.) although (+ subj.)
lilium-ii (n.) lily
linea-ae (f.) line
lingua-ae (f.) tongue, language
linteum-ei (n.) sail
liquidus-a-um flowing, liquid
lis litis (f.) quarrel
littera-ae (f.) letter, line, inscription, erudition
litus-oris (n.) beach, shore
locum-i (n.) see *locus*
locus-i (m.) place, spot, room, room for action
longe far, far away
longus-a-um long, lengthy
loquor loqui locutus sum say, speak, talk
lorum-i (n.) rein
lucerna-ae (f.) oil-lamp
ludius-ii (m.) dancer
ludo-dere-si-sum (intrans.) play; (trans.) trifle with (+acc.)

ludus-i (m.) game, show
lumen-inis (n.) eye, light, brightness
lupus-i (m.) wolf
lusor-oris (m.) player
lustro (1) purify
lux lucis (f.) light, daytime
lyra-ae (f.) lyre

madidus-a-um moist, watery
Maenalius-a-um of mount Maenalus, Arcadian (an area in Greece)
Maeonius-a-um of Maeonia (in Asia Minor)
maestus-a-um sad, dejected
magicus-a-um magic
magis more
magister-tri (m.) teacher, master, helmsman
magnus-a-um large, mighty, great, powerful
male badly, not properly
malo malle malui prefer
malus-a-um bad, wicked, harmful, ugly, poor
maneo-ere-si-sum remain, stay put
manifestus-a-um visible, manifest
manus-us (f.) hand
mare-is (n.) sea
maritus-i (m.) husband
marmoreus-a-um made of marble
Mars Martis (m.) Mars (god of war)
Marsus-a-um of the Marsi, Marsian (an Italian tribe)
mas maris (m.) male
mater-tris (f.) mother
materia-ae (f.) material, basis
maturus-a-um early
Mavors-ortis (m.) Mavors (a name for Mars)
Medeis-idos (f. adj.) of Medea (a witch)
medeor-eri heal
medius-a-um middle (of), mid
melior-ior-ius better
memini-isse remember, be sure to (+infin.)
menda-ae (f.) blemish
mendax-acis (adj.) lying
Menelaus-i (m.) Menelaus (husband of Helen)
mens mentis (f.) mind, sense, heart, feelings, intention
mensa-ae (f.) table
mentior-iri-itus sum lie, state falsely, fabricate
mereo (2) earn, gain as a reward
merito deservedly
merum-i (n.) (neat) wine
meta-ae (f.) turning-post
Methymna-ae (f.) Methymna (a city on Lesbos)
meto-ere (messui) messum reap, harvest
metuo-ere-i-tum fear
metus-us (m.) fear
meus-a-um my
miles-itis (m.) soldier
militia-ae (f.) military service
mille (indecl.) thousand, innumerable
Mimallonis-idos (f.) a Bacchante (worshipper of Bacchus)

Minois-idis (f.) daughter of Minos (i.e. Ariadne)
minor-or-us smaller, less
Minos-ois (m.) Minos (king of Crete and husband of Pasiphae)
miror-ari-atus sum marvel at, be amazed
misceo-ere-ui mixtum mix, combine, combine with (+abl.)
miser-era-erum wretched, poor
mitis-is-e kind, indulgent
mitto-ere misi missum send
modestus-a-um seemly
modo now, recently, only, just(*modo...modo* = now...now)
modus-i (m.) limit, check, tune, way, method
moenia-ium (n.pl.) walls, city
molestus-a-um troublesome, affected
molior-iri-itus sum attempt, build up
mollis-is-e soft, supple, tender, delicate, complaisant
moneo (2) warn, advise, instruct
monita-orum (n.pl.) advice, precepts
monitus-us (m.) advice
monstrum-i (n.) monster
montanus-a-um on/of the mountains
mora-ae(f.) delay
morbus-i (m.) sickness, illness
mordax-acis (adj.) abrasive
moror-ari-atus sum slow down, restrain, delay, linger
morosus-a-um bad-tempered, difficult to please
mos moris (m.) habit, custom, tradition, character,
     disposition
moveo-ere movi motum move, inspire, turn over (in the mind),
     prompt, initiate, stir
mulceo-ere mulsi (mulsum or *mul(c)tum)* stroke
Mulciber-beris (m.) Mulciber (a title of Vulcan)
multum much, to a great degree
multus-a-um much, many, many a
mundities-iei (f.) cleanliness, neatness
munus-eris (n.) function, gift, show, kindness
murex-icis (m.) purple dye
murus-i (m.) wall
Myrrha-ae (f.) Myrrha (a heroine)
myrteus-a-um of myrtle

nam for
nanciscor-i nactus or *nanctus sum* obtain, find
naris-is (f.) nostril
narro (1) tell
nascor-i natus sum be born, be formed
Naso-onis (m.) Naso (the *cognomen* of Ovid)
nato (1) swim, swim in, float about
natura-ae (f.) nature
navalis-is-e naval, nautical
navigo (1) sail
ne lest, in order that not, that not, not
nec, neque and not, nor, neither, but not
nefas (n. indecl.) crime, horror
neglectus-a-um careless, casual
nego (1) refuse, deny, say that not, say no to (+dat.)
nemorosus-a-um wooded
nempe without doubt

nemus-oris (n.) wood
nenia-ae (f.) incantation
Neptunus-i (m.) Neptune (god of the sea)
neque see *nec*
nequitia-ae (f.) naughtiness, promiscuity
nescio-ire-i(v)i-itum not to know
nescius-a-um ignorant, ignorant of (+gen.)
Nestor-oris (m.) Nestor (a Greek hero)
neve and lest, and in order that not
niger-gra-grum black
nihil, nil nothing; not at all
nil see *nihil*
nimium excessively, too much
nimius-a-um excessive
nisi if not, except, other than
nix nivis (f.) snow
nobilis-is-e noble, thoroughbred
nocens-entis (adj.) guilty
noceo-ere-ui-itum harm, impair (+dat.)
nocturnus-a-um nocturnal, at night
nolo nolle nolui be unwilling
nomen-inis (n.) name
non not
nos nostrum or *nostri* we, I
nosco-ere novi notum come to know (*novi* = know)
noster-tra-trum our, my
nota-ae (f.) signal, hint
noto (1) mark out, single out, write
notus-a-um known, well-known
Notus-i (m.) Notus, south wind
novellus-a-um young
noverca-ae (f.) step-mother
novus-a-um new, recent, young
nox noctis (f.) night
nubes-is (f.) cloud
nudus-a-um naked, bare
nullus-a-um no
numen-inis (n.) godhead, god
numerus-i (m.) number, degree
nunc now
nupta-ae (f.) wife
nurus-us (f.) daughter-in-law, married woman
nutrio-ire-i(v)i-itum feed, nourish
nutus-us (m.) nod
Nyctelius-a-um Nyctelian (epithet of Bacchus)

o (interj.) oh!
obduco-cere-xi-ctum draw over, overlay
obduro (1) be persistent, endure
obpono see *oppono*
obscenus-a-um obscene, private (applied to the private parts)
obscurus-a-um invisible
occupo (1) reach, arrive at
occurro-rrere-rri-rsum hurry to meet
ocellus-i (m.) eye
oculus-i (m.) eye
odi odisse osum hate

odiosus-a-um offensive, tiresome
odium-ii (n.) hate, dislike
odoratus-a-um smelling, fragrant
odorus-a-um fragrant
Odrysius-a-um Thracian (the Odrysae were a people of Thrace)
offero-rre obtuli oblatum put in the way of (+dat.), intrude
officium-ii (n.) courteous act, services
olea-ae (f.) olive, olive-tree
olens-entis (adj.) strong-smelling, fragrant
omnis-is-e all, every, of all kinds
onus-eris (n.) burden
operosus-a-um toilsome, laborious
oportet-ere-uit it is proper, it is right
oppono-onere-osui-ositum place against, apply, place before (+dat.)
ops opis (f.) wealth, finery (usually pl. in this sense)
optatus-a-um that one wishes for, welcome
opto (1) wish, desire (to)
opus-eris (n.) work, task, activity, handiwork, exploit
        (*opus est* (+abl.) = there is need for)
orbis-is (m.) world, part of the world
origo-inis (f.) source, start
oro (1) ask, beg
os oris (n.) mouth, face, utterance
osculum-i (n.) kiss
ovile-is (n.) sheepfold
ovum-i (n.) egg

Paean-anis (m.) Paean (Greek god identified with Apollo)
paelex-icis (f.) rival
paenitet-ere-uit it causes regret (+acc. of person and gen.
        of cause)
palam openly; (as prep. +abl.) in the presence of
Palatium-ii (n.) (also pl.) the Palatine (one of the hills
        of Rome)
Pallas-adis (f.) Pallas, Athene (= Minerva)
pallens-entis (adj.) pale, causing pallor
palleo-ere (-ui) become pale
pallium-ii (n.) cloak
palma-ae (f.) palm
palus-udis (f.) marsh
pandus-a-um bowed, sagging, curved
Paphos-i (f.) Paphos (a town on the island of Cyprus)
par paris (adj.) equal
parco-ere peperci spare, refrain from (+dat.)
parcus-a-um moderate
pareo (2) obey (+dat.)
pario-ere peperi partum produce, yield, procure
Paris-idis (m.) Paris (son of Priam)
paro (1) prepare
pars partis (f.) part, some, role (*ex magna parte* = to a large
        extent; *partem agere* = play a role)
partus-us (m.) offspring
parvus-a-um small
pasco-ere pavi pastum pasture
pascuum-i (n.) pasture
Pasiphae-es (f.) Pasiphae (wife of Minos)
passim everywhere, at large

pateo-ere-ui be obvious (as), be visible
pater-tris (m.) father
patienter patiently, tolerantly
patior-i passus sum allow, bear, put up with, suffer
paulatim gradually
pauper-eris (adj.) poor
pax pacis (f.) peace
peccatum-i (n.) misdemeanour
pecco (1) sin, do wrong
pectus-oris (n.) breast, heart, mind, character, wisdom, eloquence
pecus-udis (f.) sheep, farm-animal
Pelias-adis (f. adj.) from mount Pelion (in Thessaly in Greece)
pellis-is (f.) leather, shoe
pello-ere pepuli pulsum strike
pendeo-ere pependi hang, be suspended, overhang
Penelope-es (f.) Penelope (wife of Ulysses)
pensum-i (n.) task, stint
per (+acc.) through, along, across, by, by means of
peraro (1) inscribe
perdo-ere-idi-itum lose, forfeit, waste, destroy
perfectus-a-um perfect, fully competent
perfero-rre pertuli perlatum convey, put up with
perficio-icere-eci-ectum achieve, effect
perfidus-a-um treacherous, deceitful
perfungor-gi-ctus sum be done with (+abl.)
Pergama-orum (n.pl.) the citadel of Troy, Troy
peritus-a-um experienced, practised
periurium-ii (n.) perjury, false oath
permaneo-ere-si-sum remain, survive
perscribo-bere-psi-ptum trace
Persis-idis (f. adj.) Persian
persto-are-iti-atum persist
pervagus-a-um wandering widely
pes pedis (m.) foot
peto-ere-i(v)i-itum make for, look for, procure, seek, ask for
petulans-antis (adj.) immodest, promiscuous
Phaedra-ae (f.) Phaedra (wife of Theseus)
Phasias-ados (f. adj.) from the region of Phasis, Phasian (Phasis
        was a river in Colchis)
Pheraeus-a-um of Pherae (a town of Thessaly in Greece)
philtrum-i (n.) love-philtre
Phoebe-es (f.) Phoebe (a heroine)
Phoebus-i (m.) Phoebus (Apollo)
piger-gra-grum sluggish, torpid
piget-ere-uit it irks
pignus-oris (n.) bet, token, proof
pilus-i (m.) hair
pingo-ngere-nxi-ctum depict, sketch
pinna-ae (f.) wing
pinus-us (f.) pine, ship
piscis-is (m.) fish
placeo-ere-ui or *-itus sum* please, attract (+dat.) *(placitus*
        = favoured, agreeable)
placo (1) appease
plaga-ae (f.) net
plaudo-dere-si-sum applaud (also +dat.)
plausus-us (m.) applause

plenus-a-um full, full of (+gen.), abundant, numerous, satis-
    fied, used with full force
plus-uris (n.) a greater amount, more
poculum-i (n.) wine-cup, cup, drink
Podalirius-ii (m.) Podalirius (a famous doctor)
poeta-ae (m.) poet
pollex-icis (m.) thumb
pollicitum-i (n.) promise
pompa-ae (f.) procession
pomum-i (n.) apple
pono-ere posui positum place, arrange, lay, serve, lay aside
populus-i (m.) people, crowd
porrigo-igere-exi-ectum offer, present
porticus-us (f.) colonnade
portus-us (m.) harbour
posco-ere poposci ask for, demand
possum posse potui be able, be capable; (+acc.) manage, be
    capable of
post (+acc.) behind, after
postmodo presently
postulo (1) ask, demand
potior-iri-itus sum obtain, gain submission of
praebeo (2) provide, present
praecedo-edere-essi-essum go in front
praeceptor-oris (m.) teacher
praecipio-ipere-epi-eptum teach, advise
praecipue especially, particularly
praecipuus-a-um especial, particular
praeconium-ii (n.) announcement, declaration
praeda-ae (f.) spoil, pillage, prey
praefero-rre praetuli praelatum prefer, prefer to (+dat.),
    carry in front
praeficio-icere-eci-ectum set over, put in chage of (+dat.)
praemium-ii (n.) payment, reward
praesens-entis (adj.) present, in person
praeter (+acc.) as well as, besides
praeterea in addition, besides
praeteritus-a-um past, bygone
praevius-a-um leading the way
pratum-i (n.) meadow, meadow-grass
precor-ari-atus sum pray, beg
premo-mere-ssi-ssum grip, press, graze, conceal
prendo-dere-di-sum catch
pretiosus-a-um expensive, precious
pretium-ii (n.) reward
prex precis (f.) prayer, entreaty
Priamus-i (m.) Priam (king of Troy)
primo at first
primum for the first time, first
primus-a-um first, preceding, earliest, young
principio firstly
principium-ii (n.) beginning
prior-or-us first, earlier
prius sooner, beforehand
pro (+abl.) in the capacity of
probo (1) approve of
procul away, apart, far away

prodo-ere-idi-itum reveal, betray
produco-cere-xi-ctum produce
proelium-ii (n.) battle, dispute
profanus-a-um impious, sacrilegious
profiteor-iteri-essus sum state openly, declare
prohibeo (2) prevent, prohibit, debar from (+abl.)
promissum-i (n.) promise
promitto-ittere-isi-issum promise
propero (1) hurry, be eager
propior-ior-ius nearer, of closer importance
propositum-i (n.) purpose, intention
proprius-a-um one's own
prosum prodesse profui be of benefit/use
protervus-a-um bold, impudent
Proteus-ei (m.) Proteus (sea-god)
protinus immediately
proximus-a-um next, next to (+dat. or *a* +abl.)
publicus-a-um public, shared by all
pudens-entis (adj.) modest, bashful
pudor-oris (m.) modesty, chastity, shame, shyness
puella-ae (f.) girl, girlfriend, mistress
puer pueri (m.) boy, son
pugno (1) fight
pulcher-chra-chrum beautiful
pulpitum-i (n.) stage (also pl.)
pulso (1) beat, strike
pulvinum-i (n.) cushion
pulvis-eris (m.) dust
pumex-icis (m.) pumice
puppis-is (f.) stern, ship
puto (1) think, regard as

qua (advb.) where, to the extent that, in so far as, as, by any chance
quadrupes-edis (adj.) four-footed
quaero-rere-sivi-situm search (for), seek, ask, procure
quam how, how much, than, as
quamvis however much, although
quando at any time, ever
quantum (advb.) as much as
quantus-a-um how great, as great, how much
quasso (1) brandish
-que and (*-que...-que* = both...and)
queror queri questus sum complain
qui quae quod (rel.) who, which; (interrog.) which, what
quicumque quaecumque quodcumque whoever, whatever
quid why
quidam quaedam quoddam a certain, somebody, something
quidem certainly, truly, indeed
quilibet quaelibet quodlibet any, any at all, anyone
quin that (after a verb of doubting)
quis qua quid anyone, someone
quis quis quid (interrog.) who, what, which, what type of
quisque quaeque quidque each one, every one
quisquis quisquis quidquid or *quicquid* whoever, whatever
quo to what purpose, why, to which place
quod that, because
quoque also, too

quot as many
quotiens how often, as often as

rabidus-a-um enraged, fierce
racemus-i (m.) bunch, cluster (of grapes)
rado-dere-si-sum smooth
rapina-ae (f.) plundering, robbery
rapio-ere-ui-tum seize, abduct, carry off, seduce
raptor-oris (m.) abductor, ravisher
rarus-a-um rare, unusual
ratio-ionis (f.) reason
ratis-is (f.) ship
recalfacio-facere-feci make hot again
recedo-dere-ssi-ssum retire, withdraw
recingo-gere-ctum ungird, loose
recipio-ipere-epi-eptum receive
recubo-are recline
reddo-ere-idi-itum give back, repay
redeo-ire-ii-itum return
refero-rre rettuli relatum mention, relate, draw back
    (*pedem referre* = withdraw)
refugio-ugere-ugi flee, run away
regalis-is-e royal
regina-ae (f.) queen
rego-gere-xi-ctum guide, control, direct
reicio-icere-ieci-iectum throw away
relinquo-ere reliqui relictum leave, abandon
remaneo-ere-si-sum remain
remigium-ii (n.) rowing
remitto-mittere-misi-missum send back
removeo-movere-movi-motum remove
remus-i (m.) oar
reperio-ire repperi repertum find
repeto-ere-i(v)i-itum seek again, return to
repugno (1) fight back, struggle, resist (+dat.)
requies-etis (f.) rest, intermission
requietus-a-um rested
requiro-rere-si(v)i-situm ask, miss
res rei (f.) thing, case
rescribo-bere-psi-ptum write back, reply to (+dat.)
reseco-are-ui-tum cut, trim
resolvo-vere-vi-utum release
respicio-icere-exi-ectum look behind (at), look around (at)
resupinus-a-um supine, lying
rete-is (n.) net
retineo-inere-inui-entum hold back, keep
reus-i (m.) defendant
reveho-here-xi-ctum bring back (*revehor* = ride back)
revello-vellere-velli-vulsum or-*volsum* pluck, pull away
revoco (1) recall
rex regis (m.) king
Rhesus-i (m.) Rhesus (Thracian king)
rideo-ere risi risum laugh (at: +acc.)
rigeo-ere be hard
rigidus-a-um stiff, bristling
rigo (1) moisten, drench
ripa-ae (f.) bank

risus-us (m.) laugh, laughter
rivalis-is (m.) rival
rogo (1) ask, ask about, plead, proposition
rogus-i (m.) pyre
Roma-ae (f.) Rome
Romanus-a-um Roman
Romulus-i (m.) Romulus (founder of Rome)
rosa-ae (f.) rose
rota-ae (f.) wheel
roto (1) whirl, send spinning
ruber-bra-brum red
rubigo-inis (f.) rust, deposit
rudis-is-e crude, clumsy, inexperienced, raw, rough
ruga-ae (f.) wrinkle, furrow
rumpo-mpere-pi-ptum break off
ruo-ere-i-tum rush, hurry
rus ruris (n.) countryside
rusticitas-atis (f.) lack of sophistication, awkwardness
rusticus-a-um rustic, unsophisticated, awkward, prudish

Sabina-ae (f.) Sabine woman (the Sabines were an ancient
      Italian people)
sacer-cra-crum sacred, holy
sacrum-i (n.) ceremony, rite (*sacra* = religion)
saepe often
saevus-a-um fierce, savage
salto (1) dance
saltus-us (m.) glade, glen
sanguis-inis (m.) blood
sanus-a-um sane
sapiens-entis (adj.) wise, shrewd, knowledgeable
sapienter sensibly, wisely
sapio-ere-i(v)i be sensible
satis enough
Satyrus-i (m.) a Satyr (a minor deity)
saucius-a-um wounded
saxum-i (n.) rock
scamnum-i (n.) stool
scena-ae (f.) scenery
scilicet of course, undoubtedly
scio (4) know, know how to (+ infin.)
scribo-bere-psi-ptum write
scriptum-i (n.) composition, letter
Scyrias-adis (f. adj.) from Scyros (an island in the
      Aegean Sea)
se sui himself, herself, itself, themselves
securus-a-um free from care
sed but
sedeo-ere sedi sessum sit
sedulitas-atis (f.) assiduity, eager attention
sedulus-a-um diligent, careful
seges-etis (f.) corn, crop
segnis-is-e lazy
semel once
semper always
senatus-us (m.) senate
senex-is (m.) old man
sentio-tire-si-sum feel, notice, realize

sequor sequi secutus sum follow, pursue
sermo-onis (m.) speech, conversation, language, mode of expression
sero late
sero-ere sevi satum sow
serta-orum (n.pl.) garlands
serus-a-um late, mature
servio (4) serve (+dat.)
servo (1) watch, guard, preserve
seu if, or if
si if, even if
sic so, thus
siccus-a-um dry
sidus-eris (n.) star
signo (1) mark
signum-i (n.) sign, signal, standard
silentium-ii (n.) silence
Silenus-i (m.) Silenus (a minor deity)
sileo-ere-ui be silent
silva-ae (f.) wood
Simois-entis (m.) Simois (a river near Troy)
simplicitas-atis (f.) simplicity, artlessness
simpliciter simply, artlessly
simul at the same time
simulator-oris (m.) pretender, hypocrite
simulo (1) feign, pretend
sine (+abl.) without
sino-ere sivi situm allow, permit
sinus-us (m.) bosom, embrace
Sithonius-a-um Thracian (the Sithonii were a people of
      Thrace)
sitiens-entis (adj.) thirsty, parching
situs-us (m.) inactivity, neglect
sive if, or if
socius-a-um allied, shared, friendly
Sol Solis (m.) the Sun
solea-ae (f.) sandal
soleo-ere-itus sum be accustomed
solitum-i (n.) what is usual
solitus-a-um customary
sollemnis-is-e hallowed
sollicito (1) trouble, disturb
sollicitus-a-um disturbed, troubled, anxious, tense
solus-a-um alone, above all others
solvo-vere-vi-utum release, loosen, relax, break up, absolve
      from (+abl.)
somnium-ii (n.) dream
somnus-i (m.) sleep
sono-are-ui-itum sound, resound
sonus-i (m.) sound
sorbeo-ere-ui suck in
sordes-is (f.) dirt
soror-oris (f.) sister
spargo-gere-si-sum scatter, sprinkle, strew
spatiosus-a-um spacious, large
spatium-ii (n.) period, span
species-iei (f.) sort, species
speciosus-a-um good-looking, pretty
spectaculum-i (n.) spectacle

specto (1) see, look at, observe, examine
speculum-i (n.) mirror
spero (1) hope, hope for (+acc.)
spes spei (f.) hope
spina-ae (f.) thorn
spissus-a-um hard-packed, firm
spolium-ii (n.) spoil
sponte of one's own accord
stamen-inis (n.) thread
stella-ae (f.) star
sterilis-is-e barren, infertile
stimulo (1) arouse, incite
stimulus-i (m.) goad, incitement
sto stare steti statum stand, be situated
studiosus-a-um eager, keen
stultus-a-um foolish, silly
stupeo-ere-ui be stunned, be dazed, be stupefied
stupor-oris (m.) stupidity
stuprum-i (n.) violation, defilement
Styx-ygis (f.) Styx (a river in the Underworld)
sub (+acc.) under, shortly before; (+abl.) under, beneath,
      down in
subdolus-a-um crafty, sly
subedo-ere-i eat away below
subiectus-a-um submissive
subito suddenly
subitus-a-um sudden
subsum-esse be at hand
succingo-gere-xi-ctum girdle, surround
sucus-i (m.) juice, medicine
sulphur-uris (n.) sulphur
sum esse fui be
summus-a-um the top of
sumo-ere-psi-ptum assume, put on, take, take up
super (+acc.) above
supercilium-ii (n.) eyebrow
supero (1) remain, conquer
supplex-icis (adj.) suppliant, entreating
surdus-a-um deaf
surgo-gere-rexi-rectum rise, get up
sustineo-inere-inui-entum hold, hold out, support
suus-a-um his own, her own, its own, their own, one's own

tabella-ae (f.) writing-tablet, fan
tabula-ae (f.) will
taceo (2) be silent
taciturnus-a-um quiet, silent
tacitus-a-um silent
taedet-ere taeduit or *taesum est* it wearies
taedium-ii (n.) dislike, disgust, trouble
tam so, so much
tamen nevertheless, however, all the same
tango-ere tetigi tactum touch, touch up, handle
tantum only
tantus-a-um so great
tardo (1) slow down, delay
taurus-i (m.) bull
tecte covertly, with concealment

tectum-i (n.) roof
tectus-a-um disguised, covered
tego-gere-xi-ctum cover, conceal
Telamonius-ii (m.) the son of Telamon (= the Greek hero Ajax)
tellus-uris (f.) land, soil
telum-i (n.) weapon, arrow
templum-i (n.) temple
tempto (1) try, try out, approach
tempus-oris (n.) time, season (*tempora* = the temples, the
     head)
tendo-ere tetendi tentum or *tensum* stretch, stretch out, spread
teneo-ere-ui (trans.) hold (on to), keep, secure, possess,
     preserve; (intrans.) last, hold on
tener-era-erum tender, soft, delicate, young
tentorium-ii (n.) tent
tenuis-is-e slender, narrow, thin, small
tenuo (1) make thin, dissolve
tepidus-a-um warm, lukewarm
ter three times
teres-etis (adj.) well-proportioned, slender
tergum-i (n.) back (*dare tergum* +dat. = flee before)
tero-ere trivi tritum rub, smooth, tread, travel
terra-ae (f.) earth, ground, land
terribilis-is-e terrifying, dreadful
tertius-a-um third
testis-is (m. + f.) witness
tetricus-a-um forbidding, sternly moral
thalamus-i (m.) room, bedroom
Thalea-ae (f.) Thalea (a Muse)
theatrum-i (n.) theatre
Theseus-eos (m.) Theseus (an ancient king of Athens)
Thrace-es (f.) Thrace (a region to the north of Greece)
Threicius-a-um Thracian
thymum-i (n.) thyme, the thyme-shrub
tibicen-inis (m.) flute-player
tigris-is (m. + f.) tiger, tigress
timeo-ere-ui fear, be afraid
timide fearfully, timidly, with hesitation
timidus-a-um timid, fearful
timor-oris (m.) fear, fright
tingo-gere-xi-ctum dip, dye
Tirynthius-a-um of Tiryns (a town in Greece)
titubo (1) stagger, stumble
titulus-i (m.) glory, fame
toga-ae (f.) toga
tollo-ere sustuli sublatum lift up, pick up, remove
tonsura-ae (f.) trim
torpeo-ere be sluggish, be torpid
torqueo-quere-si-tum curl, torment
torus-i (m.) bed, couch
tot so many
totiens so often
totus-a-um all, entire
traho-here-xi-ctum drag, pull in, lead on, allure
transeo-ire-i(v)i-itum pass through
transfero-ferre-tuli-latum transfer
tremo-ere-ui quiver, tremble

tremulus-a-um shaking
trepidus-a-um anxious, alarmed
tribuo-uere-ui-utum concede
tristis-is-e sad, dismal, sombre, harsh, offensive
tritus-a-um practised, expert
Troia-ae (f.) Troy
tu tui you
tueor-eri tuitus sum defend, protect, preserve
tum then
tumeo-ere swell, be inflated with (+abl.)
tumidus-a-um swollen, haughty
tunica-ae (f.) tunic
tunicatus-a-um wearing a tunic
tunc then
tundo-ere tutudi tu(n)sum beat, strike
turba-ae (f.) crowd, band
turbo (1) drive to distraction
turpe-is (n.) disgrace
turpis-is-e ugly, disgraceful
Tuscus-a-um Etruscan (from Etruria in central Italy)
tutus-a-um safe
tuus-a-um your
tympanum-i (n.) tambourine
Tyrius-a-um dyed with Tyrian purple (from the city of Tyre
    in Syria)

uber-eris (n.) teat, udder
ubi where, when
ubique wherever
ulciscor-i ultus sum avenge, atone for (+acc.)
Ulixes-is (m.) Ulysses (a Greek hero)
ullus-a-um any
umbraculum-i (n.) parasol
umbrosus-a-um shady
umerus-i (m.) shoulder
unda-ae (f.) wave, water
unde from where
unguis-is (m.) nail
unguo-ere unxi unctum anoint, smear
unus-a-um one, one and the same
urbs urbis (f.) city
urgeo-ere ursi urge on, impel
usque continually
usus-us (m.) use, experience, exercise, sexual intercourse
ut that, in order that, so that, how, although (+subj.); as,
    just as, like (also + indic.)
uter utra utrum which of two
uterque utraque utrumque each of two, both
utilis-is-e useful
utor uti usus sum use, make use of (+abl.)
uva-ae (f.) grape, cluster of grapes
uxor-oris (f.) wife
uxorius-a-um belonging to a wife

vacca-ae (f.) cow
vacuus-a-um empty, idle
vadum-i (n.) shallows

vagus-a-um wandering
valens-entis (adj.) powerful, potent
valeo (2) be strong, be strong enough to (+infin.), be healthy
vallis-is (f.) valley
vanesco-ere disappear, vanish
vastus-a-um vast, huge
vates-is (m.) bard, poet
-ve or
veho-ere vexi vectum carry (*vehor* = ride)
vello-ere vulsi vulsum pluck, pull
velo (1) cover, dress
velum-i (n.) sail, awning
venator-oris (m.) hunter
venio-ire veni ventum come, come about
venor-ari-atus sum hunt
ventus-i (m.) wind, breeze
Venus-eris (f.) Venus (goddess of love)
venus-eris (f.) love, sexual love
ver veris (n.) spring
verbum-i (n.) word
verecundus-a-um shamefaced, bashful
verus-a-um true, genuine
vestigium-ii (n.) sign, token
vestis-is (f.) clothes, dress
veto-are-ui-itum forbid, warn off
vetus-eris (adj.) old, of former times
via-ae (f.) road, journey
vicem (f. defect.) change (*in vicem* = in turn,
     reciprocally)
victor-oris (m.) victor
victoria-ae (f.) victory, success
video-ere vidi visum see, catch sight of, perceive,
     reflect upon (*videor* = seem, appear)
viduus-a-um wifeless
vigil-ilis (adj.) awake, alert
vilis-is-e worthless
vinco-ere vici victum win, beat, defeat, win over
vinculum-i (n.) bond
vinum-i (n.) wine, dinner-party
viola-ae (f.) violet
violo (1) violate
vipera-ae (f.) viper
vir viri (m.) man, husband, boyfriend, manhood
vireo-ere-ui flourish
virga-ae (f.) twig, rod
virgo-inis (f.) virgin, girl
viridis-is-e green
virilis-is-e of men, male
virtus-tutis (f.) excellence, talent
vis vis (f.) strength, force, power(s) (also in pl.)
vitis-is (f.) vine
vitium-ii (n.) blemish, defect, fault
vito (1) avoid
vitta-ae (f.) headband
vitulus-i (m.) calf
vivo-ere vixi victum live, survive
vix scarcely, hardly, with difficulty
voco (1) call, call for, summon

volatilis-is-e flying, swift
volo (1) fly
volo velle volui wish, be willing, desire, consent,
        decide
volucer-cris-cre winged
volucris-is (f.) bird
vomer-eris (m.) ploughshare
vos vestrum or *vestri* you (pl.)
votum-i (n.) desire, wish
voveo-ere vovi votum vow
vox vocis (f.) voice, call, cry, language
Vulcanus-i (m.) Vulcan (craftsman-god)
vulgus-i (n.) crowd
vulnus-eris (n.) wound
vultus-us (m.) face, look, expression

Zephyrus-i (m.) Zephyrus, west wind

Other Textbooks from
Bolchazy-Carducci Publishers

—REFERENCE & RESOURCES—

Gildersleeve's Latin Grammar

Graphic Latin Grammar

A New Latin Syntax

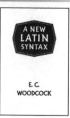

New Latin Composition

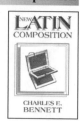

Smith's English/Latin Dictionary

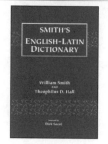

New Latin Grammar

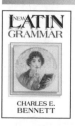

Latin Prose Composition

A Comprehensive Guide to Wheelock's Latin

38 Latin Stories
(Ancilla to Wheelock)

Key to Latin Prose Composition

*Explore **bolchazy.com** for more on **Latin** and **Greek** Pronunciation*

—Order Online Today—
www.BOLCHAZY.com

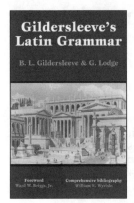

Gildersleeve's Latin Grammar

B. L. Gildersleeve and G. Lodge

The classic Latin grammar favored by many students and teachers with two new additions:

✦ Foreword by **Ward W. Briggs, Jr**.
✦ Comprehensive bibliography by **William E. Wycislo**

The 45-page bibliography that accompanies our new reprint is designed primarily but not exclusively for an English-speaking audience, comprising scholarship produced on Latin grammar in English during this century.

613 pp. (1895, third edition, reprint with additions 1997)
Paperback, ISBN 0-86516-353-7; Hardbound, ISBN 0-86516-477-0

New Latin Grammar

Charles E. Bennett

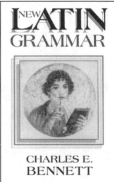

A model of clear precision, the book uses specific examples from primary sources to help students learn the inflections, syntax, sounds, accents, particles, and word formations of Latin. It also includes a history of the Indo-European family of languages, the stages of the development of the Latin language, and sections on prosody, the Roman calendar, Roman names and definitions, and examples of figures of syntax and rhetoric.

xvi + 287 pp. (1908, Reprint 1995) Paperback, ISBN 0-86516-261-1

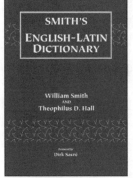

Smith's English-Latin Dictionary

An invaluable resource for Latin composition

Smith's classic
A Copious and Critical English–Latin Dictionary is again available in this reprint edition. New to the Bolchazy-Carducci edition is a Foreword by Dirk Sacré, which places Smith's *Dictionary* in its historical and pedagogical context.

Smith's English-Latin Dictionary is an invaluable resource for Latin compostion. Each entry gives an English word, its corresponding Latin equivalents, and examples drawn from a full range of classical writers. The Index of Proper Names contains Latin forms of names of thousands of persons, places, and geographical features from history and mythology, as well as the Hebrew and Christian Bibles.

xi + 1010 pp. (2000)
Paperback
ISBN 0-86516-491-6
Hardcover
ISBN 0-86515-492-4

Smith's English–Latin Dictionary. . .*is a monument all in itself and will find its place in our future classroom experiences.. . .*
—Reginald Foster, *Teresianum*

—Order Online Today—
www.BOLCHAZY.com

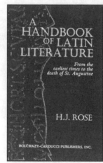

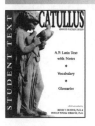

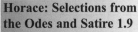

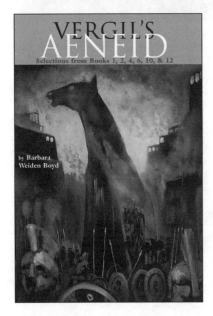
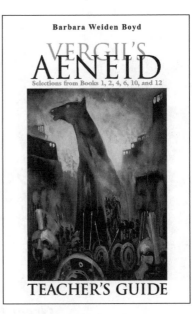

—MODERN CLASSICS—
In Classical Language

How the Grinch Stole Christmas *in Latin*

The Cat in the Hat *in Latin*

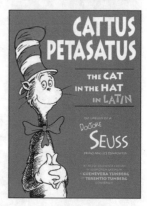

The Giving Tree *in Latin*

Shock-Headed Peter *in Latin*

"Yes, Virginia, there is a Santa Clause"...in Latin

Enjoy!
Great Gifts
Great Easy Latin Readers

*Explore **bolchazy.com** for more on **Responsible Popularization** and **Living Latin***

—Order Online Today—
www.BOLCHAZY.com

The Giving Tree* in Latin
Arbor alma

Author: Shel Silverstein

Translators: Jennifer Morrish Tunberg and Terence O. Tunberg
Illustrations: original Shel Silverstein line drawings throughout

An evocative parable, *The Giving Tree*—the story of a lifelong relationship between a boy and the tree who happily responds to the boy's every need— is retold in Latin in *Arbor alma*. This edition features the original artwork of Shel Silverstein and a translation in a style that echoes the spirit of *The Giving Tree*.

The Giving Tree is here rendered in exquisite Latin, a language whose own simple grandeur complements that of Silverstein's original story and illustrations. *Arbor Alma* adds one more dimension to this multifaceted classic. This Latin-language edition is a welcome, all-occasion gift, a delightful way to revisit a treasured tale, and an enjoyable way to refresh high school Latin. It features:

+ Exquisite Latin translation in a style that echoes the spirit of the original
+ Original artwork of Shel Silverstein
+ Latin-to-English vocabulary
+ Note on the translation and the translators

72 pp., Original Illustrations (July 2002) 7"x 9" Hardbound, ISBN 0-86516-499-1
*originally published in English by HarperCollins Publishers, New York, 1964.

Shock-Headed Peter
In Latin - English - German

Author: **Heinrich Hoffmann**
Latin: **Peter Wiesmann**
Afterword: **Walter Sauer**
New English Translation: **Ann E. Wild**

Dr. Heinrich Hoffmann's *Der Struwwelpeter,* the best known German children's book, was first published in Frankfurt in 1845. "Shock-Headed Peter" or "Slovenly Peter" (as it is mostly known in English speaking countries) has conquered the children's book market of the world not only with dozens of translations but also literally hundreds of imitations, adaptations, take-offs and parodies. These "merry stories and funny pictures for children between 3 and 6 years," as Dr. Hoffmann termed them, are cautionary tales, by turns macabre, touching, and wickedly funny. Where else does every naughty child or cruel adult get his or her deserts, and that within a few pages?

FEATURES
+ Stylistically elegant, rhyming Latin translation that is accessible to the non-scholarly reader
+ Facing page original German text and the standard popular English translation
+ Hoffmann's original illustrations, plus detailed enlargements of them
+ Afterword by Walter Sauer, on the history of the work and its Latin translations
+ Select Latin-English glossary
+New English translation, *Scruffypete*, by Ann E. Wild

66 B&W Illustrations, 72 pp. (forthcoming) 5 ½"x 8 ½" Paperback, ISBN 0-86516-548-3

—Order Online Today—
www.BOLCHAZY.com

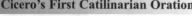

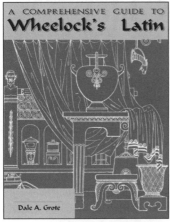
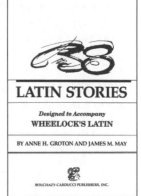

WILLIAM J. DOMINIK, EDITOR

Words & Ideas

Editor: **William J. Dominik**

Unlike most etymology textbooks, this one presents the words studied in the context of the ideas in which the words functioned. Instead of studying endless lists of word roots, suffixes, and prefixes in isolation, the words are enlivened by the social, literary, and cultural media in which they were used. Readers are introduced to a wide variety of topics from classical antiquity, entertained by clever cartoons, and are able to practice their word knowledge with exercises.

FEATURES

✦ An etymology textbook that also introduces students to a wide variety of topics in classical antiquity
✦ Chapters on mythology, medicine, politics and law, commerce and economics, philosophy and psychology, history
✦ Introduction to word building
✦ Exercises throughout
✦ Illustrations of ancient artifacts
✦ Clever cartoons on word origins
✦ Three indices: Names and Cultural Topics; Word-Building Topics; English Words and Phrases

ABOUT THE AUTHOR

William J. Dominik, Ph.D., is the author and editor of several books and numerous other publications on Latin literature and other subjects; he is also the founding editor of the journal *Scholia*. He has taught widely in Classics and the Humanities at a number of universities and is currently Professor of Classics at the University of Otago.

xxiv + 280 pp. (Forthcoming) 6"x 9"
Paperback, ISBN 0-86516-485-1

—Order Online Today—
www.BOLCHAZY.com

SERVIUS' COMMENTARY
on Book Four of Virgil's Aeneid
with notes and translation by
Christopher McDonough, Richard Prior and Mark Stansbury

Servius' Commentary
on Book Four
of Virgil's *Aeneid*

An Annotated Translation

Authors:
Christopher McDonough,
Richard Edmon Prior, and Mark
Stansbury

A unique tool for scholars and teachers, the translation of this celebrated Virgil commentary, on facing pages with the original Latin, allows easy access to Servius' seminal work on Book 4, probably the most widely read book of the *Aeneid*. Servius' commentary is important not only as a source of information on Virgil's poem but also for the countless other gems about Roman life and literature it contains. Its value has remained unquestioned. This dual-language edition is a must-have for every Classics library and the ideal ancillary text for any *Aeneid* course.

FEATURES

✦ Frontispiece: Facsimile page from the 1536 edition of Servius'
   commentary on Book 4
✦ Introduction on the life of Servius, the textual tradition
✦ Latin text of Virgil's *Aeneid,* Book 4, with Servius' commentary beneath it
✦ Facing-page translation of both Virgil and Servius
✦ Endnotes
✦ Guide to further reading

xviii + 170 pp. (2002) 6"x 9"
Paperback, ISBN 0-86516-514-9

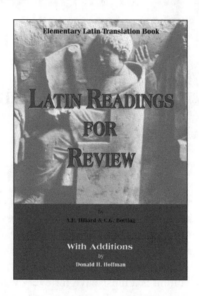

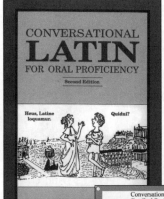

Conversational Latin
for Oral Proficiency, 2nd Edition

John C. Traupman

Text includes
+ Multi-level dialogs
+ Variety of contemporary and ancient topics
+ Topical vocabulary for each chapter
+ Authentic Roman expression
+ Comprehensive glossary
+ Appendices on colors and numbers, colloquial expressions, and sayings and proverbs
+ A chapter on transportation
+ Additional vocabulary in all categories (e.g., computer terminology)

Teachers in English-speaking countries who understand the value of active Latin in the classroom finally have the tool they need. John Traupman has given us a well-designed textbook in English for spoken Latin, which exploits a wide range of subject matter. Conversational Latin for Oral Proficiency *will help us restore an excellent tradition of instruction in Latin fluency that extends back to the* Colloquia familiaria *of Erasmus and beyond.*

—Terence O. Tunberg

Professor Traupman's Conversational Latin for Oral Proficiency *is a* locus classicus *for any teacher planning to introduce oral Latin into the classroom.*

—Rudolph Masciantonio

Who says there's no time or place for spoken Latin in the classroom? Quisquiliae *(Hogwash)!! Give Traupman's* Conversational Latin *a try. You and your students will find plenty of* hilaria mera.

—Margaret A. Brucia

256 pp. (1996, 2nd ed. 1997) Paperback, ISBN 0-86516-381-2
(2000) Cassette, ISBN 0-86516-475-4

*Explore **bolchazy.com** for other materials on **Oral Proficiency** and **Latin Pronunciation***

—Order Online Today—
www.BOLCHAZY.com